MOUNT MARCY
The High Peak of New York

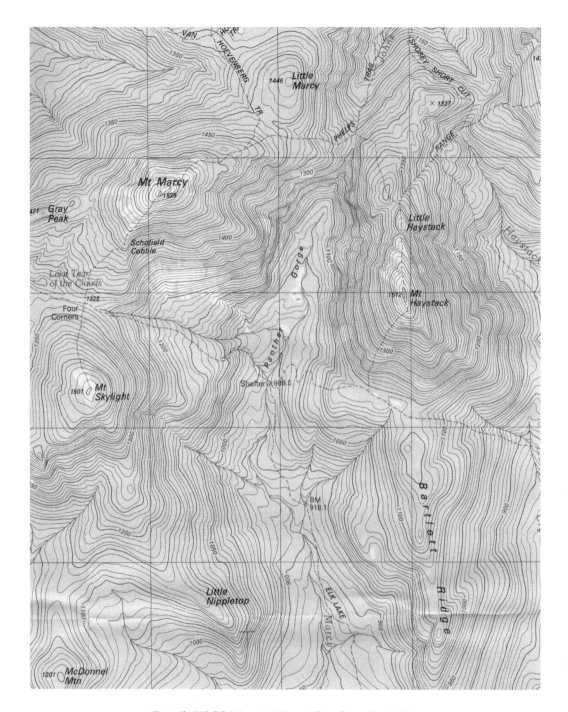

Detail, USGS Mount Marcy Quadrangle, 1979

MOUNT MARCY
The High Peak of New York

Sandra Weber

PURPLE MOUNTAIN PRESS

Fleischmanns, New York

To my daughters,
Emily and Marcy

MOUNT MARCY
The High Peak of New York

First Edition 2001

Published by Purple Mountain Press, Ltd.
1060 Main Street, P.O. Box 309
Fleischmanns, New York 12430
845-254-4062, 845-254-4476 (fax)
purple@catskill.net
www.catskill.net/purple

Photographs are by the author unless otherwise noted.

Library of Congress Control Number
2001 132678

ISBN 1-930098-22-7

Cover: Mount Marcy from Lake Tear of the Clouds. Photo © 2000 by Carl Heilman II

Manufactured in the United States of America
5 4 3 2 1

3114

Table of Contents

Mount Marcy, the highest point in New York State: 5,344 feet.

ME

VT

Mt. Marcy ▲

NH

NY

MA

CT   RI

Acknowledgments

THIS BOOK required a great deal of research and many miles of hiking. Thank you to the people who joined me on those long climbs up Mount Marcy: Bill Weber, Pete Fish, L. John Van Norden, Tony Solomon, John Lange, Emily Weber, Marcy Weber, Marsha Finnan, Terry Finnan, Vikki Finnan, Karl Clauss, and Tony Goodwin.

While the outdoor work was sometimes strenuous and other times spectacular, at least there was a trail to follow. The indoor research was, as Old Mountain Phelps would say, "a regular random scoot." Thankfully, I had four wise guides: Warder Cadbury, Mary MacKenzie, Phil Terrie, and Jim Goodwin. They gave generously of their time and their knowledge as this book took shape. Thank you also to my writing colleague, Jean Francis, who provided frequent doses of support, critique, and laughter.

Various libraries, museums, research facilities, and individuals assisted me. Thank you to Dick Tucker, Edie Pilcher, Patti Prindle, and the Adirondack Research Library; Jerold Pepper and the Adirondack Museum Library; Michelle Tucker and the Adirondack Collection of Saranac Lake Free Library; L. John Van Norden of the Adirondack 46-R Conservation Trust; Lake Placid Library; Adirondack Center Museum; Lake Placid-North Elba Historical Society; Keene Valley Library; New York State Library and Archives; SUNY at Plattsburgh Library; The Historical Society of Pennsylvania; the Library of Congress; the Princeton University Library; The Huntington Library; the Norristown Library; the Nature Conservancy; the Adirondack Mountain Club (ADK); Grace Hudowalski; Almy Coggeshall; Pete Fish; Jerry Jenkins; Carl Heilman II; and James Bailey.

I am grateful for the warm friendship and support of the members of the Hurricane Mountain Chapter of ADK. Thank you to Wray and Loni Rominger at Purple Mountain Press for your enthusiastic support of this book and New York State history in general. Thank you to Neal Burdick for your superb editing work. And, thank you to Ed Ketchledge for being a wonderful mentor and for saving the summit of Mount Marcy.

I know that my daughters, Emily and Marcy, will never forget their first climb up Mount Marcy with the weird lady in a dress. And I will never forget their strength and smiles. Over the bumps and through the muck, from my first painful descent of Mount Marcy to my recent glorious winter ascent, my husband, Bill, was there. Sometimes leading, sometimes following. Always sharing the load.

The author near the summit of Mount Marcy.

Introduction

MOUNT MARCY, Tahawus, Cloudsplitter, High Peak of Essex—by any name, it is the tallest mountain in New York State. It stands 5,344 feet above sea level, a wild mass of old rocks and earth girdled by flourishing forests and grand gorges.

There is no mountain in the world quite like it.

Of course, that may seem overstated or inflated. Mount Marcy is but a little bump when compared to the Rockies or the Alps. Even four eastern state high points—Mount Mitchell, Mount Washington, Clingmans Dome, and Mount Rogers—are taller. Yet Mount Marcy is special. It is the closest any of these tall eastern mountains comes to wilderness. It has no lodge or observation tower or road on its summit dome. The closest road is more than five miles away, the closest little village eight. Reaching Marcy's top requires a walk of at least seven-and-a-half miles through forests of birch, pine, spruce and fir, over streams and past waterfalls, around boulders and across swamps.

But even Mount Marcy is not a primeval wilderness. It is a landscape that has been abused and neglected, then protected and regenerated. It is a modern wilderness. A wilderness, in a sense, created by humans practicing restraint. A place where human activities are subdued and natural activities dominate.

Mount Marcy is a beacon for people, like me, who seek wilderness. Climbing into this high, wild place is an adventure of the body but also of the mind and soul. It hardens my body and loosens my spirit. I let go of the fast-moving, technology-oriented world and drift into another space. A space where I connect with other life forms: trees, rocks, flowers, birds, bears, black flies. A space where I touch rain, ice, wind, and mud. A space where my natural rhythms return.

I can climb the many sides of Mount Marcy and see its many moods. Whether sun-splashed, fogged over, or ice-coated, the scene at the summit is splendid. The openness is inspiring. The hard rock under my feet is infallible.

But there is so much more to Mount Marcy. Beyond the summit rock and the dirt trail, there is a post-glacial ecosystem. There is a tiny trickle of water that divides between the Ausable and Hudson rivers. There is a spring snowbowl and mountain sandwort. There are footsteps of guide Orson Phelps and mountaineer Lucia Pychowska, President Theodore Roosevelt and botanist Orra Phelps, conservationist Bob Marshall and professor Ed Ketchledge. This is also a place that has been a campground, garbage dump, and latrine. There is erosion and restoration.

The history of Mount Marcy is not dead history. It is a living history, and a broad history—about the Adirondack Park, about wildness, and about ourselves. Read its records. Sample its stories. Examine its memoirs. See if it doesn't excite your curiosity, enrich your mountain view, and make you want to split a cloud or two.

Origins

How dear to my heart are the glorious old mountains,
When for thirty years past I recall scenes to view,
Their wild mossy gorges and sweet crystal fountains
Stand out now before me as vivid as new.
Their Avalanche stript faces that glitter in sunlight
With myriads of crystals that dazzle the eyes;
Their rough ragged rocks horizontal and upright,
Proclaim their Creator must have truly been wise.
The old feldspar mountains, with their sweet crystal fountains
The evergreen mountains we all love so well.
ORSON S. PHELPS, "MOUNTAIN SONG"

Mount Marcy is a jumble of jagged rock thrust upward at the heavens. It is a cold, wet, windy wasteland—rarely noticed before 1836, and not fully explored until the 1870s. Yet it captures my attention and affection like no other mountain in New York State, or perhaps on earth.

My response is partially driven by the wildness, the beauty, and the immensity of the mountain. Yet there must be more.

Historian Alfred Donaldson wrote about Mount Marcy:

> I am tallest of the mountains where many mountains rise—
> I am Cleaver of the Cloudland and the Splitter of the Skies—
> I am keeper of the caverns where the God of Thunder sleeps—
> I am older than the waters that once hid me in their deeps.[1]

Perhaps this oldness, in geological terms, accounts for part of my affection. It has something to do with that bare gray rock exposed on the summit. "It comes as near, perhaps, to our idea of that substance upon which—there is good reason for believing—mortal eyes have never looked, known by the ideal name of Primitive Rock," reported an 1875 Plattsburgh newspaper. This rock, the newspaper story continued, shows no signs of stratification, or fossils, but exhibits a uniformity "peculiar only to those rocks which are believed to have been fused in nature's hottest subterranean furnaces, and thrown by some mighty throb against the solid crust which enveloped it, with such force as to break through, in defiance of the laws of gravity, and in such masses as are seen in this mountainous region."[2]

Mount Marcy and the surrounding mountain region are not part of the Appalachian Mountain system, as is often thought. They are geologically related

Facing page: Summit of Mount Marcy, 2000.

Mount Marcy, circa 1900, by Stoddard. Courtesy of Getman Collection, North Elba-Lake Placid Historical Society. *Facing page:* Mount Marcy, near same spot, 1999. *Below:* Aerial view, May 7, 1995. 1. Mount Marcy. 2. Lake Tear of the Clouds. 3. Mount Skylight. 4. Mount Haystack. 5. Panther Gorge. Photo by USGS *Facing page:* Aerial view. 1. Mount Colden. 2. Avalanche Lake. 3. Lake Colden. 4. Flowed Land. 5. Calamity Pond.

to the Laurentian Plateau that spreads across much of eastern Canada. They are composed of very old rock, erosion-resistant bedrock, known as anorthosite. Dated by the radioactivity of its minerals, the rock is about 1.1 billion years old.

Mountain building, like most geological processes, is slow, almost imperceptible in human terms. A billion years ago, the anorthosite that now lies exposed on Mount Marcy's summit was buried miles beneath the earth's crust. An ancient ocean called the Grenville Sea covered the rocks. After hundreds and hundreds of millions years, the rock was the first dry land to push up above the primitive ocean. The Adirondack high peaks, including Mount Marcy, were born.

Eons of erosion and uplifting worked at the raised plateau. After millions of years, erosion removed the overlying sedimentary rock, leaving the hard anorthosite. At that time, the region that is now the Adirondack mountains was flat. Sometime after the demise of the dinosaurs, the Adirondacks began to rise. Thus, the Adirondacks are young mountains made from old rocks.[3]

Over time, they were worn down and rounded. Within the last two million years, during the Pleistocene Epoch, continental glaciers reshaped the peaks. Ice advanced and melted back at least three times.

The glaciers reached as far south as Staten Island and Long Island, but were they thick enough to bury the summit of Mount Marcy? One source claims that "one continuous continental glacier covered the state, overtopping the highest mountain, Mount Marcy, and producing a nearly featureless ice surface."[4] Others believe that the evidence does not support that theory. If the great ice sheets overtopped Marcy there should be glacial marks (striae) on the summit. None have been found. There should also be glacial erratics on the summit, but as noted in 1875, "There are no rocks here but those native to the mountain—no foreign boulders which have been pushed up the sharp slope by glaciers, or dropped by icebergs."[5] Modern scientists have found glacial erratics only as high as 4,600 feet on Marcy, not on the top.

"Whether the very highest summits were ever covered is still a matter of debate," wrote geologists Jaffe and Jaffe in 1986. "Their rounded shape has been attributed to glaciation, but could just as easily be the result of normal erosion."[6]

Eventually the glacial period ended. As the last ice sheet retreated northward about 12,000 years ago, it scoured the Adirondack region of vegetation and soil. The barren, rocky slopes of Mount Marcy emerged. In a few shallow depressions, small glaciers remained. As the ice froze and thawed and froze again, it scraped at the edges of the hollows and left deep bowls known as cirques. One cirque, known as the snowbowl, is on Marcy's northeast slope at 5,250 feet. According to geologists Jaffe and Jaffe, Lake Tear of the Clouds, just south of the summit, is also a cirque, not a depression gouged out by an overriding ice sheet.[7]

The retreat of the ice had another consequence. The land, now released from the weight of the thick ice, rose several hundred feet. And is still rising. Recent studies show that "the Adirondacks may be rising at the astonishing (to a geologist!) rate of 2 to 3 mm per year. The mountains are growing about 30 times as fast as erosion is wearing them away. We suspect, however, that the present rapid uplift is a temporary spurt, and the average rate may be much less."⁸

Plants and animals moved northward onto the newly bared landscape as the climate warmed. The first immigrants to arrive were herbs, grasses, and sedges—tundra species like alpine bilberry, crowberry, and mountain alder. For a time, the whole region was tundra territory.

As the climate repeatedly warmed and cooled between 12,000 and 5,000 years ago, the tundra species were overtaken by species of trees as they advanced from the south, retreated, and then advanced. Animals such as muskox, bison, and caribou may have occupied the area.

Eventually the forests of the present age arrived. Deciduous hardwoods like sugar maple, American beech, and yellow birch dominated the valleys and lower mountain slopes. Higher up the slopes, where the temperature was cooler and the growing season shorter, balsam fir and red spruce took over. Above 4,200 feet, only balsam fir remained, though generally stunted and scrubby.

Above 5,000 feet, on the summit dome of Mount Marcy, different conditions determined what species existed. After the last glacial period ended, primitive lichen covered the summit rocks. Pioneering sphagnum mosses grew. Over the centuries, the moss made dead peat. Tundra plants, bushes, flowers, and small trees took root among the sphagnum and peat "soil." But the summit environment remained cold and wet and windy. For as many as eight months a year, the thin soil was frozen. Weathering and erosion worked at the rocks and soil and limited plant growth at the summit. Upright trees could not survive. Few new species immigrated. Only those species adapted to a tundra-like environment—those species that long ago covered the entire region—survived on the summit of Mount Marcy.

It is geology that helps the summit capture my eyes and heart. When I examine those tundra plants, I see relics of post-glacial time. When I walk on the ancient anorthosite, I feel the hardness that has preserved its elevation. When I realize that these peaks are the "truncated stumps" of former mountains whose thousands of feet of overlying rock have been elevated and eroded away, I begin to understand the longevity of Mount Marcy.

The landscape I see *from* the summit of Mount Marcy still shows the prominent geologic features, too. I look at the lakes and consider the work of the glaciers. I envision the ice sheet that exaggerated the long north-northeast valleys and made the gently curved ridge and the radial drainage patterns flowing outward from the uplifted dome. Like the first men to ascend the mountain, I marvel at the little meadow high on the slopes of Mount Marcy where "the main branch of the Hudson and a fork of the east branch of the Au Sable commence their descending course in opposite directions, for different and far distant points of the Atlantic Ocean."

Perhaps nothing is so important to Mount Marcy's short human history as its long geologic history. The topographic features of the region—the deep gorges, long valleys, and high peaks—made access to Marcy difficult from all sides.

This is its history. This is why it stood undiscovered for so long. Ironically, it was in the name of geology that Mount Marcy was first explored and ascended. But even after its discovery, it stood isolated and ignored. It took years for the first trail to be built, and many more years for the first winter ascent. Roads, villages, and commercial development stayed miles away from Mount Marcy.

This is one reason Mount Marcy is special. Unlike most of the higher peaks in the eastern United States, it still holds some wildness!

But the geological story is not over. Quite the contrary. Robert Boyle notes in *The Hudson River* that geologic and climatic evidence indicate that much of the Northern Hemisphere "is merely between glaciers." He writes that we may still be living in the Pleistocene Epoch, and the next glacier might appear in about 10,000 years, and that "Almost all the plants and animals now in the Hudson Valley, including man himself, have slipped in, so to speak, through this small chink in the enormity of time."[10]

What a grand chink it is, and how fortunate we are to have Mount Marcy for as long as we and anorthosite endure.

Summit.

Iron Works

*The Indian opened his blanket and took out a small piece
of Iron Ore about the size of a nut—"You want see 'em
ore—me know 'em bed, all same."*
                                        DAVID HENDERSON, 1826

IN the mid-1700s, the High Peaks were part of the area known as
Couchsachrage, an Indian Beaver Hunting Country. It was considered an
impassable and uninhabited "Dismal Wilderness" because of the numerous
mountains, swamps, and drowned lands.[1] But Indians hunted there and were
almost certainly the first to behold Mount Marcy.

They were also the first summer people. The region to the north, now known
as North Elba, was "traditionally the site of a Mohawk Indian summer village
before the advent of the white man," states Lake Placid-North Elba historian
Mary MacKenzie, "and numerous arrowheads and other artifacts unearthed over
the years confirm the legend."[2]

Indians continued traveling in the mountain region as late as 1826.[3] They traveled through the mountains, too. Traces of two routes have been found: one by
way of Indian Pass and the other "by way of Lakes Sanford and Henderson, and
thence to the Preston Ponds and the head-waters of the Racket."[4]

Surely, these native people saw Mount Marcy, but did they climb it? Perhaps
curiosity drew someone to the summit. Or sacred spirits kept them away. Most
historians believe they did not visit the summit. They had no reason to make the
toilsome climb. Game and fish and berries were plentiful in the lowlands.

The first men who had reason to climb near summits were surveyors. Charles
Brodhead ran the earliest survey line through the high country in June 1797, passing scarcely two miles north of Mount Marcy. But for the next forty years, while
parties climbed Mount Washington, Katahdin, and several Catskill peaks over
and over again, no one went near Mount Marcy or the other Adirondack high
peaks, with three exceptions.

A Mr. Rykert was on Dix Mountain in 1807. John Richards was on Big Slide in
1812 and possibly on Whiteface in 1814. But these men were surveyors, not
explorers. And even as surveyors, their interests were in boundary lines, not
topography. Mountains were obstacles to their work, not features worthy of
examination and measurement. Besides, why should they pay attention to these
northern mountains when it was an undisputed assumption that the Catskill
Mountains were the highest peaks in the state?

Whiteface Mountain was the only northern mountain that attracted any interest. It was a conspicuous landmark, with its bare summit, pyramid shape, and
solitary location. Thus Whiteface was presumed to be the highest in the region, at
perhaps 2,500 feet. Mount Marcy stood in the center of a jumble of peaks, miles

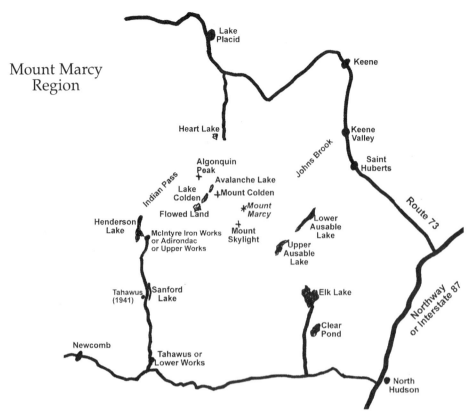

from any road or village. Still, its rocky dome projected above the other peaks. This high mountain was familiar to the people who had settled nearby.

Farmers from New England began to settle in Essex County about 1795. By 1810, the county population was 9,525. By 1825, it was 15,993 and many hamlets and villages, such as Pendleton (Newcomb), Keene Flats (Keene Valley), and The Plains of Abraham (North Elba), had formed.[5] There were plenty of people in the region to view the summit, but there was nothing to entice them to climb Mount Marcy. Hunting, trapping, and farming were best in the valleys and passes and on the low slopes.

The Plains of Abraham, on the outskirts of the present village of Lake Placid, commanded a grand view of the high peaks and provided rich soil for farming. In 1811, Archibald McIntyre,* a leading political figure and well-to-do business-man, discovered that they also held iron ore. He and his associates bought land and formed the Elba Iron and Steel Manufacturing Company, named for the island of Elba, a rich source of minerals from ancient times.** Thus McIntyre began the first of his ambitious Essex County mining ventures, both of which would prove ill-fated. Yet both played roles in the discovery and promotion of Mount Marcy.

*The correct spelling of Archibald's name is McIntyre, not MacIntyre. This book will use McIntyre for his name and for the mountain, except in direct quotes.
**In 1849, the town of North Elba was named for the Elba works.

Elba Ironworks was built along the Chubb River and added to the prosperity of the little community at The Plains for a few years. But, in 1817, many of the farmers moved away because of the disastrous effects of the "Year Without A Summer."* The same year, the ironworks closed. Competition from foreign iron and transportation problems proved too difficult.

In the fall of 1826, a party of McIntyre's relatives, including his associate and future son-in-law David Henderson, came back to the abandoned works. This time they were searching for silver. There had always been tales of precious metals being found by the natives and locals. Then, in 1825, a man named William Scott had revealed the general location of a lost silver mine in the woods to the south.

The quest for silver lured the Henderson party to the northern region. However, they quickly abandoned that folly when they discovered a bed of iron ore that appeared to be the best on the North American continent. According to Henderson's famous letter to Archibald McIntyre, it all began when a "strapping young Indian" showed up at the abandoned works where they were staying. He displayed a nugget of iron ore and offered, "You want see 'em ore—me know 'em bed, all same."[6]

Mount Marcy from Lake Placid. Courtesy of Library of Congress.

*The Year Without a Summer, 1816, was chiefly caused by the eruption of Tambora in Indonesia on April 5, 1815. It was the largest observed volcanic eruption of the previous two centureis. The debris coated the stratosphere (from about 10 to 30 miles above the earth), blocking up to one-fifth of the sun's light and heat. The reduction of light and heat played a part in the slow growth of crops, poor harvests, and unusual weather patterns in the Northern Hemisphere in 1815 and 1816.

Archibald McIntyre.
Courtesy of New York State Library

The Indian said the source of the iron was about twelve miles away, over the mountain to the southwest. The townspeople had laughed at him, thinking he had chipped it from a rock. Although Henderson and associates thought they might be led on a wild goose chase, they asked the honest-looking Indian how much he wanted for showing them the ore bed. "Dollar, half, and 'bacco," he replied. The deal was struck.

The expedition party consisted of Lewis Elijah, the Indian of the St. Francis tribe; Malcolm and Duncan McMartin; David Henderson; John McIntyre, Archibald's son; Enoch, a black man-servant; Dyer Thompson, Archibald's nephew; and Wallace, a dog. After a fatiguing journey, they arrived at the Notch, now known as Indian Pass. Henderson found it "as wild a place as I ever saw." Enoch found it dreadful and supposedly said, "What put it in your compurnihenshen ever to come in sich parts. I never thinks there be such horrificable place in all dis world."7

At last they reached the summit of the pass and then followed a stream south for a while before making camp for the night. In the morning Lewis Elijah led them to the ore deposits. Near what is now the Upper Works Trailhead parking lot, they found a surface vein of iron that formed a natural dam with a breadth of fifty feet. "Here is the great mother vein of iron, which throws her little veins and sprinklings all over these mountains," wrote Henderson.

The McMartin brothers and Lewis Elijah went down to the lake below. Most likely, at this time they gave it the name Lake Henderson. Then they rejoined Henderson and covered all traces of their marks on the ore bed.

The party hastened to return to their camp. They headed in the wrong direction for a while and then were slowed by a drenching rain, which turned to snow. Weary and hungry, they stopped for the night a mile from camp. After two more days of struggling through the woods, they arrived back at the settlement.

Henderson wanted to lose no time in procuring the iron ore property for McIntyre. And he wanted to be careful that no one found out about it. "We will take the Indian with us to Albany—dare not well leave him in this country," wrote Henderson.[8]

There were difficulties with acquiring the land known as Township 47 of the Totten and Crossfield Purchase. But McIntyre and his associates were able to purchase what is known as the Gore east of Township 47 quite easily. This tract included the westerly part of the McIntyre Range, part of Indian Pass, part of the Calamity Brook valley, Mount Adams, and the area around lakes Jimmy and Sally. A survey showed it comprised 6,080 acres and had a value of ten cents per acre. It also noted, "no oar [*sic*] in sight."[9]

McIntyre and his associates quickly developed the enterprise. They erected a forge, a boarding house, and a sawmill. They purchased more land. And, by 1830, they had built a crude version of an access road. McIntyre's enterprise seemed to have all the ingredients for great success: an abundance of iron, sources of water-power, an unending supply of timber, and a work force. The 1830 census reported almost 20,000 people living in Essex County; sixty-two lived in the Town of Newcomb, which surrounded the iron works region.

But there was no railroad or dependable road near the iron works. The access road and its connecting roads proved expensive to build and impossible to maintain. Yet that was the only transportation link. The people at the iron works could survive by growing their own vegetables, grains, and hay or procuring goods from the neighboring farmers, but the iron product had to be transported to market.

View of the Indian Pass from Lake Henderson. Courtesy of New York State Library

The Adirondack Iron-Works, circa 1853 by T. Addison Richards.

By June of 1833, Archibald McIntyre was worried about the future of the works. "I confess that I am at times alarmed & disheartened with this same concern of our's [*sic*], and afraid that it may turn out another Elba concern," he wrote to Duncan McMartin. "I cannot allow myself to believe it will be so and yet I cannot avoid sometimes of having my fears. For the ore has not yet been tested, the roads are abominable, and coal wood in the vicinity very scarce."[10]

Henderson told McIntyre that if only he would come to the region, it would benefit his health and relieve his mind. Henderson reported many improvements: an excellent road from the Sanford Lake landing to the settlement, a straight level street, a fine field of oats, excellent potatoes, and a preacher of the Gospel.

He also told about his exploration of the "East River" (the Opalescent River). Henderson, McMartin (presumably Duncan), and a worker followed the river all day and camped under a blanket at night. The next morning they came to a "splendid perpendicular fall of about sixty feet the whole river pouring over,"[11] now known as Hanging Spear Falls. A hundred paces further, they found a chute of water at an angle of about forty-five degrees. They kept climbing until they reached the still water.

Henderson wrote, "We meant to continue on to a very narrow pond between two immense precipices in the adjoining great mountain—which Judge Richards & Mr. Sanford told us, is the greatest curiosity they ever saw—but the day was wet to the skin and we travelled round the mountain, and got to the head of the Valley where the ore bed stream comes down, which we followed home & arrived at night."[12]

The "very narrow pond" that Richards and Sanford saw while surveying the land tract prior to June 1833 was likely what is now known as Avalanche Lake.[4]

If so, this would be the first recorded visit to Avalanche Lake. And since Richards and Sanford likely would have passed Lake Colden on their way to Avalanche Lake, this would be the first recorded visit to Lake Colden, too. Perhaps they made the blazes found by later explorers.

This account also shows the woodcraft of Henderson. With no path and no guide, he went off into the woods on a two-day excursion. Although he did not make it to Lake Colden, he did circle Calamity Mountain and follow the ore bed stream now known as Calamity Brook. Henderson had found the routes for entering and exiting the high mountain region.

At times, the iron operation looked promising, but by September of 1834, McIntyre had given up. "The more I think of our unfortunate concern," he wrote to McMartin, "the more I am satisfied of the egregious folly of our whole proceedings, and of the necessity of making what can be made from the wreck as speedily as possible."[13]

The proprietors stopped operation and left a caretaker to tend the farm. Meanwhile, they tried to interest wealthy businessmen in the property. In 1836, David Colden, Abraham Van Santvoord, and William C. Redfield, a scientist, visited the iron works. Geologists from the newly formed state survey planned a visit, too.

Perhaps a visit by state geologists could change the fortunes of the McIntyre Iron Works enterprise. Maybe the geologists or Redfield could ascertain other riches on their lands. Maybe the state could be convinced to improve the roads or to build a railroad through the region. Or perhaps business investors would be enticed to take an interest in the enterprise.

Hope reigned anew at the iron works in 1836, and within a few years, operations resumed. But even the enthused and energetic David Henderson could not have supposed what grand adventures lay in waiting.

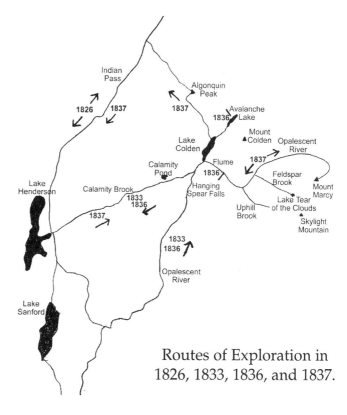

Routes of Exploration in 1826, 1833, 1836, and 1837.

The First Ascent

We reached the open rock surface covered only with mosses and Alpine plants, and at 10 A.M. I had the satisfaction of placing myself on the highest summit in the State of New York; a summit which perhaps has never before been trodden by human foot.

WILLIAM C. REDFIELD,
ON REACHING MOUNT MARCY ON AUGUST 5, 1837

ALTHOUGH the first ascent of Mount Marcy occurred over 160 years ago, some details have remained a mystery—and a source of excited debate. Who were the members of the party? What time did they reach the summit? Were they really the first? And did they name the peak? Some of the answers were provided in 1927 by Russell Carson in *Peaks and People*. Clarifications were made in Philip Terrie's "Introduction" added in 1973 and revised in 1986.

Hikers who climb the mountain and read the bronze tablet at the summit may think all the answers have been revealed to them. But the words—though set in stone—are not the truth. They only continue the conundrum.

The story begins in 1836. The growing interest in natural history and natural resources by other states pressured New York to produce a top-notch report of its own treasures. The state legislature approved $104,000 in funds for the Natural History Survey of New York. This was the first scientific agency formed by the state to study its natural resources and one of the first geological surveys in the world. The work started by the survey is carried on today by the New York State Museum.

Although the survey was to be of a general nature, its emphasis was on geology and the northern areas. Thus hunters or local settlers would not make the first known ascent of the highest mountain in the state. It would be made as part of the scientific duties of members of the Natural History Survey, who in actuality were hoping to find huge coal deposits.[1]

The influence of the survey extended far beyond coal and Mount Marcy. It was the most ambitious of the state surveys and it set the standard for all that followed. According to the American Philosophical Society, "More than any other of the surveys and explorations, with the exception of the United States Exploring Expedition, it launched notable careers in science. And it shaped the future organization of science in America, for out of the meetings of its geologists at the end of each field season (May to October) emerged in 1840 the American Association of Geologists and Naturalists, parent organization in 1848 of the American Association for the Advancement of Science."[2]

John Torrey. Courtesy of Library of Congress. Ebenezer Emmons. Courtesy of The Adirondack Museum. James Hall. Courtesy of New York State Library.

Governor William Marcy chose some of the country's most prominent scientists to work on the survey. John Torrey, the country's premier botanist, was appointed state botanist. Ebenezer Emmons, age 37, a professor at Williams College who had trained at Eaton's Rensselaer School (now Rensselaer Polytechnic Institute), was selected chief geologist in the second district, the mountain district. His former student, James Hall, age 25, became his assistant.

Emmons was sensitive, emotional, and adventurous. He would peer over the edge of Wallface's cliff and scramble up the steep, 70-foot wide rock channel on the side of Mount Colden. Hall was physically strong, tough, and ambitious. Perhaps in the classroom these personalities worked well together, but in the field they didn't. And there remained the matter of $400 that Hall had borrowed from Emmons and never repaid. Perhaps that is why, when the pair set out north, Emmons decided to make a reconnaissance of the whole district while sending Hall to the McIntyre Iron Works.

When Hall arrived at the iron works in mid-August 1836, he met William C. Redfield, an independent and self-trained scientist. Redfield had made pioneering contributions in the study of storms and had invented the "safety barges" that were once towed behind Hudson River steamboats for the safety of women passengers. In his upper forties, Redfield was physically robust and untiring in his curiosity. Nothing seemed to dampen his zeal—not rain or mud or cold.

On August 17, 1836, Redfield and Hall set out into the woods with three of the iron works proprietors: Archibald McIntyre, David Henderson, and Duncan McMartin. Their friend David C. Colden, guide John Cheney, and two other woodsmen accompanied them. Their intention was to explore up the main branch of the Hudson,[3] but it is likely that the proprietors also hoped to interest Colden or Redfield in investing in the property.

As they walked along the river, Redfield noticed traces of wolves, deer, and moose. Toward evening, they stopped to set up camp. "A shelter, consisting of poles and spruce bark, was soon constructed by the exertions of our dexterous woodsmen," wrote Redfield. "The camp-fire being placed on the open side, the party sleep with their heads in the opposite direction, under the lower part of the roof."[4] Evidently, the lean-to arrangement amazed him.

The next day, the party walked past the waterfalls and the still water that Henderson had seen on his 1833 explorations. They continued to the outlet of a beautiful lake situated between two mountains. They made camp at the lake, which they named Lake Colden.

Bark Cabin at Calamity Pond, 1859, by Lossing.

That night, Redfield realized something peculiar about the mountains: "The great ascent which we had made from our first encampment, and the apparent altitude of the mountain peaks before us, together with the naked condition of

View at Lake Colden by Charles C. Ingham. Courtesy of New York State Library.

their summits, rendered it obvious that the elevation of this mountain group had been greatly underrated; and we were led to regret our want of means for a barometrical measurement."[5]

Heavy rain fell overnight and part of the next day. Despite the poor weather that morning, Henderson and Cheney walked around Lake Colden. At noon, McIntyre, McMartin, and Hall went to examine the valley beyond the lake. They discovered another lake and named it Avalanche Lake.

Evidently, Henderson was not content to sit still and watch the rain. He and Redfield resumed ascent of the main stream. They went more than two miles, passing what is now called The Flume. Then Redfield went up a ridge to get a view. "From this point a mountain peak was discovered, which obviously exceeded in elevation the peaks which had hitherto engaged our attention," he wrote. "Having taken the compass bearing of this peak, further progress was relinquished, in hope of resuming the exploration of this unknown region on the morrow."[6]

This high peak would prove to be Mount Marcy, the highest in the state. Unfortunately, Redfield was unable to explore further; the next morning was foggy and rainy. "It was at last determined," wrote Redfield, "in view of the bad state of the weather and short stock of provisions, to abandon any further exploration at this time, and to return to the settlement."[7] On the return from Lake Colden, the party took the westerly route that Henderson had followed in 1833. This route, now known as the Calamity Brook trail, was much shorter.

That was the end of Redfield's explorations in the region for the year, but not the end of his interest in the iron works. In November, McIntyre wrote, "I saw Redfield and Van Santvoord, who seem fully inclined to take hold of our Iron Concern, and make the most of it for themselves and us."[8] For unknown reasons, nothing further happened.

As for the survey, one more event transpired in 1836. State geologists Ebenezer Emmons and James Hall ascended Whiteface Mountain and, from the summit, recognized the highest mountain that Redfield had spotted. But like Redfield, they had to postpone the ascent of the high peak. This time the deterrent was snow. "Those mountains were covered as early as the 26 of September and remained so till we left and probably [the snow] will not disappear till next June," Emmons wrote to Governor Marcy.[9]

In his report to the state legislature about the year 1836, Emmons wrote, "The highest peak among these mountains is about sixteen miles south from Whiteface, and so far as we know, has neither been ascended nor measured. Whiteface is generally supposed to be the highest, but erroneously, as is proved by leveling from its summit in range with those southern elevations."[10]

This was the first mention of "the highest peak" in published text. Even more important, Emmons estimated the height of Whiteface to be 4,855 feet above sea level, which was 1,051 feet higher than Round Top in the Catskills.[11] This proved that the northern region was far more elevated than had ever been stated. These mountains were the highest in the state.

Since waterpower and water travel were important to the state, Emmons expounded upon the discoveries of water, too. "These heights, together with the table land on which they stand, are the true water-shed of the district," he wrote. "This is known from the fact that all the large rivers flowing in the northern counties have their origin here. Their sources are either in marshes or lakes at the foot of these mountains, or they rise from springs which gush from their sides, and dash in splendid cataracts over the cliffs and rocks, as they commence their journey to the distant ocean. . . .In this region are the sources of the Hudson, Racket, Au Sable, and Black rivers."[12]

Emmons also mentioned the immense wealth of iron in the region. But while there was a great supply of timber available for fuel for working iron ore, Emmons warned about clearcutting. He suggested marking off areas to cut each year and leaving small trees to support soil and prevent its washing away. This showed great foresight; the science of forestry did not evolve for another fifty years.

Of course, Emmons recognized the harshness of the region, too: "We have spoken rather favorably of this region of country, but those who have observed the influence of elevation and latitude on climate, will not be likely to overrate the value of it, as it certainly can have no particular claim of fertility or evenness of surface, yet it is heavily timbered, and wherever it is cleared, produces the most luxuriant herd's grass and the finest of the rooted vegetables."[13]

In the spring of 1837, Emmons made plans to explore the high peaks area. In August, an eclectic group of men set out from the McIntyre Iron Works for the summit of the high peak. They included scientists, professors, an entrepreneur, an artist, and five guides. There was a boy of sixteen and a scientist who was forty-eight, rather advanced in age for those times. Those who reached the summit were William Redfield, scientist; Ebenezer Emmons, state geologist; James Hall, assistant state geologist; Charles Cromwell Ingham, artist; John Torrey, state botanist; David Henderson, proprietor of the iron works; John Cheney, guide; Harvey Holt, guide; three other guides; and Ebenezer Emmons Jr.

When Alfred Donaldson wrote *A History of the Adirondacks* in 1921, he put in print several errors in the summit roster. He listed Edward Hall instead of James Hall, and Asa Torrey instead of John Torrey. He also claimed that Professor Story of New York, Professor Miller of Princeton, and Archibald McIntyre of the iron works made the climb. But evidence shows that McIntyre, Strong (not Story), and Miller (age 18, not a professor) were not in the first ascent party. In his diary, Miller wrote that he went to the works but was prevented from going with the party because he had severe colic. His diary also records that a party composed of A. McIntyre, Mr. Strong, Mr. French and Mr. Talcot reached the iron works on the evening of August 4.[14] It is impossible that any of these men could have walked to the summit by the next morning.

In the *Journal of Commerce*, Redfield confirms that they were "a party of twelve persons."[15] And in a letter supposedly written from the summit, Hall gives the names of the party as "Professor Emmons, Dr. Torrey, Mr. Engham [*sic*], Mr. Henderson, Mr. Redfield, and myself."[16] Evidently he felt no need to list Emmons Jr. or the five guides.

View of the Adirondack Mountains by Ebenezer Emmons.
Courtesy of New York State Library.

The twelve men who left the iron works on August 3, 1837 went by way of Calamity Pond and spent the night at their old camp at Lake Colden. Redfield seems to have grown accustomed to the rustic lean-to: "We here enjoyed all the luxury of camp fare and night fires, which is realized by those who sleep in the woods, on 'feathers' plucked from the branches of the neighboring forest trees."[17]

On August 4, they resumed their ascent of the main stream, heading generally southeast, passing The Flume and the point of the 1836 explorations. They soon arrived at South Elbow (Uphill Brook), where the bed of the main stream changes to a northeasterly direction. A tributary (Feldspar Brook) entered from the southeast.

The party chose to follow the main stream, perhaps partly because they reasoned that the larger waterway led to the source of the Hudson. However, if they had chosen the tributary, they would have discovered the highest pond source of the Hudson and a shorter route to the summit. Instead, they walked north through a pass between Mount Colden and the high peak. This seems to indicate that no one in the party had ever been on the high peak. However, even after people stood atop the peak, the shorter and more direct route went unused for over thirty years.

About half way up the pass, they stopped for the night. While the guides prepared camp, Redfield and Emmons could not contain their adventurous spirit. They continued for half a mile. With their barometers, they determined the elevation to be 4,200 feet.[18]

Imagine the jubilation that this news brought to the expedition. Nevertheless, it was likely not enough to keep them warm through the brutally cold night. Nor was it enough to shield them from the cries of the panther. According to Redfield, "It was expected at one moment that the glare of his large eyeballs would be discovered by the reflection of the fire light, and fire arms were placed in requisition, but his cat-ship showed more of his native caution than to singe his whiskers in the blaze of our camp fire."[19]

In the morning, it was thirty-three degrees. The party hastily resumed their ascent to the east. The stream diminished and became somewhat concealed under boulders. At 8:40 a. m. they arrived at the head of the stream.

The scientists found this spot quite remarkable—for three reasons. First, they noted the "beautiful and open mountain meadow" wedged between two mountain ridges. Then, the elevation was found to be more than 4,700 feet, "being more than nine hundred feet above the highest point of the Catskill mountains, which have so long been considered the highest in the state."[20] Last, from the high meadow, they saw the dividing of waters. From this spot, droplets began their long downward courses in opposite directions: to a branch of the Hudson River and south to New York City, or to a fork of the Ausable River and north to the St. Lawrence River.

This spot is generally accepted as the place now known as Plateau. The course of the stream, the elevation, and the dividing waters all point to this location. In addition, Redfield's sketch of the region shows the "Source" precisely at Plateau.

Despite their interest in this meadow, Redfield, Emmons, and the other men marched toward the mountain summit. "Its ascent now promised to be of easy accomplishment by proceeding along its ridge in a W.S.W. direction," wrote Redfield. "On emerging from the pass, however, we immediately found ourselves entangled in the zone of dwarfish pines and spruces. . . .These gradually decreased in height, till we reached the open surface of the mountain, covered only with mosses and small alpine plants, and at 10 A.M. the summit of the High Peak of Essex was beneath our feet."[21]

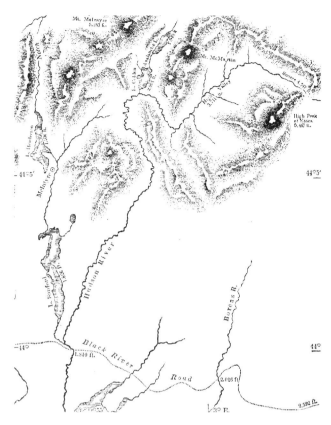

Sketch of the Northern Sources of the Hudson, 1837, by William Redfield.

The exact time that the party reached the summit has been in doubt. Redfield's published account, as excerpted above, gives ten o'clock but his field notes say, "Top of central peak at Noon."[22] Hall's letter from the summit is marked two o'clock.

Actually, all of these accounts come into agreement when considered in concert with Redfield's statement in the *Journal of Commerce*: "We spent five hours upon this summit."[23] Thus they likely arrived upon the summit about ten o'clock and left about three o'clock in the afternoon.

What did they do for five hours?

Their first order of business was to enjoy the view. James Hall first published a description of that scene:

> The summit is a naked rock and for many feet below the vegetation is moss and lichens with a few stinted spruces and alpine plants. . . .From this mountain we have one of the grandest views imaginable on the south, east, and west and to a considerable distance on the north we have mountains extending before us;

sometimes for a little distance they appear to form ranges, and again and for the most part, they are irregularly disposed, and present all the appearance of the ocean in a violent storm. Some of these mountains are clothed in evergreens to their summits, others are laid bare by slides leaving a crest of naked rock. Innumerable little lakes and streams are seen in all directions—Lake Champlain is visible on the east, and beyond that the Green Mountains, and beyond the low parts of this chain, we see the White Mountains, extending along the horizon like a dark cloud.[24]

Hall wrote this passage in a "private letter" to an editor friend; it was not intended for publication. But, the editor decided the information was so interesting that he resolved to "take the responsibility" and publish it.

William Redfield's account was published a few days later as a series of letters to the *New York Journal of Commerce*. Another version of his account appeared in *American Journal of Science and Art* in January 1838, and then was reprinted in *Family Magazine*. The text appears strikingly similar to Hall's. "The air on the mountain top was found to be cold and bracing," wrote Redfield, "and the aspect of the morning was splendid and delightful. Around us lay scattered an unnumbered multitude of mountain peaks of various magnitude and elevation, like a vast sea of broken and pointed billows." He also mentions the distant mountain ranges, "the glistening of the beautiful lakes," and "the white glare of recent mountain slides as seen on the sides of various peaks."[25]

This is one of the most eloquent and striking descriptions of Mount Marcy's summit—if you end the quote right there, as most citations do. But that creates the erroneous perception that the first explorers stood in a pristine wilderness. Redfield continues, "To complete the scene, from one of the nearest settlements a vast volume of smoke soon rose in majestic splendor, from a fire of sixty acres of forest clearing, which had been prepared for the 'burning,' and exhibiting in the vapor which it imbodied, a gorgeous array of the prismatic colors, crowned with the dazzling beams of the mid-day sun."[26]

No matter how comforting and beautiful Redfield found the first sights from Mount Marcy, they included settlements and sixty burning acres. Even in 1837, all about Mount Marcy was not wildness.

Nor was it desired to be, at least by Redfield. He wrote, "In future prospect, this region may be considered as the Wales of America, and under the fostering enterprise of our State government and people, it will ere long resound with the noise of the ponderous hammer, and the hilarity of a hardy and industrious population."

On August 5, 1837, the summit resounded with the noise and hilarity of twelve hardy men. They placed a small red and white flag on the southwestern end of the peak, and on its northeastern end they erected a pyramid of rock about six feet in height.

The scientists examined the summit surface and found it to consist of labradoritic rock and a few specimens of hypersthene. At noon, they found ice, half an inch thick on small deposits of water. Redfield recorded a temperature of forty-seven degrees. He also took a barometric reading but noted "Bar. bad."[27]

At one o'clock, Redfield and Emmons took another barometric reading. From these measurements, Hall calculated the mountain's height to be 5,300 feet. Initially, Redfield deduced it to be "not far from 5,700 feet." Later he and Emmons reported it to be 5,467 feet.

Botanist John Torrey found the geology of the region "uncommonly interesting." Like the others, he was fascinated by the ice, but of course, he was most excited about the mountain flora. "I found many interesting alpine plants never before seen in the U[nited] States, except on the White Hills of NH [New Hampshire]," he wrote.[28]

Artist Charles Cromwell Ingham barely made it to the summit. It is said that he "fainted a number of times in making the ascent, but became so excited with all that he saw, he determined to persevere, and finally succeeded in accomplishing the difficult task."[29] It is unclear what Ingham did on the summit for five hours. No summit sketches or paintings have been discovered. Perhaps he simply rested.

At some point during the day, Professor Emmons became convinced that they were the first men on this summit. "The region in which the east branch of this river [the Hudson] rises, it seems had never been explored previous to our visit;" he wrote, "and it is not unreasonable to suppose this, for all our writers on geography have uniformly underrated its height, have made incorrect statements in relation to the origin and course of the principal branches of the Hudson, and also in relation to the character of the whole mountain group in which they rise."[30]

Almost a hundred years later, author Russell Carson theorized that Harvey Holt had climbed Mount Marcy prior to the 1837 ascent. Carson had always been perplexed by Redfield's comment that "At Keene, Mr. Harvey Holt, an able woodsman, who was attached to our party, will cheerfully act as guide and assistant, in reaching the mountain."[31] Carson wondered how Holt knew how to reach the peak from Keene. But Redfield also wrote that the peak could be ascended from Johnson's at Clear Pond, southeast of Marcy. There is no evidence that either of these routes had been used. I suspect that Redfield was just proposing routes and being courteous in recommending Holt.

But another piece of evidence indicates that Holt might have climbed from the Keene Valley side before 1837. In her reminiscences, Nettie Holt Whitney, Harvey Holt's daughter, recalled the times when her father and Uncle John Cheney used to hunt together. She wrote, "They were the first to cut a trail up this side of Mt. Marcy, which was in 1836, to accommodate their hunting expeditions."[32]

It sounds convincing. But there is much contradicting testimony.

Emmons, Redfield, and Torrey were present on the ascent with Holt in 1837. All of their accounts state that even the hunters of Essex County, implying Holt and Cheney, knew of no one's having ascended the peak before. As Redfield said, "Even the more hardy huntsman of later times, who, when trapping for northern furs, has marked his path into recesses of these elevated forests, has left no traces of his ax higher than the borders of Lake Colden."[33]

Holt knew the woods. No doubt he had led hunting expeditions on the lower slopes of Mount Marcy. But even Whitney's account does not state that he climbed to the top. Since Whitney was not born when this trail was supposedly cut, it is likely that she erred slightly in the details or dates as she retold the story.

I believe August 5, 1837, is the date of the first ascent, and the men on the summit that day believed it, too. As customary with first explorers, they began conferring names on the peaks. About two o'clock, Hall wrote a letter, stating: "We have just given the name of Marcy to the highest mountain in State, and another about the same height, a few miles east [*sic*] of it, we have called Mount McIntyre."[34] These names were chosen to honor Governor William Marcy, who instituted the survey, and Archibald McIntyre, who hosted the gentlemen at the iron works.

This letter provides strong evidence that the name of Marcy was first applied to the peak on August 5, 1837. A letter written by botanist John Torrey confirms this. On August 23, 1837, Torrey wrote, "The peak which we named Mt. Marcy is full 5,300 ft. above the level of the sea."[35] Despite the mountain having been given the name Marcy, Redfield continued to use the descriptive name, The High Peak of Essex. To add to the confusion, the name Tahawus was applied to the peak a month later.

From Hall's letter, it is also clear that the name McIntyre was applied to an individual peak, not to a range of mountains. Emmons substantiates this in his 1838 report, stating that "Another remarkable mountain, bearing N.47 degrees W. was named Mount McIntyre." But Russell Carson relied entirely on Redfield's account, which is unclear about whether the name referred to the highest peak of the ridge or to the entire ridge. Thus, McIntyre now refers to the range and is usually spelled MacIntyre. Algonquin refers to the highest peak in the range.

It has also been considered whether the name "Adirondacks"* was given on August 5, 1837. Two pieces of evidence indicate that that occurred later. In Emmons' report of 1838, he wrote, "The cluster of mountains in the neighborhood of the Upper Hudson and Ausable rivers, I proposed to call the Adirondack Group, a name by which a well known tribe of Indians who once hunted here may be commemorated."[36] His choice of words seems very deliberate. He did not say, "I named" or "has been named," as he did in other instances. He said, "I proposed."

Once again, it is Hall's letter that supplies additional proof. "We have not yet determined upon a name for this group of mountains," Hall wrote from the summit on August 5. The name "Adirondack" may have been discussed that day but evidently no decision was reached.

---

*Emmons spelled *Adirondack* with a "k" on the end. Others did not, particularly when referring to the village near the iron works. This book will use *Adirondac* when referring to the village and *Adirondack* in other references, except in direct quotes.

Note that both quotes indicate that the name "Adirondack" was intended to apply to the "cluster of mountains," not to the entire region. That cluster is now called the High Peaks, a variation of Redfield's descriptive name for Mount Marcy.

About half past three on the afternoon of August 5, the party descended the upper slopes, choosing a more direct and far steeper route than that by which they had ascended. The descent to their

Adirondack Pass (Indian Pass) by Charles C. Ingham. Courtesy of New York State Library.

camp took a little more than an hour. The next day, August 6, they descended to Lake Colden. Two men joined them at their Lake Colden camp on the following day.[37] Who were the two gentlemen? Miller's diary mysteriously ends on August 5. Could Miller and Strong have walked to Lake Colden? Perhaps this accounts for Redfield including them as members of the party in his article for the *American Journal of Science and Arts*.

The party made a visit to Avalanche Lake. Professor Emmons, with his untiring curiosity and vigor, climbed about 1,500 feet up the Colden dike. On the morning of the eighth, they went up a steep ravine to the summit of Mount McIntyre (now Algonquin). This was the first recorded ascent of the second highest peak in the state.[38]

After an abrupt descent into Indian Pass, the party made camp. The next morning, they walked to Lake Henderson and then on to McIntyre Iron Works. They may have been tattered and tired after being in the forest for seven days, but John Torrey wrote, "I look back on that expedition as one of the most memorable and gratifying events of my life."[39]

The personal letters and articles written by Hall, Redfield, Emmons, and Torrey all attest to the thrill of the expedition. Accounts of the view, the ice, the panther, and the alpine plants call attention to the wonderment the scientists felt at finding this high mountain within the rapidly developing state of New York. This region "presents all the rugged characters and picturesque features of a primeval wilderness," wrote Redfield.[40]

Newspapers and journals were quick to print such remarks, for the publishers themselves were genuinely amazed at these discoveries. Benjamin Silliman, publisher of the *American Journal of Science and Art*, wrote to Torrey, "It is strange indeed that of all things high mountains should find a hiding place—but so it seems with your Essex Mountains which are now for the first time really *brought to light*."[41]

For Marcy's Sake

If the fairest features of landscape are to be named after
men, let them be the noblest and worthiest men alone.
HENRY D. THOREAU, 1854

IMAGINE YOURSELF standing atop a glorious mountain, a mountain no one has ever stood atop before. Barometric measurements indicate it is the highest mountain in the state. A botanist discovers rare alpine vegetation. Even the old guides stare in awe at the sprawling landscape.

As the exhilaration relaxes, you realize that there is no name for this mountain. It has been described only as the central peak or the high mountain. As the first explorers, it is your honor to give it an official name. And as is the common custom, you think of the man you wish to honor. Of course, it cannot be anyone in the expedition party because it would be disgraceful for a gentleman to name a mountain for himself.

Faced with just such circumstances, the 1837 ascent party stood atop the highest peak in the state and named it for Governor William Learned Marcy. Perhaps State Geologist Ebenezer Emmons suspected criticism of the choice for he wrote that the privilege of naming the peak "is of but little consequence."

He then defended the designation: "As this tour of exploration was made by gentlemen who were in the discharge of their duties to the State, and under direction of the present Executive, whose interest in the survey has been expressed both by public recommendation and private counsel and advice, it was thought that a more appropriate name could not be conferred on the highest summit of this group than Mount Marcy."

No doubt, Emmons promoted the choice to honor the man who enabled him to be there, the man who supported the geological survey and selected the best men for the job, putting aside political affiliations. And it must have seemed fitting to name the highest mountain in the state for the highest executive in the state, his Excellency.

In the ensuing years, Emmons continued naming peaks for governors, e.g., Seward and Dix. Years later, state surveyor Verplanck Colvin would do the same with Wright, Seymour, and Clinton. As recently as 1999, Governor George E. Pataki continued the tradition by designating a previously unnamed peak near Mount Marcy "TR Mountain" to honor Theodore Roosevelt, New York's thirty-third governor and the United States' twenty-sixth President.

Despite the custom of naming peaks for statesmen, scores of people singled out Emmons and faulted him for choosing the name Marcy. Criticism bustled about this particular name because the pretty name "Tahawus" was suggested shortly thereafter and said to be an old Indian name for the peak—which it was not.

In defense of Emmons, he alone did not choose the name Mount Marcy. Both Hall and Torrey wrote that "we" named the peak, implying an agreement of the entire party. In addition, the name appears to have been chosen with the highest integrity and good intentions. The men did not go to a book and look up lists of Presidents and Congressmen and stump-speakers, as has been accused of those who chose names in the White Mountains.[1] Emmons and the party chose the name out of allegiance.

Still, was Marcy worthy of the honor? Did he meet Thoreau's criteria of noblest and worthiest?

Consider some evidence from Washington. The Marcy Papers at the Library of Congress contain boxes and boxes of Governor Marcy's journals, correspondences, and speeches. A journal entry from August 6, 1836, deserves particular notice. Marcy had just finished reading the first volume of Charles Lyell's *Principles of Geology* and found it of great interest. Marcy wrote, "Things that were to me strange and unaccountable appear less so, but others that excited no attention become objects of curiosity and nice speculation."[2] He regretted only that he was not twenty years younger so he could give the study of geology more attention.

Governor William Learned Marcy.
Courtesy of Library of Congress.

This was William Marcy! A reader, an explorer, a dreamer. An old man of fifty years. A man who wished he could be exploring the north country with geologists Emmons and Hall.

Marcy must have told David Henderson of his wish because on March 27, 1837, Henderson wrote to McIntyre: "So it appears, Gov. Marcy has some idea of camping it with us next time we visit the upper Hudson."[3]

Although it appears that Marcy never made the visit, he managed to capture the essence of mountain exploration. *Things that were to me strange and unaccountable appear less so, but others that excited no attention become objects of curiosity and nice speculation.* His expedition wasn't up the highest peak but he clearly comprehended the experience.

This makes him appear worthy enough to be awarded the mountain's name. But if this fanciful romantic notion seems flimsy, there are ample practical reasons to honor William Marcy. According to his biographers, William Learned Marcy stood among the most important men of his generation. He served three terms as

Governor of New York, from 1832 to 1838; was Secretary of War in the Polk cabinet from 1845 to 1849; and was Secretary of State in the Pierce cabinet from 1853 to 1857. He barely lost his party's nomination for President of United States in 1852.[4]

Unfortunately, this most capable and eminent leader died just a few years before the Civil War. History does not seem to remember men whose public careers ended before the war, except those who brought about the war. Thus, Marcy's life has not received much attention.

His life started on December 12, 1786, in Sturbridge (now Southbridge), Massachusetts. His father was Jedediah, a farmer, and his mother Ruth Learned, a husbandman's daughter. Marcy studied for a while at Leicester Academy and then entered Brown University, graduating with high honors in 1808. Relying upon his own resources, he moved to Troy, where he worked at a store and studied law. Eventually, he was admitted to the bar. From the very first, Marcy took an interest in politics, contributing columns to the Troy *Budget*. He supported the principles of the Republican (Jeffersonian) party, afterwards called the Democratic party.

In June 1812, when war with Great Britain broke out, Marcy joined a military company, which was later dispatched to French Mills, now Fort Covington, north of Malone, New York. On the night of October 22, 1812, they went to capture Canadian militia encamped at the nearby St. Regis Indian reservation. Marcy, at the head of the file of men, broke open the door. He later confessed that he regarded himself as "un enfant perdu," a soldier in ambush.[5] But Marcy survived and the troops inside the house were captured.

Besides demonstrating his bravery, this event documents William Marcy's first—and, presumably, his only—experience in the north country of New York. It has often been pointed out that there is no record that Governor Marcy ever saw, much less climbed the mountain that was named for him. But he may have seen the mountain as he traveled from Troy to Fort Covington in 1812.

After the war, Marcy was appointed to a series of positions: Recorder of Troy, Adjutant General of the State, and State Comptroller. In 1829, he was appointed a justice of the Supreme Court of New York. He presided over one of the most celebrated criminal trials ever held in the United States: that of the alleged slayers of William Morgan, of Batavia, New York. Morgan allegedly revealed secrets of the Masonic Order and was promptly found dead. Marcy's handling of the case required courage and fairness in the face of popular prejudice. He is regarded as having conducted the proceedings "with distinguished ability and entire impartiality."[6]

However, a trivial incident associated with the case caused Marcy great embarrassment. A special circuit of the Supreme Court in Niagara County heard the Morgan case. All of Judge Marcy's expenses were to be paid while he presided at the special circuit. One day Marcy tore his pants while getting out of a stagecoach. He hired a tailor and, since he strongly objected to lumping charges, he itemized his accounts, including the item: "For mending my pantaloons, 50 cents."

When he ran for Governor of New York in 1832, someone scrutinized his accounts and found the item and exposed him to public ridicule. It worked. All serious issues were forgotten and the story of "the patch on Marcy's pantaloons" was taken up. Cartoons pictured pantaloons with a white patch on the seat bearing the number 50 on it. At Rochester, a huge pair of patched trousers was displayed atop a fifty-foot pole. However, the incident did not always work to Marcy's detriment; a rural citizen fondly remarked that "if Bill Marcy wore patched clothes," then Marcy was the man for him.

Cartoon showing Marcy's patched breeches. Courtesy of Library of Congress.

To counter the attack, Marcy found among the accounts of the Morgan case a charge for the "transportation" of his political enemy Thurlow Weed to Auburn, the seat of the state penitentiary. Marcy wrote an article for the Albany *Argus*, stating that the state could well afford to transport Weed to Auburn, if he had only been permanently detained there. Marcy had turned the laugh on Weed and the situation was mitigated. Marcy won the election.

Just prior to the pantaloon incident, Marcy uttered the words that would win him lasting fame and infamy. Although he disliked to speak in public, especially in debate against more tried speakers, Marcy addressed the Senate on January 25, 1832, in regard to the confirmation of the appointment of his friend Martin Van Buren as minister to England. Several speakers had accused Van Buren, as Secretary of State, of introducing to national affairs the system of rewards and punishments notorious in New York State (a reflection on the methods of the

Albany Regency). In defending Van Buren, Marcy said that he could see "nothing wrong in the rule that to the victor belong the spoils of the enemy."

The seemingly harmless phrase caught the ears of the public and made Marcy famous. "To the victor belong the spoils" has passed down through the decades.

Despite the sound bite, when William Marcy became governor, he showed no favoritism in his appointments to the Natural History Survey. He was uninfluenced by party and political considerations. He chose the most qualified and highly recommended men. And they produced important scientific observations.

On February 20, 1838, Governor Marcy said, "The results of their labors in developing our internal resources, and adding to the wealth of the State, will be quite equal to the high expectations which have been formed of the usefulness of the public enterprise." He was correct about the results of their labors "adding to the wealth of the State"—just not in the way he thought they would. He thought wealth would come from developing the natural resources, not from making them a park.

Naming the high peak Mount Marcy did not work the way Ebenezer Emmons thought it would, either. What should have brought honor to William Learned Marcy brought controversy, and few people remembered who he was or why the mountain honored him. However, in 1919, when there was a movement to rename the peak Victory Mountain, those people spoke. See "Victory Mountain Park" chapter.

The editor of the *The Sun* said, "it would be ill-advised to strip that name from the peak."[7] And John Bassett Moore wrote, "Such an act would be worse than vandalism. I do not hesitate to declare that in all the history of the United States there is no name that more fully typifies the glory, the progress and the ideals of the great original American Republic than does that of William Learned Marcy."[8]

Although William Marcy never had an opportunity to visit the slopes of Mount Marcy, he did enjoy a taste from them. At Archibald McIntyre's home in Albany, Marcy feasted on a dinner of fresh trout and moose meat brought from the iron works by guide John Cheney.[9]

Call It Tahawus

Before going one step further I must allude to what I deem the folly of a certain state geologist, in attempting to name the prominent peaks of the Adirondac Mountains after a brotherhood of living men. If he is to have his way in this matter, the beautiful name of Tahawus will be superseded by that of Marcy, and several of Tahawus' brethren are hereafter to be known as Mount Seward, Wright, and Young. Now if this business is not supremely ridiculous, I must confess that I do not know the meaning of the word. A pretty idea, indeed, to scatter to the winds the ancient poetry of the poor Indian, and perpetuate in its place the names of living politicians. For my part, I agree most decidedly with the older inhabitants of the Adirondac wilderness, who look with decided indifference upon the attempted usurpation of the geologist mentioned. CHARLES LANMAN, 1847

THIS "NAME BUSINESS" is "supremely ridiculous" but also titillating. It stirs sentiment and arouses passion. Reverend Joel Headley quipped that Mount Marcy, "as it is foolishly called," should be "properly Mount Tahawus."[1] And, novelist Richard Henry Dana noted that it was "profanely called Mt. Marcy, by some sycophant of a state surveyor."[2]

Such accusations and insults dictate that this ridiculous "name business" be addressed (by some sycophant of an author).

If Lanman's assertion that the peak was originally named Tahawus is correct, then the name Mount Marcy may be profane and foolish. But was the name Tahawus being "superseded" by that of Marcy? Was Tahawus an "ancient" name given by the local Indians?

No! It was a farce.

Poet and author Charles Fenno Hoffman visited the iron works in September 1837, one month after the first ascent. He attempted to climb Mount Marcy despite having an amputated leg. Guide John Cheney said Hoffman "would not be persuaded by words that he could not reach the summit; and when he finally discovered that this task was utterly beyond his accomplishment, his disappointment seemed to have no bounds."[3]

Hoffman penned accounts of his trip, skillfully masking his failure to reach the summit of Marcy. In the *New York Mirror*, he wrote, "The highest peak. . .was measured during the last summer, and found to be nearly six thousand feet in height. Mount Marcy, as it has been christened, not improperly, after the publick [*sic*] functionary who first suggested the survey of this interesting region, presents

a perfect pyramidal top, when viewed from Lake Sanford. The sharp cone was sheathed in snow on the day I took a swim in the lake; the woods around displayed as yet but few autumnal tints, and the deep verdure of the adjacent mountains set off the snowy peak in such high contrast, that soaring as it did far above them, and seeming to pierce, as it were, the blue sky which curtained them, the poetick Indian epithet of TAH-A-WUS, *He splits the sky*, was hardly extravagant to characterize its particular grandeur."[4]

Plaque at Summit of Mount Marcy.

This lovely last sentence caused widespread confusion. Since Hoffman was an authoritative Indian scholar and antiquarian, the public warmly received the name Tahawus and the picturesque translation, Cloud-Splitter. It soon came to be believed that the mountain was originally named Tahawus and the foolish geologist Emmons had changed the name to Mount Marcy.

Possibly Hoffman did not intend this to happen. He did not suggest *naming* the mountain Tahawus; he simply evoked a poetic phrase and neglected to clarify its origin. But Hoffman should have been more astute. Surely, *he* understood the bewilderment concerning Indian names.

In an appendix to his poem "Vigil of Faith," Hoffman wrote, "It is very difficult even with the aid of the straggling Indians who still hunt the wilderness around the sources of the Hudson, to recover the aboriginal terminology. . . . [T]he geographical names, therefore, often traceable to at least four languages, are necessarily much confused."[5] Indeed, they are, Mr. Hoffman, and your inexactness has added to the confusion.

It seems Hoffman never came forward to correct his oversight. Thus, in 1846 author Joel Headley popularized "Tahawus" in his articles. The name of the Lower Works was changed to Tahawus in 1847. And, that same year, some mountaineers formed the Tahawian Association.[6] To complete the contrivance, someone chiseled TAHAWUS into the rocks at the summit.

The nonsense was perpetuated because of growing public sentiment for Indian culture. According to Philip Terrie, Professor of English and American Culture Studies at Bowling Green State University, the growing trend was to transform the image of the Eastern Indian from a devilish presence obstructing American civilization to a figure of myth and romance. Once the Eastern Indians no longer posed a real threat, they began to be romanticized and idealized. It was all part of an unconscious process of idealizing Indians, allowing whites to feel a bit less guilty for having stolen their land.[7]

This sentiment was glaringly evident in author Wallace Bruce's argument for the use of the name Tahawus. He wrote, "There is no justice in robbing the Indian of his keen, poetic appreciation, by changing a name. We have stolen enough from this unfortunate race, to leave, at least, those names in our woodland vocabulary that chance to have a musical sound to our imported Saxon ears."[8]

What an insensitive gesture Bruce made—names in exchange for land, wild game, and a way of life. And who cares if they are authentic names, so long as they are pretty names?

The overwhelming public support for the so-called "aboriginal" names squashed the truth-seekers. In 1865, Alfred Street wrote, "This name was either discovered or invented by that fine poet and profound Indian scholar and antiquarian, Charles F. Hoffman."[9] An 1875 newspaper also reported that the aboriginal origin of Tahawus was "doubtful."[10] Yet, the supposed aboriginal name was firmly established and, as late as 1919, reputable organizations pronounced that

Lake Sanford, circa 1853, by T. Addison Richards.

"the Indians revered it as something sacred and they gave it the name Tahawus."[11]

Finally, in 1921, the truth began to emerge. Alfred Donaldson, in *A History of the Adirondacks*, examined many of the "musical Indian names" in the region. He found that in nearly every case they were recent applications and seldom the names that natives used for the places. In regard to Tahawus, he wrote, "It was probably invented or first applied by Charles Fenno Hoffman, the versatile Indian scholar, who devised and compounded many another Indian name to meet the needs and whims of his poetic fancies."[12]

A few years later, historian Russell Carson found that the name Tahawus was not from the local Abenaki. According to Mitchell Sabattis, "Mount Marcy in the language of the St. Francis tribe was known as Wah-um-de-neg, meaning that it was always white."[13]

So where did the word Tahawus come from? "It is perfect Seneca," according to Dr. Arthur C. Parker, a full-blooded Seneca Indian and the state archeologist in 1924. "Tahawus; he splits the sky," was listed in the 1827 book, *Account of Sundry, Missions performed among the Senecas and Munsees; in a series of Letters.* According to this book, it was not a place name but an abstract word of religion.[14] Hoffman transplanted a picturesque Seneca name to Mount Marcy. "The ancient poetry of the poor Indian" was a farce. Hoffman, not the local Indians, was the first to apply the name Tahawus to the mountain.

As for the usurping of the name, all evidence points to the fact that the name Mount Marcy was given one month before Hoffman used the word Tahawus. Thus, the name Mount Marcy clearly preceded Tahawus.

But the widely read account of William Redfield obscured this fact. It referred to Mount Marcy as the High Peak of Essex. Redfield was on the summit when the peak was named, so why didn't he mention the name Mount Marcy?

Although Redfield said nothing publicly, he may have been miffed about the name. Years later his son wrote, "Certainly it was hardly just that the explorer [Redfield]. . . should not have been honored by its name. . . . At this day it is acknowledged that mountain summits should commemorate the names of scientists rather than those of politicians, or even statesmen."[15]

Regardless, in 1837, Hoffman himself acknowledged that the name had been conferred, "not improperly," after the promoter of the survey. It seems he agreed with the reasons for naming the mountain in honor of Governor William Learned Marcy. Years later, surveyor Verplanck Colvin concurred, noting in his 1874 report: "The titles, Mt. Marcy, Mt. Seward and Mt. Dix, were given years ago by the State Geologists to the peaks which now bear those names. . . . The titles of Mounts Marcy and Seward, though generally accepted, are objected to by many who prefer the 'cleaver of the clouds,' and *Ou-kor-lah,* or the 'great eye.' It seems appropriate, however, that we should have among our mountains, such majestic monuments to those who have so often received the public trust, and in that manner give a peculiar and historical character to our geography."

However, by 1886, Colvin seems to have changed his mind and added to the name confusion. He used "the Marcy group" and "the McIntyre range" to refer to groups of peaks and supplanted the original summit names with "Mt. Tahawus" and "Mt. Algonquin."[16]

In the 1920s, author Russell Carson was greatly disappointed to discover that Tahawus was not the original name and seemed to put forth the same ambiguity as Colvin. "Personally I like the name Tahawus best," wrote Carson. "But really it should make no difference for both names will always exist and we should not forget that Gov. Marcy, while not an Adirondacker, was the originator of the Emmon's [*sic*] survey which was the first great step in opening the Adirondacks to the people, and as such is worthy of such an honor."[17]

Despite the intense historical research Carson conducted in his search for the truth, he allowed the name chaos to continue. In 1937, a plaque was erected to honor the centennial of the first ascent of the mountain. The top portion reads:

1837 - MARCY - 1937
ALSO KNOWN BY THE INDIAN NAME
TAHAWUS MEANING CLOUD-SPLITTER

Of course, the words do not say the Indians used to call the mountain Tahawus. But anyone might interpret it as such. And so, until the forces of nature wear away at man's bronze words, the mountain shall have two names, neither being an aboriginal name for the mountain. One bestows a fitting, poetic platitude and the other honors a man responsible for its exploration.

Tahawus
by Dan Berggren

Some of us are valley dwellers. We never seem to thirst.
Others work upon the prairie where consistency comes first.
But living in the mountains takes strength in every way.
To rise above the timberline is a challenge every day.

chorus:
Tahawus, that's what the natives called it.
Tahawus, the highest of the high.
A mountain that could split the clouds, the wind, the rain and time
And rise above the timberline.

There are men and there are women who stand above the rest.
When clouds of gloom and sorrow put us to the test
They're strong and they're determined to see the light of day.
They rise above the timberline pointing to the way.

The earth is made of water. The earth is made of stone.
It's shared by plants and animals; we do not live alone.
And if we work together who knows what can be done
As we rise above the timberline reaching for the sun.

There are clouds of hate and anger. There are clouds of poverty.
There are those in clouds of sickness, those who are not free.
We need the strength of mountains to see what we can do.
To rise above the timberline and split a cloud or two.

Measuring Up

It is not difficult to imagine, that Mr. Emmons's baro-metric measurement of Mt. Marcy may be farther from the truth than he is willing to admit.

E. F. JOHNSON, 1839

FOR YEARS, the best geographers estimated the northern mountains at something more than a thousand feet. James Macauley, in 1829, in *Natural, Statistical, and Civil History of New York*, asserted that some of the mountains might reach 2,500 or 3,000 feet, but this estimate was not widely accepted.[1] An 1836 State Gazetteer stated that the summits reach heights only "from 500 to 1500 feet above their bases."[2] The northern peaks just did not measure up to the lofty Catskill Mountains, which were confidently maintained to be the highest mountains in New York State. When Ebenezer Emmons came along in 1837 and claimed that Mount Marcy was over 5,000 feet, the figure must have been unbelievable.

Literally unbelievable, according to some. In 1839, Edwin F. Johnson, a civil engineer of the Ogdenburgh and Champlain railroad, reported Mount Marcy to be 4,907 feet tall.[3] He made the calculation without going near the mountain; he used a method of triangulation. By measuring the angle of the summit above a known elevation near Lake Champlain and using the distance to the summit as given on a map, he applied trigonometry to determine the height of Mount Marcy.

Emmons reacted defensively to Johnson's lower altitude for Mount Marcy. Emmons wrote, "I shall merely remark that it is quite doubtful whether the mountain in question is distinguishable from those of the same group, especially by one who has never visited the interior of this section; and if visible, his measurement is not entitled to consideration except as a very imperfect approximation."[4]

Johnson returned the harsh criticism in a long article printed in the prestigious *American Journal of Science*. He defended his instruments as well as his measurement and pointed at possible problems with Emmons' instrument, time and number of observations, and formulas. Johnson claimed that he merely wanted his measurements to be given consideration. It was not his intent "to disparage, in the least, the labors of Mr. Emmons."[5]

Emmons wasted no time in substantiating his measurement. He enlisted the services of Farrand N. Benedict, a professor of mathematics and civil engineering at the University of Vermont. Benedict was a highly respected scientist and no stranger to the Adirondack mountains. Starting in 1835, he had spent a month every summer exploring the region, particularly the rivers, lakes, and ponds.

In the summer of 1839, Benedict promptly set off to climb Mount Marcy, taking with him George McRae, a young botanist. Benedict's barometric readings from the summit began at 6:07 a. m. on August 14 and continued until 10:30 a. m. The day was windy and the summit was engulfed in clouds and rain. McRae and guide John Cheney retreated to a sheltered spot, leaving Benedict alone on the summit to take his readings in the rain.[6]

What did Benedict experience in that solitude atop Mount Marcy's summit as the storm moved away and the sky cleared? Benedict was not one to express such sentiments. But his cousin, Joel T. Headley, was. Evidently, Benedict told his story to Headley, who later printed an embellished version: "He was in the clear sunlight, while an ocean of clouds rolled on below him in vast white undulations, blotting out the whole creation from his view. At length, under the influence of the sun, this limitless deep slowly rent asunder, and the black top of a mountain emerged like an island from the mighty mass, and then another and another, till away, for more than three hundred miles in circumference, these black conical

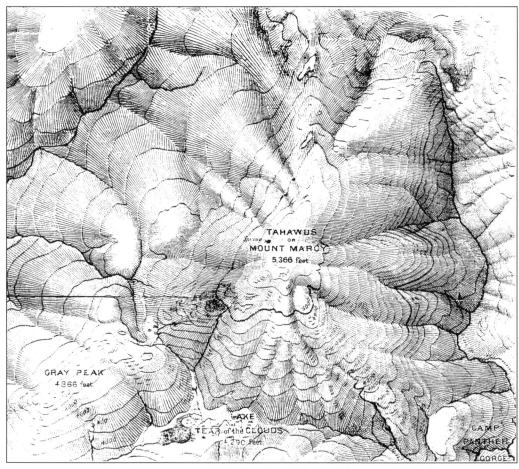

Adirondack Survey, 1873. Sketch of Mount Marcy and Pond
Source of the Hudson River by Colvin.

islands were sprinkled over the white bosom of the vapory sea. . . .It is impossible to conceive anything half so strange and wild."[7]

In Benedict's long technical report to Emmons, there are no such flowery passages. Benedict chose to pass over every personal circumstance connected with his ascent.[8] Instead, he reported in detail how his ten barometric measurements determined the mean height to be 5,344.69 feet. Benedict's measurement not only validated Emmons' calculation but has proven to be amazingly precise—to within one foot.

Despite repeated measurements, skeptics kept challenging the results. "The right of Mount Marcy to chieftainship was even disputed by some, who thought Mount MacIntyre the highest," wrote surveyor Verplanck Colvin in 1874, "and I decided to settle this vexed question by comparative measurements made at the same instant of time on both mountains." Using the triangulation method, he determined Mount Marcy to be the highest and to have a mean altitude of 5,402.65 feet. This was determined "from 222 selected observations."[9]

Still, the only way to truly settle the question was by level and rod. This meant running a line of levels over every inch of every mile from a known benchmark in Westport to the summit of Mount Marcy. The vastness, difficulty, and danger of such an undertaking were tremendous. But Colvin attempted it in 1875.

It was late September before Colvin received funds to take to the field that year. He left the selection of the route mostly to guide Orson

Colvin Survey Crew Measuring with Spirit-Level and graduated Rod, on Whiteface Mountain by Colvin.

"Old Mountain" Phelps, who worked his way through the thick forest with a bush-hook, clearing a sight line for the leveling team. "Of course there was but little in the way of two surveyors running the line of levels west from Westport to the head of the [Keene] Flats," wrote Phelps, "but from the head of the Flats to the summit of old Tahawus was a different thing."[10]

While Phelps did his work, Colvin made a march for the summit of Marcy. On October 22, he wrote, "Now we saw above us the strange, cold, ashy dome of the mountain, alpine, in the deep, yellowish patches of snow, which, mixed with tints of gray and green, gave the wild peak a weird contrast with the deep-blue sky. The soft snow in the upper forest was here trampled by the footprints of wild beasts; above the timber line hundreds of snow birds (Plectrophanes) rose fluttering at our approach, and two eagles, rising from the gulf at the east, soared past us majestically, unmindful of revolver shots. At 3 P. M. we stood again upon the well-remembered summit."[11]

On Wednesday, October 27, it snowed all day to a depth of eight inches. By Thursday, provisions were running short and a guide was sent to Keene. The leveling party made it to the notch below the summit, but Phelps warned about poor prospects for further work due to bad weather. That night, the men supped on bear meat. The next day, the guide returned with provisions from Keene—more bear meat.

Colvin climbed to the summit again and noted the leveling progress. They had reached an altitude of 4,799 feet above tide—"already the highest point so far reached by any regular leveling work in New York."

That wasn't enough for Colvin. He wanted to push upward. The next morning, the party faced dense fog and icy ledges. "The black cliffs of Haystack are grim with monstrous yellowish icicles," wrote Colvin. Old Mountain Phelps warned again that they should retreat, "fearing least [sic] we may be entrapped in the deep snows in the gorge."

Colvin would not relent. He carried forward with his mission.

November 1 was bitterly cold. The winds were seventy miles per hour. One man froze both his ears. The temperature at mid-day was zero. Phelps left for home.

Two days later, Colvin got a break; the weather turned bright and clear and still. The party hurried to re-ascend Marcy, now deeply drifted with snow and coated with ice. As they approached timberline, Colvin took charge of the level. "Determined the timber line on Marcy at this point to have a height of 4,890 feet above tide," he wrote. "At evening I had run the line upward to within two hundred feet of vertical height of the summit."

The next day, November 4, was somewhat cloudy and cold. The barometer indicated an approaching storm. "Without rest, without food, we worked, eagerly, fiercely, determinedly all day," wrote Colvin, "and at length as evening approached we could see our goal just above us, and at 4:50 p.m. I placed the level on the summit of Marcy. . . and then the party broke out spontaneously into hurrahs! But their voices and revolver shots sounded weak and faint in that thin, frosty atmosphere, and in the increasing duskiness, the men with moustaches, and eyebrows, and clothing white with frost—the instruments also frost encrusted—had a wild and singular appearance, in consonance with the place, season and occasion."

They determined the height of Mount Marcy to be 5,344.311 feet above mean tide. Colvin wrote, "The last entries made—the field-books closed—we commenced the descent of the peak, the darkness of another severe storm closing in as we descended. But storms were no longer fearful to us, for the much needed work was done. Our vertical angles and hypsometrical work could now be computed on an accurate basis, and I had the satisfaction of having made the first positive measurement with level and rod of the highest land in New York—the summit of *Ta-ha-wus*."

That night, Colvin and his men celebrated their accomplishment. In honor of the event they ate a choice supper of bear's meat "fried, boiled and stewed." Then, unmindful of the snow storm that had arrived, they fell fast asleep.

On November 6, they broke camp and set out to leave, but found Upper Ausable Lake frozen. They broke a passage through the ice for their boat to reach open water. Then they found that Lower Ausable Lake was a sheet of ice, "too thick to break a passage with boat, apparently too thin to hold a man," while the rocks along the shore were combed with ice and made walking impossible.

They had no choice. They loaded their baggage into a heavy boat and chopped the ice with the weight of the boat. "At length the ice refused to yield," wrote Colvin, "and cautiously stepping from the boat, the water rising above the ice we drew the boat up, and turned it into a sled; then led by one of the guides, who far ahead selected a safe route on firm ice, we drew our uncouth craft along the frozen lake."

They reached the outlet safely, having accomplished the most daring measurement of Mount Marcy ever made. No one came forward to challenge the work of these men. Even today's surveyors, who use metric measurements, have found Mount Marcy to be 1,629 meters, which is 5,344 feet—the same height calculated by Colvin's men, and by Farrand Benedict in 1839.

Colvin Survey Crew Crossing Lower Ausable Lake, 1875. Detail of a drawing by Colvin.

Trips Up the Opalescent

The bed of the stream is full of that exquisitely beautiful mineral [opalescent feldspar]. We saw it glittering in splendour, in pebbles and large boulders, when the sunlight fell full upon the shallow water. A rich blue is the predominant colour, sometimes mingled with a brilliant green. Gold and bronze-coloured specimens have been discovered, and, occasionally, a completely iridescent piece may be found. It is to the abundance of these stones that the river is indebted for its beautiful name.
BENSON LOSSING, ABOUT THE OPALESCENT RIVER, 1859

IN HIS 1838 REPORT to the Governor of New York, geologist Ebenezer Emmons remarked that the heights of these mountains "gave an unusual interest to this section, and has induced already many gentlemen to visit. . .this region of mountain; and it will undoubtedly in a few years become a favorite place of resort to persons of leisure."[1]

Emmons was correct. Scientists, writers, botanists, poets, painters, and just plain hikers did come to the region. Many visited the McIntyre Iron Works, which had resumed operations and become known as Adirondack Iron Works. Some even went up Mount Marcy, following the river filled with opalescent feldspar.

Poet and author Charles Fenno Hoffman wasted no time; he came in September 1837, just one month after the first ascent party. His accounts were published in *The New-York Mirror* and, later, in *Wild Scenes in the Forest and Prairie*. Although he failed to ascend Mount Marcy, Hoffman attempted to describe the summit. He quoted a "hunter," presumably guide John Cheney: "It makes a man feel what it is to have all creation placed beneath his feet. There are woods there which it would take a lifetime to hunt over, mountains that seem shouldering each other to boost the one whereon you stand up and away, heaven knows where."[2]

The next gentlemen known to make an ascent of Mount Marcy were Professor Farrand Benedict and botanist George McRae. As discussed in the previous chapter, Benedict measured the peak on August 14, 1839, to settle the squabble over Marcy's height. Years later, Benedict wrote an account of their climb up the "zigzag path" to Mount Marcy. He said he had "passed by, through, and around lakes, over hills, gulfs and streams, taking water-beds for paths and guides, tumbling over logs and through swamps" to get to the foot of the mountain. Then, the real ascent began. He crawled on his hands and knees, wedged his way through the thick brush, leaped a chasm, and trod on a frail tree bridge.[3]

As he climbed higher, he noticed that the trees grew thinner and smaller: "The pines and firs that below were one hundred feet high, are now but fifty." Farther along, "the tall fir tree has dwindled down to a pigmy of a few inches in height." Near the top, all vegetation ceased. The rocks were bare.

Benedict remarked that it was summer at the foot of the mountain, but at the top it was almost winter. "We have gone back two seasons in a few hours," he wrote.

Then he described his experience of being on the summit as a storm cleared away.

> What a landscape is here! [W]e bound the horizon on either side with a circle of four hundred miles. A dense fog has settled down between the hills and filled up the valleys; nothing visible but the tops of the mountains. It looks like a vast ocean, with numberless pyramidal islands scattered about. . . . But the curtain of fog is being lifted up; rents here and there give a glimpse of the green forests below. A little while and the sky is clear; we look down now upon the wide forests, extending as far as the eye can reach. . . . An interesting feature of the view is the number of lakes that are reposing quietly, protected by walls of rock and forest, that, near at hand, are spread out like sheets of silver, clear and unbroken, while at a distance they become mere white specks or lines, surrounded by deep green. The different species of trees display a varied foliage, mingling a dark row of evergreen with the orange and golden hues of the deciduous, while the tall tops of the pine and fir shoot above the rest, to tell of their locality and first greet the sun. We can see the light cloud beneath us, while its shadow moves over the forest tops like a thing of life; nature is here in her primeval beauty and splendor.[4]

In 1846, Benedict's cousin, author Joel Headley, climbed Mount Marcy. Headley was a Protestant minister but had suffered a nervous breakdown in 1842. He sailed to Italy to recover his health and discovered that people would pay to read about his travels.

Headley came to the Adirondack wilderness to refresh "an unsteady and an unusable brain."[5] His account, published in book form in 1849 as *The Adirondack; or, Life in the Woods*, was the first piece of popular romantic travel writing about the Adirondacks. "Here there are no mule paths, as in Switzerland, leading to the bases of mountains, whence you can mount to the summits; but all is woods! woods! woods!" he wrote. "The highest and most picturesque of the Adirondack peaks lie deep in the forest, where none but an experienced guide can carry you."[6]

His Mount Marcy adventure began on July 12. "Hurrah! we are off," he wrote, "and crossing a branch of the Hudson near its source, enter the forest, Indian file. . . . [W]e strained forward—now treading over a springy marsh—now stooping and crawling like lame iguanas, through a swamp of spruce trees, and anon following the path made by deer and moose. . . until, at length, we reached Lake Colden."[7]

It was almost impossible to walk through the forest. So instead, they kept to the Opalescent River, "so called from the opals found in its bed." After tramping five miles, they emerged at the base of the bare, naked pyramid of Mount Marcy. From there, they climbed until, "At length we reached the top; and oh, what a view spread out before, or rather below us. . . . It looked as if the Almighty had once set this vast earth rolling like the sea; and then, in the midst of its maddest flow, bid all the gigantic billows stop and congeal in their places. And there they stood, just as He froze them—grand and gloomy."[8]

"Man is nothing here," continued Headley, "his very shouts die on his lips. One of our company tried to sing, but his voice fled from him into the empty space. We fired a gun, but it gave only half a report, and no echo came back, for there was nothing to check the sound in its flight. . . . And this is New York, I at length exclaimed."

According to this account, Headley made it up in one day, starting at seven in the morning and reaching the top at four in the afternoon. Quite a feat! A good start at the record-breaking game that some hikers would play in future decades.

A guide named Thompson said that Headley left an unfavorable impression and that some of his stories were greatly exaggerated.[9] This leaves us to ponder the truths we read, especially in popular accounts. Yet many of these accounts are genuine and insightful. Headley's story about the accidental death of David Henderson is such a piece.

"We came to the rock where he was shot," wrote Headley. "It stands by a little pond, and was selected by them to dine upon. Cheney was standing on the other side of the pond. . .when he heard the report of a gun, and then a scream; and looking across, saw Mr. Henderson clasp his arms twice over his breast, exclaiming, 'I am shot!'"[10]

This first "calamity" associated with Mount Marcy occurred on September 3, 1845. Henderson was not climbing mountains; he was looking for a water supply for the Adirondack Iron Works. Henderson dreamed that he could make the iron works produce a fortune if he could find a more powerful waterway to drive the blasts for the furnaces and to turn the wheels of the forge. He knew there was an endless supply of iron ore below the forest—if only he could make better use of it.

The company's engineer, Daniel Taylor, thought he could build a half-mile canal to connect the Opalescent with the branch of the Hudson now called Calamity Brook. So off through the woods went Taylor and Henderson to investigate the site. They took along Henderson's ten-year-old son, Archie, and guides John Cheney and Tone Snyder.

Upon arriving at the pond at the head of the brook, Henderson spotted some ducks and told Cheney, "Take my pistol and kill some of those ducks." The birds flew off before Cheney had a shot. He handed the pistol, still cocked, back to Henderson.

Cheney and Archie circled to the other side of the pond to go fishing. Then they heard the fatal shot. Ducks circled high in the sky. The guides ran from the woods. Archie ran to his father's side. It appeared that as Henderson threw his knapsack and pistol belt onto a rock at the water's edge, the cocked pistol struck the rock. The ball entered his side and passed upwards through his heart.

"What an accident, and in such a place!" Henderson said. A moment later, he added, "Archie, be a good boy, and give my love to your mother." A few minutes later he died.

Tone Snyder hurried back to the village to get men to help carry out the body. On their way up the narrow path, they cut bushes and branches and small trees to clear a trail. At the pond the other men built a crude stretcher of poles and balsam boughs. When the village men arrived, they placed the body on the stretcher and began making their way through the woods.

The *Plattsburgh Republican* remarked that "this dreadful calamity occurred in the woods."[11] The word stuck. Shortly afterwards, author Richard Henry Dana Jr. referred to "Calamity Pond."[12] Later, the stream took the name Calamity Brook and the nearby hill became Calamity Mountain.

Scientists and authors were not the only visitors to the Mount Marcy region in the 1830s and 1840s. Several artists came, too. The artist Charles Ingham, who was a member of the first ascent party, returned in 1838 with another artist, James Linen.[13] But Ingham probably did not struggle up Mount Marcy again.

In late September of 1846, the artist Thomas Cole visited the area, sketching the scenery of Indian Pass, Adirondack Iron Works, and other spots.[14] Guide John Cheney said Cole climbed to the top of Marcy.[15] Cole did paint a scene in 1847 that has been titled "Mount Marcy from the Opalescent River (Indian Pass-Tahawus)".* But the scene is not an accurate rendition of any real location, so it is unclear if Cole ever climbed along the Opalescent, let alone up Marcy.

It is certain that artist and writer Charles Lanman climbed Mount Marcy in June of 1847. "I ascended Tahawus, as a matter of course," he wrote, "and in making the trip I traveled some twenty miles on foot and through the pathless woods, employing for the same the better part of two days. My companion on this expedition was John Cheney."[16]

"We only spent about one hour gazing upon the panorama from the top," wrote Lanman, "and then descended about half way down the mountain where we built our watch fire." Apparently, Lanman had wished to spend the night on the summit, but Cheney had not thought it prudent. Cheney proved wise, as during the night "a regular built rainstorm" arrived.[17]

Both men were drenched to the very skin. The thunder bellowed and "the lightning seemed determined to root up a few trees in our immediate vicinity, as if for the purpose of giving us more room. Finally Cheney rose from his pillow (which was a log of wood), and proposed that we should quaff a little brandy, to keep us from catching cold, which we did, and then made another attempt to reach the land of Nod."[18]

Regarding Cheney, Lanman said, "He is a remarkably amiable and intelligent man, and as unlike the idea I had formed of him, as possible. I expected, from all that I had heard, to see a huge, powerful and hairy Nimrod; but instead of such, I found him small in stature, and bearing more the appearance of a modest and thoughtful student."[19]

Henderson Monument at Calamity Pond.

---

*The painting is now at the Museum of Fine Arts in Houston.

John Cheney had developed a reputation that evidently was larger than life. Author Charles Fenno Hoffman had called him a mighty hunter and a real-life version of Cooper's Leatherstocking.[20] Cheney became the first of a long line of local men and women being employed as professional mountain guides, hired not only as hunters and fishermen but also to lead parties to the top of Mount Marcy.

Guide John Cheney by Stoddard.

He guided scientist Farrand Benedict in 1839,[21] was Cole's "guide and entertainer" and Headley's "experienced guide" in 1846, and now was Lanman's "companion."

Travelers definitely needed a woodsman guide for the trip up Mount Marcy. But even with a guide, the Opalescent route was rough and difficult. Did it need to be so? Trails had been built up Mount Washington. Could there not be a decent trail up Mount Marcy?

The first known proposal for an Adirondack Mountain trail was made on October 18, 1847. The Tahawian Association, a group that included town and county supervisors, met at the Essex County courthouse in Elizabethtown. Archibald McIntyre, proprietor of the Adirondack Iron Works, presided. The group approved a project to build "a pedestrian road through the wilderness in the western section of Essex County to the tops of TAHAWUS and WHITEFACE."[22]

It was quite an ambitious plan. The trail was to go "from Keene Flats, westward to the summit of Tahawus, estimated distance ten miles; thence down to the Adirondac and Tahawus Iron Works, fifteen miles; thence northward through the Adirondac [Indian] Pass to Lake Placid, seventeen miles; thence eastward to the top of Whiteface and down to Wilmington, eight miles—the whole distance estimated fifty miles."[23]

This plan is quite surprising. There is no record of any of the officers having climbed Mount Marcy. And no known ascent had ever been made from the east side. How did these men think it could be done? And who did they think would use this trail? Cheney said that no one had climbed Marcy from 1840 to 1846. Yet the association discussed "the advantages, which would accrue to the health seeking pedestrians of our Literary Institutions, and other classes of the cities and villages of the land."

Perhaps they were referring to the major promoter of this project, Dr. David P. Holton, Superintendent of Schools for Essex County. It was claimed that Holton climbed Mount Marcy in 1840 and cut "phonographic" characters into the summit rock. However, according to author George Marshall, the text of the original account was unclear; it looks as though they may have been "pornographic" characters.[24]

It is quite doubtful that Holton cut into Marcy's summit rocks in 1840, but he did engrave phonetic symbols on Whiteface Mountain in July of 1847. A month later he led a "Tahawus Celebration" at the Adirondack Iron Works. A poem titled "Comstock Phonetic Alphabet" was written especially for the celebration and included, as Marshall called it, "one of the earliest descriptions in bad verse of the view from Tahawus."[25]

> We stand and look down on the Empire State!
> Girt by the Clinton range which doth await
> Upon Tahawus; We rejoice to see
> Our mountain mid his giant family.
> Explode the elements of our nervous speech
> Which all the tongues of man combine t'enrich!
>
> —
>
> Ring out the Saxon consonated cry
> And let the iron-echoed crags reply.

The ceremonies were followed by an ascent of Mount Marcy where Holton and his party engraved the phonetic alphabet. Old Mountain Phelps said the characters were visible in 1849, but another visitor that year did not notice any phonetic characters. Instead, he found that someone—perhaps from the Tahawian Association—had chiseled the word TAHAWUS into the granite.[26]

Despite Holton's energetic spirit, the grand trail project stalled at the planning stage. It would be more than ten years before the first formal trail was built on Mount Marcy. Yet the pathways must have been improving, because in 1849 a party made the fastest trip ever—and without Cheney. A participant in this ordeal was the famous author Richard Henry Dana Jr.

Dana was feeling run down and his physician advised him to journey to the mountains. So he left Boston and came to the Adirondacks with Theodore Metcalf as his traveling companion. At Westport, a friend introduced them to Villeroy S. Aikens, an experienced woodsman and sportsman, who joined the group. The party rode westward to Keene and stopped at a cabin for breakfast. It turned out that the cabin was the Flanders house along present-day Route 73 and the man living there was John Brown, the abolitionist.

The party then proceeded through Indian Pass, carrying little more than overcoats. Dana wrote, "In the pocket of my coat I had a knife, a comb & a handkerchief, & these were literally all I had. No change of dress of any kind, & nothing for toilet but a comb. Our guide took some crackers & a flask of brandy, & we set out."[27]

After seventeen miles of walking, they found their way to the village of Adirondac. "Here was no attempt at taste, hardly any at neatness or even comfort," wrote Dana.[28] The accommodations consisted of a bath in the stream, a place to sleep on the floor of the boarding house, which lodged ninety-six iron-workers, and a poor supper of milk, bread, pork, and potatoes.

About six o'clock on the morning of June 25, Dana, Metcalf, and Aikens set out for Marcy. Since Cheney was busy, their guides were Dan Gates, John Might, and a tall Vermonter. The six men walked rapidly along a good path to Calamity Pond. Then they passed over rocks and through swamps until they reached the Opalescent River. "Its course is very irregular, & often broken by cascades, rapids, deep basins, & gorges," wrote Dana. "In one of these Metcalf & I bathed, stripping & plunging in from the rocks, & swimming up under the fall."

They found an old camping spot, ate dinner, and then marched on. Dana wrote, "The ascent of this summit for the last mile is probably the most difficult mountain ascent in America, owing mainly to the dense growth of scrub cedars and spruces, almost impenetrable, which must be struggled thro', every step being a strenuous effort. This could be avoided by a few hours' work of half a dosen men with axes."[29]

It had taken the party about eight hours to go fifteen miles. That is three hours faster than Headley's ascent, if anyone was keeping records. They stayed on the summit for an hour and then descended to the Opalescent River. After walking a couple of miles, they camped for the night. They left at five o'clock the next morning and returned to the village at nine o'clock, having made "the shortest passages both up & down which have ever been made." Evidently Dana was counting.

The party ate lunch at Adirondac, had a farewell drink, and set off through Indian Pass with Mr. Aikens serving as their guide. He had never been through the pass except in coming over, but being a good woodsman, he thought he was able to find

Fall in the Opalescent River.
The Flume by Lossing.

the way. He wasn't. They became lost and spent the cold night in an old, deserted shanty. Dinner was one small trout, which Aikens caught using a piece of his red shirt for bait.

In the morning, as they left the clearing, they found a trodden path and followed it. Eventually they arrived at Brown's house. "Three more ragged, dirty, & hungry men seldom called at a house for breakfast," Dana wrote.[30]

But they held the honor of the fastest trip up Marcy. And the first known ascent made by a party from North Elba. Of course, many followed their footsteps. Years later, a trail was cut directly from North Elba to the summit. Eventually, this became the most popular trail to Marcy.

Meanwhile, the pathway from the Upper Works along the Opalescent to the summit seemed to improve. Perhaps a few men with axes did a few hours' work as Dana suggested because, in 1851, a party made it seem like a simple walk in the woods.

Artist Jervis McEntee, his friend and artist Joseph Tubby, and Joseph's son Josiah came to visit the region. Before going up Marcy, they stopped at the village of Adirondac (or Upper Works), which was enjoying its heyday as an iron operation and as a tourist spot. Steel made from Adirondack Iron Works ore had just won first place at the 1851 World's Fair. The village now had about twenty houses and its own post office.

After several days of sightseeing, the party felt ready to ascend Marcy. Their guide was a man named Puffer, who had never been up Marcy. So before they left, they obtained directions from two men. Mr. Wright at the boarding house discussed the route with them. The next morning, a Mr. Clark gave them further directions and walked with them for half a mile to make sure they had a fair start.

The fair start turned into a bad start for McEntee. He fell while fishing at Calamity Pond and badly bruised his knee. "I felt very faint for a moment," he wrote in his journal. "It pained me very much so that I thought strongly of going back which I afterwards regretted I did not do."[31]

The party continued around the pond and came to a path, which they followed to Lake Colden. From there, they followed the streambed of the Opalescent until they came to the camp at the foot of the mountain. They spent the night and then started climbing again at 4:30 in the morning.

"Ascending the stream a few rods above the camp we struck a trail which we followed to the top of the first ridge and above vegetation. . .The ascent had been very easy so far and we were now at the foot of the bare rocks which composed the summit and which rose a thousand feet above us grim and terrible," McEntee wrote.[32]

They drank from a good spring and continued to the summit.

The ease with which this party ascended the peak is surprising. Unlike previous parties, they had no difficult climbing or struggling through pathless woods. They found a path from Calamity Pond to Lake Colden. They had no trouble following the streambed and finding the old camp. Most incredibly, they found a trail up the ridge, avoiding the "scrub cedars and spruces" that had plagued Dana's party. For some strange reason, subsequent parties did not find this trail.

McEntee's party stayed on the summit for five hours, warming themselves with a fire built "from the stumps of the low and ragged spruces." As for the view, McEntee wrote, "Gleaming lakes and dim vallies [*sic*] stretched far away and the sad and solemn gloom of the unbroken forest sent not a sound from its vast abodes below to that still summit where we stood. I shall never forget that desolate mountain top with its frowning rocks and the deep impressive silence of its summit."[33]

Wind and mist moved over the summit as they descended. The fog became so thick that they could not find the place where they came up the rocks—a frequent, and often disastrous, situation that occurs on Mount Marcy. This party was lucky. They finally discovered the path they had followed on the way up and were soon safely down to the ridge. Here they struck another "more distinct trail" and in a very short time were at the foot of the stream. They continued all the way back to the village that day.

"My knee was painful and very much swollen," wrote McEntee, "and our clothes were torn almost off our bodies so that being ashamed to go ourselves we sent Puffer to the post office while we sat down by the road and awaited his return."[34]

Despite his pain and shame, McEntee climbed Mount Marcy again in 1866. Artist Sanford R. Gifford accompanied him, and sketched several scenes along the way.[35]

The drawings and paintings of Gifford, McEntee, Cole, Ingham, and other artists showed the mountain region to the world. The travel narratives of Hoffman, Headley, and Lanman enchanted city folks. The romantic ornamentation of the language of the sublime that filled their writings—the "grand and gloomy" mountains, "frowning cliffs," and "solemn woods"—appealed to the popular interest in nature.

But the urban population was interested not only in reading about the wilderness; they wanted to go see the glories of nature. The Adirondack region was a ready-made retreat. "We can retire from the busy world, away from its noise and tumult, its cares and perplexities," wrote Farrand Benedict in *Putnam's Monthly*. "We can here invigorate the body with healthful and pleasant exercise, with the pure air and the fresh breeze. We can charm the imagination with beautiful scenery, the calm lake, the towering mountain, the gorgeous sunset, the wave tops of the forest ocean. We can feast the intellect on the sublimity of the heights and depths, on the displays of the mighty power of nature, on the works of an artist, that has just put the finishing on and spread over them the canopy of heaven."[36]

Who could resist that feast? More tourists visited the region. And, soon, it was not only gentlemen tourists who were induced to follow the Opalescent River to Mount Marcy. Women were on their way, too.

Coming Round the Mountain

When we at last reached the crown of the mountain,
Marianna herself, who was our standard-bearer, solemn-
ly declared that she would not make the ascent again
[even] if the Queen of Sheba were coming up on the other
side to meet her.

T. ADDISON RICHARDS, 1859

IN HIS 1857 BOOK, *Appleton's Illustrated Hand-Book of American Travel*, author and artist T. Addison Richards encouraged tourists to allow forty-eight hours to do the tramp—"par excellence, of the Adirondack"—to the summit of the Mount Marcy. He also warned that it was a twelve-mile trip and extremely toilsome.[1]

In a later essay, published in the September 1859 issue of *Harper's Monthly*, Richards told the story of his own toilsome trip to Mount Marcy. The startling part was that his party included four women. If McEntee's and Tubby's clothes were torn almost off their bodies, how could women possibly survive a mountain excursion?

Richards' article speaks to the question:

"Such a life is not exactly the thing for women," said we [Richards and his companion, Westcott], in conclusion.

"Stuff!" interrupted Tahawus [the guide]. "They come here safely enough sometimes, and I often wonder we don't see many more of them. . . for the women has got more grit than the men, after all, when you put them to their trumps."

"And by the Commodore," cried Westcott, "some of 'em seem to think so, for yonder's a camp and I thought I heard a woman's rattle!"[2]

This playful dialogue sets the scene for the arrival of three ladies, their maid Marianna, three gentlemen, and two guides. Richards' party joined this party and the next day, they set out together for the village of Lower Works (Tahawus).

The ladies trolled for pickerel in Lake Sanford and fished for trout in Lake Henderson. Later, Marianna earned the "laurels of the day." When the guide wounded a deer, she quickly lifted a rifle and shot the deer dead.

Finally, the ladies felt ready to venture upon "the supreme exploit of our Adirondack travel—the ascent of the great Mount Tahawus." The journey proved difficult, especially for the men who, "dreaming that their strength was inexhaustible, spent it prodigally in every frolicsome feat which the changing way and their exuberant spirits invited." The ladies proved to be more provident but were "well contented with the length and labor of the walk."

One of Richards' engravings showed a lady clinging to a branch and gentlemen assisting two ladies as they clamber up a steep gully. The fourth lady, presumably Marianna, the "standard-bearer," stood atop the knoll triumphantly waving a flag.[3]

The entire party finally reached the summit. Did the ladies enjoy the view? I do not know; I only know that Marianna said she would not make the ascent again "if the Queen of Sheba were coming up on the other side to meet her."[4]

Historian Russell Carson discounted this tale since in one of his books Richards admitted that he wrote "to relieve the gravity of fact with the grace of fiction, as to present at the same time an instructive topography and an entertaining romance."[5]

The Ascent of Mount Marcy, circa 1853, by T. Addison Richards.

But Richards' accompanying sketches show women shooting deer and mounting a summit. Since no other women had ever climbed Marcy, why invent such a scene? Perhaps Richards enhanced the story but I believe the events actually happened, although not in 1859. The sketch "The Great Indian Pass," which accompanies the article, is dated September 23, 1853. Thus it seems likely that the climb occurred in 1853, making it the first known ascent of Mount Marcy by women.

History tells us that many men thought women were too weak or frail to climb mountains. Perhaps their aversion to climbing had more to do with fashion. Corsets, girdles, petticoats, and heavy floor-length skirts hampered women like Marianna and her lady friends. And society hampered them even more. The prevailing notion was that women should show no athletic vigor or adventurous spirit.

Richards expressed the same notion in *The Romance of American Landscape*. In a chapter about the Adirondacks, he wrote, "What can our drawing-room belles do in a country which can be traversed only on foot, or in boats. . . and which must always confine their wardrobes to the narrow limits of a carpet-bag or a knapsack; and where, too, the paths, when such blessings are found at all, are over jagged rocks."[6]

More women stepped forward to show exactly what belles could do. In 1858, Mary Cook and Fannie Newton climbed Mount Marcy from the east. And on August 31, 1859, Helen Lossing followed the footsteps of Marianna up the Opalescent to the summit. Her husband, Benson J. Lossing, described and illustrated the feat in *The Hudson from the Wilderness to the Sea*: "Indeed it was a triumph for us all, for few persons have ever attempted the ascent of that mountain, lying deep in the wilderness, hard to penetrate, the nearest point of even a bridle path, on the side of our approach, being ten miles from the base of its peak. Especially difficult is it for the feet of woman to reach the lofty summit of the *Sky-piercer*—almost six thousand feet above the sea—for her skirts form great impediments."

Climbing Tahawus, 1859, by Lossing.

Afterwards, John Cheney supposedly told Mrs. Lossing that she was "only the third woman who has ever accomplished the difficult feat."[7] Then, presumably, Mary Cook and Fannie Newton were the first two women up Marcy, and Richards' account about Marianna and her friends must be pure fiction. That has been the long-held conclusion, as printed in *Peaks and People*.[8]

New evidence raises perplexing questions about this claim. When did Cheney make this statement? After the climb, Lossing stopped by Cheney's house but found Cheney was not home. Did he talk to Cheney later? Examination of Lossing's field notebook shows no mention of meeting Cheney. Lossing's reputation for sometimes enhancing facts to make the story more interesting— one author even dared to call him "a mere hack"[9]—brings into question the origin of this statement.

Helen Sweet Lossing.
Courtesy of
New York State Library.

And what women preceded Helen Lossing up Marcy? The *Essex County Republican* reported Cook to be "the first woman that ever stood upon its summit." But the next week they printed a retraction: "I wish to correct an error. Miss Mary Cook was not the first woman to ascend Tahawus. She was the second."[10]

If Cook was not the first woman up Marcy, who was? We'll probably never know for sure, but Marianna and her friends made the earliest ascent discovered so far. And, even though Helen Lossing was not the third woman up Marcy, hers was the first well-documented climb.

Benson Lossing is wholly guilty of making this story "interesting." His details of everything from the intolerable mosquito to maple sugaring to dwarf balsam enhance the narrative and provide valuable historical information. Of particular interest is his description, the first printed description, of a woman's outfit for a Mount Marcy excursion. Lossing wrote, "A woman needs a stout flannel dress, over shortened crinoline,* of short dimensions, with loops and buttons to adjust its length; a hood and cape of the same materials, made so as to envelop the head and bust, and leave the arms free, woolen stockings, stout calfskin boots that cover the legs to the knee, well saturated with beeswax and tallow, and an india-rubber satchel for necessary toilet materials."[11]

What about supplies? Lossing said provisions should be simple. Some salted pork should be brought to use for frying the fish, birds, and game that the guides would provide. And, a short-handled frying pan, a tin pan, tin tea or coffee pot, tin plates and cups, knives, forks, and spoons would be needed.

*A petticoat of coarse, stiff, cotton fabric, formerly made of horsehair and linen.

Lossing gave a word of advice as to when to visit, cautioning "never enter this wilderness earlier than the middle of August. Then the flies and mosquitoes, the intolerable pests of the forests, are rapidly disappearing, and fine weather may be expected." He undertook his own trip on August 29.

Once again, Lossing provided striking details in his description of the route to Marcy. He wrote that the walk from Lake Henderson to Calamity Pond was on a "sinuous mountain path" that "lay along the track of a lane" cut to erect a monument at the pond. A few years after Henderson's death the family put a sandstone monument, eight feet in height, upon the rock where he was shot. The heavy monument was transported through the woods in wintertime on a sled drawn by oxen.

The party of Lossing and his wife; his companion, Mr. Buckingham; and the guides, Mitchell Sabattis and William Preston, camped by the pond and continued climbing at eight o'clock the next morning. Between Calamity Pond and Lake Colden, "there was nothing but a dim and obstructed hunter's trail to follow."[12] From there they followed the streambed of the Opalescent River. Lossing noted the size of the stones in the river ranged from tiny pebbles to huge boulders. He remarked about their color, too, noting the rich blue, brilliant green, gold, and even iridescent pieces.

It took the party four hours and little exertion to climb high up the valley to the foot of Mount Marcy. "The water is very cold, the forest trees are somewhat stunted and thickly planted, and the solitude complete," wrote Lossing. Yet, there were signs of civilization, even in this remote and silent spot. They found "an excellent bark 'camp,' and traces of recent occupation. Among them was part of a metropolitan newspaper, and light ashes."[13]

After a snack, they climbed toward the summit. "The journey upward was two miles, at an angle of forty-five degrees to the base of the rocky pinnacle," wrote Lossing. "We had no path to follow. The guides 'blazed' the larger trees (striking off chips with their axes), that they might with more ease find their way back to camp."

Why didn't the guides Mitchell Sabattis and William Preston follow the ridge route that McEntee had taken in 1851? Evidently, there was not a favored route over the last one or two miles to the summit. Most parties blazed a direct, but difficult, path while others, like McEntee, took a longer route that proved to be much easier and faster. Perhaps the guides tended to take the steep and strenuous route to impress their clients. Maybe the guides feared that their services would be unwarranted if they showed their clients the easy route. Dangerous, pathless woods meant job security.

Every danger and fatigue was forgotten when Lossing set foot on the summit. "Our view from the summit of Tahawus will ever form one of the most remarkable pictures in memory;" wrote Lossing, "and yet it may not properly be called a *picture*. It is a topographical map, exhibiting a surface diversified by mountains, lakes, and valleys."

Departure for Tahawus, 1859, by Lossing. From left, Sabattis, Preston, Mrs. Lossing, Mr. Buckingham, Mr. Lossing.

He appears to recognize that although the view from the summit is expansive, perhaps a better "picture" is obtained from a lower vantage point. Thus, Lossing did not attempt to describe the close-up scenery; he expounded on the sights viewed through his telescope. He saw smoke from the settler's cabin, the sails of watercraft, and the houses of Burlington on the eastern shore of Lake Champlain.

More important, historically, Lossing documented the existence of a stone hut and the ascents of several people. In a nook on the south side of the summit, Lossing found a small hut made of loose stones and covered with moss. Inside the hut, he found a piece of paper that said, "This hospice, erected by a party from New York, August 19, 1858, is intended for the use and comfort of visitors to Tahawus.—F.S.P.— M.C.— F.M.N."

These initials correspond to artist Frederick S. Perkins, Mary Cook, and Fannie Newton, who climbed from Keene Valley. The piece of paper proved that the party reached the summit, and that others climbed, too. Alfred G. Compton and Theodore R. Davis, of New York signed the paper on August 14, 1859. Charles Newman of Stamford and Charles Bedfield of Elizabethtown signed on August 16, 1859.

Davis was still in his teens when he made this climb, but he would soon become a notable illustrator and artist. Some of his sketches of Indian Pass, the iron works, and other Adirondack scenes appeared in *Harper's Weekly*. It seems quite remarkable that he and Lossing stood on top of Mount Marcy within days of each other.

Above: The Deserted Village of Adirondack. *Below:* Indian Pass from Lake Henderson. Both by Theodore R. Davis, who climbed Mount Marcy in 1859.

Mount Marcy had certainly become a favorite destination. And, for twenty years, the Adirondack Iron Works (Upper Works) was the starting point for almost all ascents. But things were changing. Women climbed the mountain now. New routes were being discovered. And the days of producing iron at the works were over.

By 1850, the works, shops, and houses had grown into a busy little settlement. In 1854, a huge new blast furnace was put into operation. Plans for a plank road and a railroad line were conceived. But all was not good. The iron market was depressed. There were impurities in the ore. A flood in 1856 broke the upper dam at Adirondac (Upper Works). The rushing waters demolished the dam and sawmill at Tahawus (Lower Works). The death of Archibald McIntyre, in 1858, was the final blow.

"All was left a desolation," wrote Lossing. "We saw white skeletons of trees which had been killed by the flood, standing thickly, and heightening the dreary aspect of the scene." But Lossing predicted that "the projected railway will yet be constructed" and the "forest village will be vivified, and the echoes of the deep breathings of its furnaces will be heard in the neighboring mountains."[14]

This vision proved unduly optimistic. It was almost ninety years before that railway was built and the village was reborn. Ironically, this 1940s operation mined the titanium once considered an impurity in the iron. As for those old furnaces, they still only echo the "Halloo" of curious tourists.

In the summer of 1863, naturalist John Burroughs spied blue jays, small hawks, a wild pigeon, and ruffed grouse as he marched along the dilapidated corduroy road past dilapidated houses to the Upper Works, now known as Deserted Village. He wrote, "It was a curious and melancholy spectacle. The remoteness and surrounding wildness rendered the scene doubly impressive."[15]

Despite this scene of decay, Burroughs found it "an admirable place to go to." He said, "There is fishing and hunting and boating and mountain-climbing within easy reach, and a good roof over your head at night, which is no small matter. One is often disqualified for enjoying the woods after he gets there by the loss of sleep and of proper food taken at seasonable times. This point attended to, one is in the humor for any enterprise."

Fog shrouded Burroughs' view of the mountains, but finally "the wind changed, the fog lifted, and revealed to us the grandest mountain scenery we had beheld on our journey. There they sat about fifteen miles distant, a group of them,—Mount Marcy, Mount McIntyre, and Mount Colden, the real Adirondack monarchs."[16]

There is no indication that Burroughs climbed Mount Marcy. "But better than fish or game or grand scenery, or any adventure by night or day, is the wordless intercourse with rude Nature one has on these expeditions," he wrote. "It is something to press the pulse of our old mother by mountain lakes and streams, and know what health and vigor are in her veins, and how regardless of observation she deports herself."[17]

Although the Deserted Village held a special appeal for Burroughs, mountain climbers no longer had to content themselves with it. Shorter routes, faster routes, easier routes up Mount Marcy came into favor. People found routes from Keene Valley and Elk Lake. (See following chapters.) People also went south from North Elba through various mountain passes to connect with the Opalescent route.

As nearby Lake Placid developed into a tourist spot, transportation to the North Elba area became easier than the rough wagon ride to the Deserted Village. A new road was built from Keene to North Elba, going through Cascade Pass. More people began to travel to Mount Marcy from the north.

Local men often served as guides. A farmer named Nash (probably Timothy Nash) guided Dana's party in but not out, and as a consequence, they lost their way and had to spend a night in the woods. North Elba farmer Henry Thompson, son-in-law of abolitionist John Brown, guided "some gentry" up Mount Marcy in August 1859.[18] Merrill and Robert Blinn guided author Alfred Billings Street from North Elba through Indian Pass to the Upper Works and up Mount Marcy in 1865. Street's party went over Marcy and down to the Ausable Lakes, out to Keene Valley, and then to Jay, Wilmington, and back to North Elba. The "round trip" had been done in the other direction, but Street is the first to report doing it from the north.

His account suggests that the North Elba guides did not know the Opalescent route very well. "Although we supposed ourselves on the slope of Old Tahawus," wrote Street, "neither of the guides, this visit being their first on this side, could indicate the fact with certainty."[19]

Several times Street mentions a "trail." It is the first substantial evidence of a cleared trail up the Opalescent River from Lake Colden. But though he was following a trail, he declared that climbing Mount Marcy was not easy. "No! it is stern, persistent work;" he wrote, "work that calls upon your mightiest energies! In attempting its ascent, strong, hardy trampers have given out, and lain down helpless in an attack of wood-sickness. And here is a new disease! I first heard of it in the Adirondacks! Wood-sickness! a sea-sickness on land! brought on by excessive fatigue, or by being buried, day after day, in the greenness of the woods—these tremendous, tangled, sun-concealing, weltering woods!"[20]

At last Street reached the summit and was lucky to find a clear and bright view. It was magical, savage, and wild. "Where there wasn't a big peak, a little one was stuck up," he quoted a guide having said.

Then, Street fell into a trance, imagining that the mountain was talking to him. He heard the mountain asking why the vain mortal wailed in despair, for the mountain had sat unnoticed and unknown for years and years without sinking into despair. The mountain had kept hope that one day it would be known among men and no longer be lonely. "And true, O mountain, true is the lesson thou hast taught me," wrote Street.

Street explicitly demonstrated the prevailing belief that nature had no purpose until man "discovered" it. And the desire to conquer it, to declare one's sovereignty over it was marked by Merrill Blinn. With his hammer, he chiseled his name, and the names of Street and Robert, into the summit rock. Of course, Old Mountain Phelps reportedly cut his name into the rock atop Mount Marcy, too.[21]

"And thus do we all seek to foil forgetfulness," wrote Street. "Here, on the top of this savage peak, we hoped to rescue our memories from inevitable fate. A few seasons of rain and frost, and though deep the characters be cut, moss and lichen will creep into them, and, at last, bury them as securely as the grave will bury our frames of a day."[22]

Street almost buried his frame in the "grassy carpet" as he attempted to get a better view of the gorge he soon christened Panther Gorge. As he descended an innocent-looking slope, Merrill yelled, "Don't go there, I entreat!" But Street ignored the warning.

The "grassy carpet" turned out to be the sharp needles and stiff branches of balsam bushes. Street persevered until he met "the most terrible twine of bayonet-pointed chevaux de frise" he ever met. He made little headway and finally turned back. Suddenly, the descent seemed easy compared to the ascent. Such is the fate of many a hiker who ventures toward Panther Gorge.

He struggled through the shaggy foliage, then up sharp gullies of rock, and finally "up over or rather half wading through the stiff layers of balsam." He was glad to plant his feet on the peak previously termed "savage" but now called "the friendly peak."[23]

Next, Merrill and Robert demonstrated the great height of the mountain by performing the customary act—they fired their rifles to listen to the echo. "The sounds were like two short taps, or rather asthmatic coughs," wrote Street. "A minute followed of blank silence—then a faint tone struggled from a distant gorge. And such is fame."[24]

The party longed to spend the night, "to lie here on the brow of the stately Titan," but were forced to make camp down in the forest. Evidently, the stone hut that Lossing found in 1859 was gone. The next morning they walked up Marcy to watch the sunrise and then headed down Panther Gorge, over Bartlett Ridge, out to Lower Ausable Lake, and continued their round trip.

North Elba guide William "Bill" Nye developed his own version of the round trip. He took parties from North Elba through Indian Pass, up Mount Marcy, and back through Avalanche Pass. He even took women on this adventure.

In 1868, he guided a rather "ample" woman named Matilda Fielding. She climbed Mount Marcy but nothing is reported of her ascent, only of her mishap on the trip back. Bill Nye told the story to Seneca Ray Stoddard, who put it in his guidebook.[25]

Mrs. Fielding, her husband, and their teenage niece named Dolly, came from somewhere on the Hudson. Their trip was to be from Nash's in North Elba through Indian Pass to the iron works, then on to Mount Marcy and back by way of Avalanche Pass. It was late in the day when they left from Nash's, and all the boarders told Mrs. Fielding she could not go through the pass that day. She said, "you'll see I shall, if the guide will show me the way."

They did make it through, traveling the last three or four miles by torchlight. The next day they went to Lake Colden and camped, and the next day to Mount Marcy and back to Lake Colden. The following day they started through Avalanche Pass. "You will remember the walls," said Bill Nye, according to Stoddard's guidebook, "hundreds of feet high on either side, that you can neither get over nor around without going around the mountain, well, along one side is a shelf from two to four feet wide, and as many under water, and when we got there they wondered how we were to get past. I said I could carry them or I could build a raft, but to build a raft would take too much time while I could carry them past in a few minutes. Provisions were getting short and time set to be at North Elba, so Mr. Fielding says, 'Well, Matilda, what say you? Will you be carried over, or shall we make a raft?' Mrs. Fielding says, 'If Mr. Nye can do it, and thinks it safe, I will be carried over, to save time.'"

Nye said it was "perfectly safe" and after testing the depth of the water, he came back for his passengers. But Mrs. Fielding said she did not see how he was

"Hitch-up, Matilda!" by Stoddard.

going to carry them across and keep them out of the water. Nye said, "I will show you," and he did.

> I set down with my back against a rock that came nearly to the top of my shoulders, told her to step on the rock, put one foot over one side of my neck, the other over the other side, and sit down. *That* was what she did not feel inclined to do, and was going to climb on with both feet on one side, but her husband told her to "throw away her delicacy, and do as I told her," reminding her of her word, which was enough; she finally sat down very carefully, so far down on my back that I could not carry her, I told her it wouldn't do, and at last she got on and I waded in.

"Hurrah! There they go!" "Cling tight, Matilda!" shouted the young lady and the husband in the same breath. "Hold your horse, aunt!" laughed Dolly. "Your reputation as a rider is at stake. . ."

I had just barely got into the deep water, steadying myself with one hand against the rocks and holding on to her feet with the other, when, in spite of all I could do, she managed to work half way down my back.

"Hitch up, Matilda! *hitch up*, Matilda! Why *don't* you hitch up?" screamed Mr. Fielding, and I could hear him dancing around among the rocks and stones, while I thought Dolly would have died laughing, and the more he yelled "hitch up," the more she hitched down, and I began to think I would have to change ends, or she would get wet; but by leaning way over forward, I managed to get her across safe and dry. Then "how was she to get off?" I said, "I will show you." So I bent down until her feet touched the ground, and she just walked off over my head, the two on the other side laughing and shouting all the time.[26]

Matilda showed women how to abandon society's fetters and, in the process, became an Adirondack legend. Today there are two wooden walkways along the west side of Avalanche Lake called "Hitch-up Matildas." But the flat rock shelves are still there.

Lest this story seems a little too fanciful, an unpublished manuscript at the Adirondack Museum in Blue Mountain Lake tells of a similar adventure. Bill Nye guided a party of three men on his "round trip." The account is undated but indicates the Henderson calamity occurred twenty-two years earlier. This places the trip in 1867.

The men walked through Indian Pass and then up the Opalescent River to the summit of Mount Marcy. They make no mention of a stone shelter, although they report "examining the formation of the top most fully."[27]

Their return route was by Avalanche Lake. Nye did not offer to carry this party; he made them wade. "There's a ledge only three or four feet under water on which we can cross by keeping close to shore," he told them. They didn't much care if they got wet; they were already well soaked from a rainstorm.

When they reached the end of the lake, the clouds rolled away and revealed the Avalanche Pass. "We all thought it much finer than the far famed Indian Pass and left it with much regret," wrote the unknown author.[28]

By 1871, a guidebook stated, "Mt. Marcy is frequently ascended from North Elba."[29] It doesn't specify the route as via Indian Pass or Avalanche Pass. Certainly the fine scenery of Avalanche Pass attracted visitors, but they found a tough walk. Surveyor Verplanck Colvin visited the pass in 1869, and when he returned in 1873, he found a way to avoid it. He climbed through a pass between Avalanche (or Caribou) Mountain and Mount McIntyre (Algonquin).

"Deep in the defile we were surprised to find a rich little oasis meadow of 'blue-joint' grass, which, thick and rank, rose to our elbows," wrote Colvin. "It was full of paths made by deer, and cozy beds from which they had only risen at our approach. A discussion which ensued as we climbed the mountain side in regard to the American reindeer or caraboo [*sic*], was the occasion of our naming the new pass after an animal which once inhabited the region, but which is now, probably, here extinct."[30]

When they ascended Caribou Pass, Colvin determined the height to be 3,662 feet above tide. They marched down the north side through the unknown forest until they reached the main branch of the West Branch of the Ausable River. Then they found the "trapping line (marked trees)," the course they had followed in 1869 when marching from Avalanche Lake.

A trail was made in 1874, and in 1876 the name "Caraboo Pass" appeared on the Essex County map. No matter how you spell it, this pass was once part of a route from North Elba to Lake Colden and up Mount Marcy.

Throughout the 1870s and 1880s, more routes developed and more people came to climb Mount Marcy. Of course, after they came, some wanted to own a piece of it.

A group of hikers who descended to the Deserted Village in 1879 were surprised to find the principal house, a large two-story building, literally crowded with city guests, some fifty men, women and children. One of the hikers wrote, "On further inquiry we ascertained that this unusual gathering consisted mostly of the Adirondack Club," which was composed chiefly of "men of wealth or distinction."[31]

A room was finally found for the tired hikers in the "haunted house," across the road. As soon as they went to bed, the "ghosts and ghostesses" came out from their rooms. They ran back and forth, from room to room, making the old house shake from cellar to garret. "When heavy men, worth four or five hundred thousand dollars, 'come down,' it makes things jar!"[32]

A few years later, Stoddard's guidebook said, "This is now the headquarters of the Adirondack Club [predecessor of the Tahawus Club], who have leased and hold the surrounding territory as a game and fish preserve for the use of themselves and friends, where, it is understood, uninvited guests are not welcome."[33]

Private clubs. New trails. Women. They were all coming round the mountain.

Mercy Climbs

He has long acted as a guide up Mount Marcy (Mercy as he always calls it) and has come to regard it as something nearly human and kin to him. He has no patience to hear any other mountain preferred to it, and listened skeptically to all I had to say about the New Hampshire hills. "You've never been on top of Mercy, I reckon."
REV. JOSEPH TWICHELL ABOUT OLD MOUNTAIN PHELPS

JOHN CHENEY AND HARVEY HOLT were among the first locals to ascend Mount Marcy and the first professional mountain guides in the Adirondacks. They took many parties up and down the mountain, but always retained their roles as woodsmen, hunters, and fishermen. They attained mild notoriety compared to guide Orson Schofield Phelps, who built a reputation as a mountain climber, a nature lover, and a self-made poet and philosopher.

Orson "Old Mountain" Phelps (1817-1905) claimed to have been alone in his love of mountain scenery. He told his Keene Valley neighbors that if only they would expend a little sweat and money, hundreds of people would come every summer. The neighbors laughed and said he was demented. Somehow he did manage to get a promise of $6 to hire an assistant for cutting a trail to Mount Marcy. But some of the money was never paid. "And now," said the old fellow, "men who never cut a stick on the mountains to make a trail are reaping the benefit of those I made, and they are all down on old Phelps."[1]

Part of Phelps' charm was his bickering about others reaping benefits from his efforts, his intol-

Orson "Old Mountain" Phelps, 1888, by Stoddard. Courtesy of New York State Archives.

75

erance of folks who didn't properly appreciate the scenery, and his bending of the truth as much as a willow bough in a typhoon. Most charming was his invention of language.

"Mount Mercy" became his quaint name for Mount Marcy. He described it as "a mountain on top of mountains" and said that the view from the top always gave him a feeling of "heaven up-h'isted-ness." Of course, it was his favorite peak.

"He heard with impatience that Mount Washington was a thousand feet higher, and he had a child-like incredulity about the surpassing sublimity of the Alps," wrote Charles Dudley Warner. "Praise of any other elevation he seemed to consider a slight to Mount Marcy, and did not willingly hear it, any more than a lover hears the laudation of the beauty of another woman than the one he loves."[2]

Phelps reportedly climbed Mount Marcy more than one hundred times, much more than anyone of that period. He probably guided more than five hundred people to the summit. Some never ventured into the woods without Phelps, "for a ramble without him would be like, 'Hamlet with Hamlet left out.'"[3]

"I guess I am about as well known as I ought to be;" he said, "there is nothing historic about me except making a road to the top of Mt. Marcy from the south and east. Twenty-two years ago I climbed Old Tahawus from the E. and descended it to the S., and from all I can learn I was the first man that traveled either of those routes."[4]

It is generally accepted that Phelps made the first climb of Mount Marcy from the east in August 1849 with Almeron Oliver and George Estey, both of Schroon. Most accounts say he climbed from the Ausable Lakes, while some claim he went up Johns Brook. As for Phelps' road to the top from the south and east, he was bending that willow bough a bit. He meant trail, not road. By south, he probably meant Elk Lake; he did cut most of that trail. As for the trail from the east, he is credited with cutting the first trail in 1861, although some accounts erroneously date the trail to 1849.

But even before he cut proper trails, Phelps guided tourists to the top.

One of Phelps' first clients was the artist Frederick S. Perkins. In 1857, Perkins and Phelps purportedly named Skylight, Basin, and Saddleback Mountains. Phelps would later claim that they also stood atop Mount Marcy and named Lake Perkins, the pond later christened Lake Tear of the Clouds.

The next summer, Perkins brought an artist friend named Mary Cook to Keene Valley. "Long skirts and portly proportions notwithstanding," wrote one historian, "she climbed the highest of the Adirondacks and refused the aid of a rope around her waist to help her up the slide."[5]

Although not the first woman to ascend Mount Marcy, she was "the first that went over the mountain; and thro' the Indian Pass, and took what is called the 'Round Trip.'"[6] With Frederick Perkins, Fannie Newton, and Old Mountain Phelps, she built a small stone hut on the top of Mount Marcy. And Mary Cook climbed Marcy again. In 1861, Phelps guided Cook and two Keene Valley sisters,

Orpha and Teresa Bruce, up Mount Marcy.[7] This is the first known ascent of the mountain by local women and one of the first ascents by Phelps' trail.

In 1861, Phelps had built the first trail up Mount Marcy, marking it with cairns and ax blazes. The route started at Shanty Brook, on the carry trail between the Ausable Lakes. It followed the south fork of Shanty Brook, cut across Crystal Brook, and went

Artists at Keene. From *Daily Gazette*, 1877.

over Bartlett Ridge. Then it curved around the southwesterly side of Haystack (at the 3,900-foot level) and descended into Panther Gorge about its center. The trail went up the great slide on Marcy and on to the rocks a few hundred feet south of the summit. It turned straight north and continued to the top.

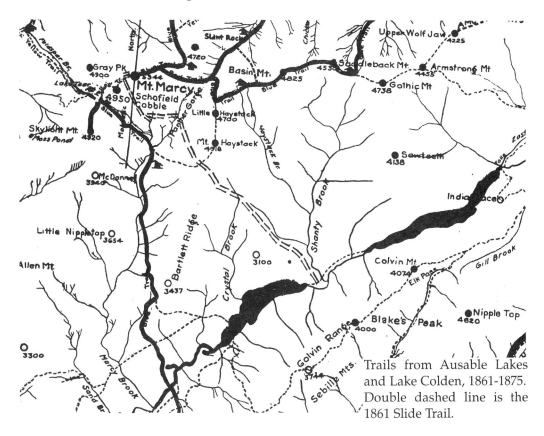

Trails from Ausable Lakes and Lake Colden, 1861-1875. Double dashed line is the 1861 Slide Trail.

Rev. Joseph Twichell observed that Phelps had a certain devoutness to the slide: "Our guide was at home when his feet struck this rock, and there was something touching in the simplicity with which he hailed a beautiful stream which spread itself like a thin veil over its surface at one place, as he stopped to gaze up the steep: 'I've come to meet ye again, old friend.' And he stooped and took a draught of the cold stream."[8]

Visitors found the slide daunting. One wrote, "This rock is steep, like the roof of a cottage, and you hesitate before trusting yourself upon the apparently slippery surface, lest you should lose your foothold and find yourself shooting with a fearfully accelerated velocity down the slope, a thousand or fifteen hundred feet, into some unknown abyss below. But once upon the rock, you soon gain confidence as you find that its surface is like coarse sandpaper."[9]

Why would Phelps route the trail across the slide, some thousand feet in height? The open slide may have been a bit precarious, but it was a ready-made trail. Call it astuteness or laziness; Phelps saved time and effort in his trail-building by avoiding a long stretch of thick, stunted, twisted, torturous trees.

Perhaps the Marcy slide, like the steep upper slope on the Opalescent side, was also a means of job security—an easy, cleared trail meant doom to the guide, but a critter from the city could not cross the Marcy slide without one.

In August 1864, another lady came to try Phelps' slide. Her name was Lucia Pychowska and she was the first woman to publish an account of her trip up Mount Marcy. She filled a twelve-page article in *The Continental Monthly* with nature observations, humorous anecdotes, and womanly advice. "There had been no fatigue and no difficult climbing. Indeed, it would be no very serious matter to go one day and return the next," she wrote. "And hence we advise all travelers in that region with sound lungs, moderate strength, and any love for forest life and magnificent scenery, to make the ascent."[10]

Lucia Duncan Cook Pychowska—a restless, agile, little lady—was married to John Nepomucene Pychowska, a famous Polish musician, who was tall, slim and rich, but not a hiker. So Pychowska's hiking companion was her brother, Eugene Cook, or in later years, her daughter, Marian. In the 1880s, they became the leading hikers, trail builders, and explorers in the White Mountains of New Hampshire.

On her hike up Marcy, Pychowska took her brother and a lady companion named Elsie. They hired three guides, including "an old pioneer, short, slight, weather-beaten, and sunbrowned"—Phelps. The party carried axes, blankets, and other provisions, including a pint of brandy and the same of whiskey "to meet emergencies of cold or weariness."

For women's attire, Pychowska recommended broad, thick-soled, low-heeled boots of soft leather, woolen stockings, an underskirt made of gray flannel and hemmed just below the knee, and an outer skirt of winsey or Kentucky jean. In places of unusual steepness along the trail, where a temporary shortening of the dress was required, "a strong clasp pin, easily carried, will in a moment fasten up the outer skirt, washwoman fashion."[11]

In addition, Pychowska recommended bringing a light umbrella in case of sudden rain or very hot sun. And, each person should carry such toilet arrangements as necessary, "only let them be as light as possible, every ounce on such a tramp soon becoming a matter of serious consequence."[12]

Wasn't she concerned about proper appearances and popular fashions? Hell, no. She wrote, "The wind may toss the locks, the sun brown the skin, and the brambles tear the garments, but there are none to cavil, none to count the gray hairs or the freckles, or see that said garments are of last year's fashioning."[13]

Yet she also maintained that a woman could still wear "pretty" things in the woods. "Why should the female figures in the landscape spoil it by ugliness in color or repulsiveness in form?" she asked. "It is indeed a mistake to imagine that, to walk rapidly and safely through steep and pathless wilds, a woman must don a garb suggestive only of a 5th of November procession."[14]

One gentleman agreed with this philosophy; he added one pretty item to a woman's garb. "It is a good habit of the ladies in the Adirondacks to wear pretty hunting knives or daggers in their girdles," he wrote—for protection against bears.[15]

Lower Ausable Lake, 1889, by Stoddard. Courtesy of Library of Congress.

Upper Ausable Lake, 1887, by Stoddard. Courtesy of Library of Congress.
Below: Camp at Upper Ausable Pond. From *Daily Gazette*, 1875.

Under Phelps' guidance, Pychowska and her party made their way from Keene Flats to Lower Ausable Lake. Then, they were rowed up the pond. The path to Mount Marcy turned off to the right, but the party walked along the carry path to Upper Ausable Lake. They rowed across the pond to some bark shanties to eat and to enjoy the scenery.

"The lake is about two miles long, and one broad," wrote Pychowska. "Its shores are gently sloping, and wooded with splendid trees of the primeval forest, beech, birch, maple, and spruce. The soil is excellent, and the wild flowers and mosses are luxuriant and abundant. . . . [T]he clear water gives back the most wonderful reflections, and those 'ladies of the forest,' the white birches, could ask no more transparent mirror. There is nothing to mar the effect of the whole, no driftwood, no burnt patches, no ragged-looking clearing—all is harmonious and entirely satisfactory."[16]

The party went back up the lake and started along the pathway to Mount Marcy. Phelps took the lead, sweating and grumbling under his load. "Fortunately, he was not a very rapid walker, making only from two to two and a half miles per hour," wrote Pychowska, "so there was no danger of fatigue to any of the party, except to our Diogenes [Eugene Cook], who measures weariness by time and not by miles, walking more easily eight miles in two hours than in four."

On and up they went, ascending and descending Bartlett Ridge. There they made their first acquaintance with the renowned black fly. Pychowska remarked, "We had heard so much of this pest, and seen so little of him, that we began to think his existence somewhat mythical, in short, a traveller's tale, invented by men to keep women from venturing beyond the well-beaten track of ordinary journeying. At this, our second halt, however, he assaulted us so vigorously that we were glad to take refuge in the smoke of a smudge our guides had lost no time in making. . . . We saw the creatures, and found them somewhat troublesome (especially when, later in the day, they insisted upon spreading in with bread and butter), but suffered no pain or even inconvenience from their bite. This may have been owing to the lateness of the season, or to the non-inflammatory condition of our blood." If the thick smoke of a smudge was undesirable, a recipe

"Punkies About" by T. B. Thorpe, 1859.

of "a coating of grease mixed with essence of pennyroyal" could be used. However, the party felt that the results of a vigorous attack would be preferred to the greasy safeguard.[17]

They walked a short distance farther and then halted to make camp and eat supper. A few vigorous, well-directed strokes of the axe and soon a great circle of bark, six feet high and nine feet in breadth, stood ready for use. Wigwams were soon made ready for sleeping. And supper was ready for eating.

"Our bill of fare consisted of hasty pudding (corn mush)," wrote Pychowska, "eaten with butter and maple sugar (a dish for a king, and therefore well suited to sundry of the sovereign people, only Elsie and I, having no vote, cannot in any sense be called sovereign), bread and butter, crackers, and toast."[18]

Pychowska was quite an inventive and independent character. What other writer managed to weave women's rights into a description of a woods dinner? She had a sensitivity to nature, too—almost a modern environmental concern. When she woke in the morning and looked around their camp, she was grieved. "The girdled trees standing near our camp looked at us reproachfully in the morning light," she wrote, "ten giants doomed to death to furnish a night's covering to six pigmies! Our fires, too, were they safe, or might they not run along the inflammable turf and perhaps destroy acres of beautiful, precious timber?"[19]

Phelps wasn't happy in the morning either. He looked up toward the mountaintops and shook his head ominously. "Indeed," he said, "it won't be much use to go on up, for the Haystack looks so blue that *durn'd* haze must have come back again, and you'll have no view from *Mercy* today."

"Well, it can't be helped, but we'll try it anyhow!" was the unanimous response.

The party crossed a little stream, climbed half a mile, and came to the foot of the great slide. Pychowska found the pathway somewhat steep but not difficult. "Excelsior is the cry and the top of the slide the next goal to be won," wrote Pychowska. Then came the last steep cliffs and the summit was achieved.

"Here we are among the clouds," she wrote, "the wind blowing freshly, and the mists sweeping past, obscuring every object below. In this wind lay our hope, and scarcely less in the mists, for they might be the means of dispersing the haze. There went a rift, a patch of blue sky—and there a bit of green mountain! Then again all was leaden, damp, and cold. We seemed to have reached the Ultima Thule, to be the sole living creatures in some far-away corner of the earth gone back to chaos and mysterious twilight. Again a break, and again appeared a stretch of dark fir-covered mountain tops, an avalanche-riven peak, a bright, green field, or a corner of some far-away blue water. This hide-and-go-seek between landscape and mist lasted some half hour, when the clouds all rolled away, and left us with bright sunlight and the most glorious view our eyes had ever rested upon."[20]

Pychowska sat in the warm sun, sheltered from the wind by a rock, and wrapped in a shawl. Lemons, added to some maple sugar, a block of chocolate, and a few crackers, furnished a delightful treat.

They had been on the summit about two hours when the sky threatened rain. They hastened down the rocky slope and gathered things from camp. Then they proceeded down to the Upper Ausable Lake. Although it was only three in the afternoon, they did not care to walk through the wet woods, so they stayed at the bark shanties on the lake.

By morning, the rain stopped and Phelps showed Pychowska the sights. "Our pioneer, who loved every peak and pond in the neighborhood with the affection of a discoverer, took advantage of the charming morning to row us all round the lake, to show us the pretty inlet with its beaver dam, and help us gather the singular leaves of the pitcher plant, and the beautiful, fragrant white water lilies riding at anchor in the lucent stream," Pychowska wrote.[21]

Phelps seemed to have enjoyed guiding Lucia Pychowska and Mary Cook, but he did not enjoy all women hikers. "Women, some women, never ought to come into the woods," said Phelps. "There was a lot of 'em I took up *Mercy* last summer, went gigglin' all the way up, talking of their beaux, and ribbons, and when they got up didn't see nothing. I wanted to kick 'em off the *mounting*."[22]

Phelps wasn't very pleased leading "an eccentric lady tourist" and her companion up Mount Marcy either. Miss Sundry and Miss Slow, as Phelps called them, required guides, packmen, and waiters—seven in all.

Miss Sundry, Phelps wrote, was "less than 30 years old, of medium size, fair form, rather dark complexion, sharp features, rather plain looking in the face, has a peculiar wild stare at times when she might be taken for a maniac, the next you may see a face full of malicious mischief. . . . Another moment she will bring on to her face a reverential stare that would make one think of an Angel. . . . The thought of any masculine as a social companion is a horror to her. If the most polite gentleman in the world should offer to take her hand to help her over a log she would snarl as bad as an old cat with her tail under a chair-rocker. . . but she is an enthusiastic admirer of nature's wildest scenery, in her peculiar way."[23]

The party went over Bartlett Ridge to Panther Gorge camp, where all expected to stay for the night. Except Miss Sundry, who said, "It is only 2 o'clock, let's have a lunch, and go up to the head of the slide to camp. It looks like being a pleasant night, what say you Philosopher?"

"It looks fair enough for it now," said Phelps, after looking up at the calm blue sky. "But it's some work to take these loads 15 to 18 hundred feet up into the air, and over that horrid steep rough trail."

"Never mind, I can do it," said Miss Sundry. And so off they went to the head of the slide.

Though Phelps had seen the sun set and rise from the summit of Mount Marcy many times, he saw a sight unlike any other the next morning. "It was the morning star just coming over the crest of the bare rock on the north slope of

Haystack Mt., a little below the level of our camp," wrote Phelps. "It was not a twinkling spark as we see stars from the valleys, but an orb with an apparent surface of a 4 inch ball, and instead of little weak twinkles it shot off streams of liquid fire for many yards in all directions."

After daylight, fog moved in, but the party climbed to the summit anyway. They stood and watched as the clouds opened and the whole western horizon was clear. Then all the fog lifted and gave them a "first class view." After a while, they climbed down the mountain toward the Opalescent valley.

The next day, bad weather forced them toward the Deserted Village. The party marched over brooks and fallen treetops, when suddenly "Oh! help me up," was heard. Phelps looked around and saw Miss Sundry sitting splash down in a mud pool. "It was a little place of mud and water," said Phelps, "the water perhaps three or four inches deep and then black soft mud as deep as any reasonable person could ask for, for an easy place to sit." But Miss Sundry was calling a man to help her. Phelps hauled her out, as he said, "like pulling a pig out of a scalding tub."[24]

From Phelps' description, the woman appears to have been the notorious Anna Newman of North Elba. Like Mary Cook, she was an artist and a single woman. Some said she was a man-hater. She "never allowed a man to touch her."[25] (Well, maybe if she was sitting in a mud pool she could make an exception.)

Newman was from a wealthy Philadelphia family. She started coming to Keene Valley about 1866, drawn to the region by the gathering of artists. But soon painting and drawing became secondary to mountain climbing and lakeside camping. Her cousin, Henry van Dyke, wrote of her: "Something in the outline of those mountains and in the fragrance of those woods seemed to attract her and give her great content." But he also remembered her as "a very original and interesting person."[26]

After summering in the area for several years, she purchased a house in North Elba in 1872. Of course, her eccentricity brought her notoriety in the small community. But she was also kind and generous, and when she died, the lower end of Lake Placid Village came to be known as "Newman."

Phelps guided other distinguished people, many of whom he liked better than Anna Newman. For example, he enjoyed the company of Rev. Joseph Twichell, who understood the essence of life in the mountains. "One of the first things to do, when you are installed in a farm house at Keene Flats," wrote Twichell, "is, nothing. It is about the only thing that does not require a guide. . . . But it requires genius to do nothing, or to 'loaf your soul,' for any considerable length of time."[27]

Keene Flats was not the place for very proper people or for mere sportsmen. They could go elsewhere. The "Flats" was the place for people who loved the mountains and mountain air and mountain scenery. "Keene Flats is the gateway to the mountains," wrote a *New York Times* correspondent. "Like Chamounix, it is a *cul de sac*. The road stops here, and the 'trails' go off to the various points of interest. As people start from Chamounix for the ascent of Mont Blanc, and the tour of Mont Blanc, so they start from this place for the ascent of Marcy, and the tour of Marcy and Dix."[28]

And here was the home base of Phelps. "That grand old guide, Phelps, the hero of this region, says, in his homely way, that there are beauties among the mountains which you can't 'hog down' as if they were acorns under the oak tree in the valleys; you must climb and work to get glimpses of them," wrote the correspondent. "Such a life of mountain climbing undoubtedly seems very stupid to the vast multitude of Summer tourists; but there are people to whom it has a perfect fascination. . . . The natives, meanwhile, look on the 'city critters' with silent wonder as if they were a sort of mild lunatics."[29]

Maybe the natives understood a short visit in August or September to laze in the late summer shade. But who would voluntarily come during the height of the black fly season of late June or early July? Were they madmen? Perhaps some were, but one lady botanist found mosquitoes, midges, and black flies to be "necessary evils, thorns in the side to prevent our being 'exalted above measure,' when weighed against the many pleasures of this free and independent life they count absolutely as nothing. Stinging vexations, some of them are; the midge hurts the pride as well as the flesh; one dreads to be eaten by a microscopic foe. The bite of the black fly, less painful at the time, is somewhat serious in its results. Often, your first notice of its presence is the blood dropping from a wound, which takes days in healing."[30]

From the landing on Upper Ausable Lake, this author, her lady friend, and other companions walked through wet bushes and marshy ground until the ascent of Bartlett Ridge began. At first they thought it seemed a great waste of time and strength to go up with the expectation of going down again; but they found the descent "a grateful change, a rest to limbs wearied with climbing."[31]

The climb then proceeded up the side of Marcy, and the author wrote:

The great slide is grand, awful. . . . We crossed this slide diagonally, finding our hob-nailed shoes a great assistance and comfort in doing it—stopping only to gather the sundew (Drosera rotunaipolia), a rare and beautiful plant which we found nowhere else, that with the red peat-moss (Sphagnum acutifolia and Sphagnum Sedoides) in two varieties, finds a lodgment on these wet and slippery rocks.

Beside a boulder covered with curious lichens in endless variety, and near a spring, we rested and lunched. We then addressed ourselves anew to our task. This is no Monday play. Up, up, the eye seeks in vain for the end; but weary though we are, we have a glance and a welcome for the beautiful dwarf cornel (Cornus canadensis), that in this high mountain region is in its Springtime freshness, when in the valleys below, it has put off its snowy blossoms, and clothed itself in dazzling scarlet. Beyond any flower I ever saw, this has an almost human expression of cheerfulness; it is a literally laughing blossom. The beautiful

Linneatoo, or twin flower (Linnea borealis), taking name from from the great botanist, being his favorite flower, is here one mass of blossoms; when below its flowering time is over. The creeping crowberry (Chiogenis hispidula), the child of the Adirondack, with its delicate trailing vine, its tiny evergreen leaves, and waxen berry of purest white, nestled lovingly in the moss beside our path. We passed the sheep laurel (Kalmia angustifolia) with its whorl of rosy blossoms. Afterward all these were left behind and we came to the upper line of trees; gnarled old balsams, the very embodiment of toughness and obduracy, as my tattered dress soon indicated. . .

Before noon we stand on the topmost stone of Marcy 5,400 feet above sea level. A countryman on first reaching this point exclaimed, "By golly, there's nothing but mountains, and where they couldn't get in a big one they sharpened up a little one and stuck it in." No language can describe the glory and magnificence of the view. . .

Here, on the mountain-top, we find a little Alpine flower, the mountain sandwort (Alsine Greenlandica), with tufts of white blossoms, and the mountain cranberry (Vaccinium oxycoceus), dwarfed to such fairy proportions that one scarcely recognizes the tiny, rosy flower. These, with curious lichens, found only here, and a few mosses, redeem this lofty peak from utter desolation.[32]

The party returned to their camp on Upper Ausable Lake, though the excitement of the day kept some from sleeping. When at last one lady slumbered, a toad, "miscalculating a jump," landed on the middle of her forehead, and wakened her "effectually."[33]

Here is yet another writer given to humorous and insightful descriptions of woods life. According to historian Russell Carson, this anonymous writer produced "the most vivid and interesting account of a trip up Marcy by the old route." While Carson was admiring the writing, he seemed to miss the clue—the "tattered dress"—that implies this writer was a woman.

Even with all the guides and tourists going up and down the mountain, the trails were not improving. Reverend Twichell blamed the guides. He said, "Trails were bad and the last idea of the guides was to improve them."[34]

A *Times* correspondent discovered that in several places there were "blind trails leading nowhere in particular, made by older guides for the purpose of misleading and perplexing the green guides from the hotels."[35]

And guides did not recommend the shorter routes, such as the Johns Brook trail. Instead guides recommended the Ausable Lakes route which generally took three days in the coming and going. Other parties stayed longer and completed the round trip to the Deserted Village and through Indian Pass. Again they bypassed the shorter route, through Avalanche Pass. Was this choice of longer routes the desire of the clients to see the scenery or the canniness of the guides to get a bigger fee?

When Alfred Billings Street descended Marcy, he noted that there were no markings at the spot where the trail turned toward Bartlett Ridge. "One would as soon have turned aside, unless conscious of its existence."[36] Street stared into the chasm, named it Panther Gorge, and continued down the trail. Until they came upon a strange new object—a trail sign! "A fractured stump, like a post, stood at the intersection,—most picturesque of sign-boards,—and on a rough shingle were two lines, at first difficult as a Delphic oracle. 'Tou reite Mount Mairc, lefft Upr Ousobl Pond. Reite onn Sothe Lour Ousobl, aynd thin ovr Pond tou Keyne Flatt.'"[37]

Pond was the only word spelled right. Yet Street's party determined that they should turn left to go to Upper Ausable Lake (Pond).

In 1872, Phelps proposed a solution to the bad trails: build a road up Marcy and make money from the tourists!

"I am satisfied there can be a wagon road up Marcy from the north-east or south-west," wrote Phelps. "Of course it would take capital to make it. But if the people of the White Mountains are doing a business of $2,000,000, with no better natural inducements, I think it is time the Western part of Essex County should begin to break through that old petrified covering of selfishness and try to make their localities what they should be—a place where millions of dollars circulate—instead of twenty or thirty thousands, as it now is."[38]

The discovery of Lake Tear and the Marcy-Skylight pass changed Phelps' plans. In 1875, he cut an important new trail from Panther Gorge up to the top of the pass. From there, trails led south to Mount Skylight, west to Lake Colden, and north to the summit of Mount Marcy.

His skill as a trail-builder, combined with his primitive charisma, made Phelps a welcome companion. His associates included surveyor Verplanck Colvin, theologian Dr. Horace Bushnell, Rev. Joseph H. Twichell (pastor of Mark Twain), and Dr. Noah Porter (the President of Yale). These distinguished men earned him some attention in the press, but fame really came when Seneca Ray Stoddard gave a detailed profile of Phelps in his 1874 Adirondack guidebook.

Stoddard described Phelps as a little old man, "muffled up in an immense crop of long hair, and a beard that seemed to boil up out of his collar band; grizzly as the granite ledges he climbs, shaggy as the rough-barked cedar, but with a pleasant twinkle in his eye and an elasticity to his step equaled by few younger men, while he delivers his communications, his sage conclusions and whimsical oddities, in a cheery, cherripy, squeaky sort of tone—away up on the mountains as it were—an octave above the ordinary voice, suggestive of the warblings of an ancient chickadee."[39]

When Stoddard asked Phelps to guide him up Mount Marcy, Phelps replied, "Well, I s'pose I kin do it. I'll be along as soon as the old woman'll bake me a short-cake."

For some reason, Phelps did not take this party up the usual trail. Instead, he led them on a bit of a "random scoot" up Panther Gorge and onto the side of

Haystack. Perhaps he took this route in order to show them a sight "that is worth seeing." He pointed out a wall of rock on the side of Marcy and said, "That is one of the wildest places in the Adirondacks, where, after a heavy rain or in the spring, streams pour down it from all sides. You see that water-course over there in the centre? I have seen an almost unbroken sheet of water, six feet wide, pouring over that to the bottom of the gorge, almost a thousand feet below."[40]

Phelps then led the Stoddard party to the upper end of the gorge, where they joined the Johns Brook trail coming from Keene Valley. (See "Johns Brook" chapter.) They came to a little marsh where branches of the Hudson and Ausable started. Presumably this was the same spot that the Emmons party found in 1837—the spot now called Plateau.

Mount Marcy from Haystack Mountain, circa 1920. Courtesy of New York State Archives.

They climbed through stunted trees to the bare top of Marcy and relished the view. Phelps told about being on the summit at sunset and watching the clearing of a thunderstorm. "There was a tornado sweeping over the top of the mountain and the fog-clouds, broken into patches, were running at lightning speed," he recalled, "and when one of those clouds would strike the mountain all would be shut in with fog for perhaps two or three seconds when it would open, giving a view to the west of a dazzling brilliant orange-tint over the whole western sky.

This could be enjoyed from two to four seconds more when the enveloping fog would come again to save one from going crazy, I suppose."[41]

He told of another time when he saw a thunderstorm from the summit. "I once saw one at near midnight," he said, "approaching from the west, when it was all below me, and I could look on the top of the cloud and see the streaks of lightning darting in every direction; it appeared like a mountain of serpents writhing in every conceivable manner."[42]

Stoddard's profile of Phelps was fascinating, but other, more exuberant essays soon appeared. On August 20, 1875, *The New York Times* printed an article about Phelps. "He is a true child of the woods—another 'Leatherstocking,'" wrote the correspondent. "To me he is as full of interest as the mountains themselves. . . though his thoughts are clothed in homely language, he often surprises me by their appropriateness and their real delicacy."[43]

In 1878, "A Character Study," by Charles Dudley Warner, appeared in the *Atlantic Monthly* and then in the book *In the Wilderness*. Warner called Phelps "a real son of the soil," because of his peculiar relation with soap. Supposedly Phelps' philosophy was: "Soap is a thing that I hain't no kinder use for."[44]

Warner wrote that Phelps' clothes "seemed to have been put on him once for all, like the bark of a tree." But under this uncouth exterior, Warner claimed there was an internal fineness. "Perhaps his most characteristic attitude was sitting on a log, with a short pipe in his mouth," wrote Warner. "If ever man was formed to sit on a log, it was Old Phelps."

Warner claimed that "Phelps was the ideal guide: he knew every foot of the pathless forest: he knew all wood-craft, all the signs of the weather, or, what is the same thing, how to make a Delphic prediction about it."[45]

As Phelps grew older, he seemed to grow less tolerant of his clients and more willing to talk about the woods life rather than swing an axe or tote a pack. These were not the conventional qualities of an "ideal guide." His critics said, "Old Phelps is a fraud."[46]

Even today, Phelps is a hard man to reckon with. Charles Brumley, author of *Guides of the Adirondacks*, calls Phelps "a mountain renaissance man."[47] But historian Mary MacKenzie says he became "something of a humbug as a guide—lazy and inefficient, more entertainer than woodsman—whose flamboyant personality cancelled out his sins of omission."[48]

It is often claimed that Schofield Cobble, the rocky hump on the south slope of Mount Marcy, is named for Orson Schofield Phelps. It is not. Others have thought it was named for Josephine Scofield, lady friend of Henry Van Hoevenberg. It is not. Schofield Cobble is named for Peter F. Schofield, an ardent hiker and proponent of Section 7, Article VII, the "forever wild" provision.[49] A high peak north of Mount Marcy is named Phelps Mountain in honor of Orson "Old Mountain" Phelps.

Lake Tear of the Clouds

*But how wild and desolate this spot! It is possible that
not even an Indian ever stood upon these shores. There is
no mark of ax, no barked tree, nor blackened remnants of
fire; not a severed twig nor a human footprint. . . . First
seen as we then saw it, dark and dripping with the moisture of the heavens, it seemed, on its minuteness and its
prettiness, a veritable Tear-of-the-Clouds, the summit
water as I named it.*

VERPLANCK COLVIN

YOUNG VERPLANCK COLVIN yearned for a different career. He wasn't sure
what he wanted to do, but he knew he didn't want to keep working in his
father's law office. Soon he met Alfred Billings Street, chief librarian at the New
York State Law Office and author of *Woods and Waters* (and later *The Indian Pass*).
He corresponded with writer Charles Fenno Hoffman, who coined the name
Tahawus. He met Dr. James Hall, prominent paleontologist and one of the men
who had made the first ascent of Mount Marcy.[1]

These influences encouraged Colvin, at age 22, to begin exploring the
Adirondacks. During 1869 and 1870, he took many trips into the wilderness,
always bringing a barometer, compass, and hand level to attempt to measure the
heights of peaks and ridges.[2] As he was measuring, he was also observing the
forests, the waters, and the lumbering destruction. Colvin wrote, "It is impossible
for those who have not visited this region to realize the abundance, luxuriance
and depth which these peaty mosses—the true sources of our rivers—attain
under the shade of those dark evergreen forests. . . . With the destruction of those
forests, these mosses dry, wither and disappear; with them vanishes the cold, con-
densing atmosphere which forms the clouds."[3]

Colvin realized that the loss of the mosses meant nothing could hold the
water. Without the water supply from the north, the lower Hudson would be a
slough of salt water and the canals would become empty ditches. He proposed a
solution: an Adirondack Park, where the forests were protected.

It took years for the park idea to take hold. Meanwhile, Colvin's zeal for surveying led to a new career. In the spring of 1872, the state legislature appointed
Colvin, age 25, Superintendent of the Adirondack Survey and appropriated
$1,000 to aid in the completion of a survey and map of the Adirondack wilder-
ness.

On September 14, 1872, Colvin and his survey party began one of their most
famous exploits. In a gray, icy mist, they climbed Mount Marcy only to find that
work was impossible with numb fingers and no visibility. They retreated from the
summit and stumbled down to their old camp in Panther Gorge. The next day

dawned sunny and absolutely cloudless and the crew placed their surveying instrument, the theodolite telescope, on the summit of Mount Marcy for the first time.[4]

It was probably later the same day that Colvin put Bolt No. 1 into the summit of Mount Marcy—"the center of the mountain system, and of the great quadrilaterals of this triangulation." The inscription on the copper bolt read: "Tahawus or Marcy, N.Y.S., Adirondack Survey, 1872, No. 1, Verplanck Colvin, D.I.R." It would permanently show where the theodolite had been placed.[5]

The next day, September 16, work stopped at eleven o'clock, when a severe storm set in. While most of the party returned by the trail to Lake Colden, Colvin would not waste the day on account of a storm. He wrote, "Taking with me one guide, I descended the south side of Mt. Marcy, with the intention of climbing and barometrically measuring Skylight Mountain and Gray Peak, and to visit a little lake lying in the chasm between the mountains. . . . The cloud was so dense that we could see nothing a hundred yards distant, yet we were able to reach the Gray Peak and measure it."[6]

Colvin and guide Bill Nye then went to find the hidden little lake. All the guides had avowed that the lake "must go to the Ausable," though they never took the trouble to explore that valley and be sure.[7]

"About 4 P.M. we stood on the shores of the little lake in a deplorable plight," wrote Colvin, "our boots full of water and clothing torn and dripping. . . . The little pond was a red-letter point in this survey, for we found it, as I had long surmised, not flowing to the Ausable, as has been represented, but to the Hudson river—an inaccuracy of the maps, which is perhaps the best proof that we were the first to ever really visit it."[8]

Lake Tear of the Clouds, 1879, by Colvin.

"This pond, with its elevation of 4,293 feet, will be interesting to the physical geographer," wrote Colvin. "It is, apparently, the *summit water* of the State, and the loftiest known and true *high* pond source of the Hudson river."[9]

Despite the importance of this discovery, Colvin noted that something was missing. In the stream flowing from the lake, "there were seen pools that a trout might lie in, but no fish are here."[10] Later writers have surmised that the stream is too steep to support aquatic insect life and that spring meltwaters scour the streambeds.[11]

Besides the absence of fish, Colvin noticed the beauty of the pond. He described it as "a minute, unpretending tear of the clouds—as it were—a lonely pool, shivering in the breezes of the mountains, and sending its limpid surplus through Feldspar brook to the Opalescent river, the well-spring of the Hudson."[12]

Colvin and Nye were wet and chilled after exploring the lake, so they abandoned the attempt of Skylight. Following the outlet of the lake, they made a descent down the ravine of Feldspar Brook, reaching the shores of the Opalescent River about dark.

Finally, someone had discovered a new route across the mountains. For 35 years, parties had been climbing *over* Mount Marcy; now there would be a route that allowed parties to go from Lake Colden to Ausable Lakes without ascending the high peak.[13]

Colvin regarded the discoveries of this new pass and of the summit water as among his most important achievements. The new pass would facilitate travel and the pond settled an important geography question.

Old Mountain Phelps scoffed at Colvin's claim of discovering the pond and at his name, Lake Tear. Phelps claimed the pond was named Lake Perkins and told this story to a party he was guiding on August 23, 1874.

Phelps led the party of men on the "Round Trip," starting at Keene Flats, going over Mount Marcy, and out through Indian Pass. After they had plodded down the west side of Marcy into the Opalescent Valley—"over the roughest mountain trail known in the whole wilderness"—the question was raised by some member of the party whether there was no better route for getting up to or down from the summit of Marcy westward.[14]

> "Of course there is," said Mr. Phelps.
>
> "Then why in the name of wonder did you tumble us down like a load a pumpkins over that terrible place?"
>
> "Because there is no other trail cut out. I've talked and talked till I'm tired of trying to get a little help to cut a new trail but it's all of no use. Do you remember the stream we crossed back about two miles coming into the Opalescent on the left side, the bed of which was full of opals? Well, that's Feldspar Brook which comes down from Lake Perkins, I call it, after the man who first discovered it thirty years ago, although Mr. Colvin who 'discovered' it two years ago calls it Street's namby-pamby name 'Tear of the Clouds.' No great feat to discover it, I should think. No one could help seeing it from the top of Marcy unless he shut

his eyes, or was in as thick a fog as there was up there this morning. You know, Marcy and Skylight are twins; separated by only a slight depression. Well, near the summit of the depression, but a little over to the westward is Lake Perkins, and its outlet is Feldspar Brook, down which there is a very comfortable grade. That's my route for a trail over Marcy and there ought to be a camp up there half way between Marcy and Skylight, on the trail."[15]

Phelps always told a good story, but sometimes he fabricated details or down-right fibbed. Perkins' first visit to Keene Valley was 1857, only fifteen, not thirty years before Colvin's arrival. It does seem easy to spot the lake from the top of Marcy, but no one ever mentioned it. Besides, Colvin did not claim to be the first to see it, he claimed to be the first to visit it. As for the "namby pamby" name, Lake Tear of the Clouds was not the name Colvin used for the lake. In his 1873 report, he repeatedly called the pond Summit Water. It was the legislature who adopted the pretty name Lake Tear of the Clouds.

The only supporting evidence of the name "Lake Perkins" is in Stoddard's 1874 guidebook.[16] Of course, Stoddard's guide was Old Mountain Phelps.

Although Phelps resented the name of the lake, he wrote these lines in one of his poems:[17]

> The little clear lakes are so peacefully sleeping,
> At the feet of these giants so tall and so grand,
> That they look like the tears of many years weeping,
> That have flown down their cheeks and have mingled with sand

Phelps gathered the funds necessary to clear a trail to Lake Tear. On June 21, 1875, he set out with two guides, L. J. Lamb and Ed Phelps (his son), for work on the Marcy trails. On the 22d, Phelps reported that they "cleared a fair trail to Lake Perkins (Colvin's Tear of the Clouds); returned to Panther Gorge at night and soon found ourselves in a terrific thunder shower."[18]

The next day they built a shanty called Summit Camp between Skylight and Marcy. The following morning they cut the trail up Marcy, completing it by 10:30. They then proceeded to cut a trail up Skylight and completed that by three in the afternoon. But they weren't done! They decided to start cutting the trail down Feldspar Brook. They cleared the route to within about two hundred yards of the Opalescent valley and the old trail, when the booming of thunder was heard over McIntyre and Wallface. With that warning, they stopped work and returned to camp.[19]

At first Colvin supported this blazing of new trails and building of shanties. He even asked the state to erect a hut atop Mount Marcy—for protection and to "induce more tourists to visit the summit."[20] But by 1879, he seemed to change his mind. Colvin wrote that Tear of the Clouds was "a gem more pure and more delightful to the eye than the most precious jewel," but that "close behind our exploring footsteps came the 'blazed-line,' marked with axe upon the trees; the trail, soon trodden into mire; the bark shanty, picturesque enough, but soon surrounded by a grove of stumps. . . . [T]he first romance is gone forever."

As Colvin predicted, the trail through the Skylight-Marcy col soon became the main route up Mount Marcy from Upper Works, from Elk Lake, and from Ausable Lakes. The intersection of the trails at the foot of Marcy became known as The Junction and then Four Corners. Most hikers made the short trek from Four Corners to pretty Lake Tear. As more people came, more trails were marked and trampled. And more shanties were built.

Colvin's dream for an Adirondack Park came, too. In 1892, the Adirondack Park was established. It contained 2.8 million acres, a mixture of Forest Preserve (state) land and private land. Preserve lands received protection from timber cutting and development in 1894 with the passage of Section 7, Article VII, (now Article XIV) of the State Constitution, the "forever wild" provision.

Author Wallace Bruce wrote, "Let us rejoice, therefore, that the State of New York is waking at last to the fact, that these northern mountains were intended by nature to be something more than lumber ranches, to be despoiled by the axe, and finally reverted to the State for 'taxes' in the shape of bare and desolate wastes. Nor can the most practical legislator charge those, who wish to preserve the Adirondack Woods, with idle sentiment; as it is now an established scientific fact that the rainfall of a country is largely dependent upon its forest land. . . . Our age is intensely practical, but we are fortunate in this, that so far as the preservation of the Adirondacks is concerned, utility, common sense, and the appreciation of the beautiful are inseparably blended."[21]

Rejoicing was appropriate. But the protection was limited. Mount Marcy and Lake Tear were privately owned in 1894; they were not part of the Forest Preserve and thus not protected by the "forever wild" provision. The state finally purchased them in the 1920s. (See "Victory Mountain Park" chapter.)

Today the terrain surrounding Lake Tear is nearly as wild as when Colvin found it almost 130 years ago. It remains of interest to scientists, too. Recent measurements reveal that Colvin's elevation estimate of 4,293 is very close to recent figures of 1,320 meters (4,330.7 feet). Other studies show that Lake Tear's depth is less than three feet maximum, the same estimate made by Old Mountain Phelps in 1875. However, Phelps' estimate of the pond's length was fifteen rods (247.5 feet), less than half the recent measurements.[22] During dry weather in 1879, it was said to be only four rods wide and eight rods long.[23] The differences in these three measurements might be explained by what was defined as "pond" and by fluctuations in weather conditions.

Scientists would not expect the area of open water on Lake Tear to be increasing. Basically, it is a bog and bogs tend to slowly cover open water with a mat of moss and other plants. Lake Tear of the Clouds may one day become dry land.

Mountaineer Jim Goodwin wonders when that "one day" will come. He observed the lake in 1919 and again in the 1990s. "I couldn't see that it had changed very much in almost 80 years," he said. "Perhaps altitude is a factor or it

Lake Tear from Summit of Mount Marcy and Lake Tear of the Clouds, 2000.

takes longer for the process to work than we had assumed."[24] Or perhaps some beavers have lent a hand.

Another quirk concerning Lake Tear is the designation "highest source of the Hudson River." Many consider Lake Tear of the Clouds the source of the Hudson. Yet some people point out that its waters do not become the Hudson, in name, until ten miles below Lake Tear. The lake flows into Feldspar Brook, which flows into the Opalescent River, which then meets the Hudson.

But the "Hudson River" that begins at Lake Henderson and flows through Lake Sanford is purely a matter of labeling. The early explorers called it the north branch of the Hudson or simply the outlet of Lake Sanford. They considered today's Opalescent to be the main northern branch of the Hudson. And on the first map of the high mountain region, William C. Redfield's map of 1837, the stream flowing from Mount Marcy was clearly labeled the Hudson River.

Regardless of the names applied by humans, geography says Lake Tear of the Clouds is the highest pond source of the Hudson River. And from its lofty pool, the water descends, "gathering volume at every brook, till in full breadth it swells before the wharves and piers of the metropolis, floating the richly burdened ships of all the nations."[25]

Heart Lake

*The purity and rarity of the atmosphere instills new life
and vigor in the system, while the blood dances so merrily through the veins that one could almost imagine the
long intervening years since childhood to have vanished
into dreams. Here. . . is a physical and mental tonic, far
more potent than can be found in drugs.*
PLATTSBURGH REPUBLICAN, ABOUT MOUNT MARCY, 1875

HEALTH-SEEKING PEOPLE quickly discovered the benefits of the
Adirondacks. Consumptives, hay fever sufferers, and other sick people
found that the mountain climate, especially the invigorating air, improved their
conditions. As early as 1859, Benson Lossing reported, "Invalids go in with hardly strength enough to reach some quiet log-house in a clearing, and come out with
strong quick pulse and elastic muscles. . . . and women begin to find more pleasure and health in that wilderness than at fashionable watering-places."[1]

No example could be more manifest than that of Miss Jenks. When she married John Moore, she could not walk two miles in a day. Moore brought her to the
woods and she could soon walk twenty. It was reported that, "Mrs. Moore can go
with her husband to almost any place, go with him to Mt. Marcy, go trapping
sable, go hunting deer on snowshoes, go in the boat for a buck in the lake, go fishing in the lake or the brooks, in fact anywhere she pleases."[2]

From her home at Upper Works, Mrs. Moore tended a line of traps sixteen
miles long, making her rounds alone on snowshoes. And she even guided, when
ladies desired company on their mountain excursions. "Think of that ye city
weaklings as you take your airings on soft cushions," wrote Stoddard, "and then
wonder if a life among the mountains is beneficial."[3]

By the end of the 1870's, more and more health-seekers visited the mountains.
Some sat in rocking chairs on hotel porches; but many camped in the open air and
climbed mountains.

Inventor Henry Van Hoevenberg came from New York City to seek the mountain's healing powers. "I owe everything to the Adirondacks," he wrote. "In 1877,
I was prostrated after a very busy summer, during which I suffered severely from
aggravated hay fever. Visiting the AuSable Lakes with a party of friends, I found
that my hay fever had left me, and during the two weeks that I spent there I was
perfectly well."[4]

At the same time, Jane Scofield, who suffered from consumption, was camped
on Upper Ausable Lake. Scofield and Van Hoevenberg took a mountain walk
together; legend says that on top of Mount Marcy, Van Hoevenberg pledged his
love to Scofield. The couple looked out over the magnificent landscape and
searched for a site to build a grand home. They chose a spot on the shore of a

heart-shaped lake beside a craggy mountain, which was immediately named Mount Jo, in honor of Miss Scofield.

Van Hoevenberg said that he then "journeyed over the top of Mount Marcy and across country to Clear Lake,"[5] which is now called Heart Lake. Did he really go directly north from the summit of Mount Marcy? This is the first hint of anyone making that trailless journey. Perhaps he really meant that they went down to Lake Colden and out to Heart Lake via Avalanche Pass.

After their two weeks in the mountains, Scofield and Van Hoevenberg separated and returned to New York. Soon, Scofield took ill again and decided to return to her home in Toronto. On her way, she detoured at Niagara Falls. She walked out to the edge of Horseshoe Falls and was never seen again. Van Hoevenberg returned to the Adirondacks the next year, he purchased the land they had admired and began constructing the grand Adirondack Lodge.[6]

Even before he finished the lodge, Van Hoevenberg began constructing trails, and forever changed mountain hiking in the Adirondacks.

The existing trail from North Elba to Mount Marcy was thirteen-and-a-half miles. The route apparently went seven and a half miles through Avalanche or Caribou Pass to Lake Colden, and then six miles along the Opalescent trail to Four Corners and the summit. Van Hoevenberg's new trail was only seven miles long—"the *shortest* and *easiest* route to the top of 'Old Tahawus,'" said Wallace's guidebook.[7]

According to one report, the new trail was scouted under Van Hoevenberg's watchful eye. The chief guide, Peter McCree, burned a birch tree here and there along the route while Mr. Van, as Van Hoevenberg was affectionately called, watched with binoculars from the summit of Mount Marcy. By following these smoke signals, Mr. Van made sure the guides stayed on course.[8]

After the trail was scouted, it had to be cut. Wallace reported in his guidebook, "'Old Bill Nye,' the intrepid guide and mountain explorer, has cut a trail directly to the summit of Mt. Marcy, enabling one to make the ascent from the 'Lodge' within 5 hours. An exquisitely beautiful cascade (discovered by Nye, and christened 'Wallace's Falls,') is encountered *en route*."[9]

As with most of his trails, Mr. Van did not simply choose the shortest path. He routed his trails past magnificent scenery, in this case, Wallace Falls, which Mr. Van called Crystal Falls and is now Indian Falls. He also built shelters at picturesque spots, such as Tahawus Cabin (Marcy Camp) near present-day Plateau.

Ad in Wallace's *Descriptive Guide*, 1875.

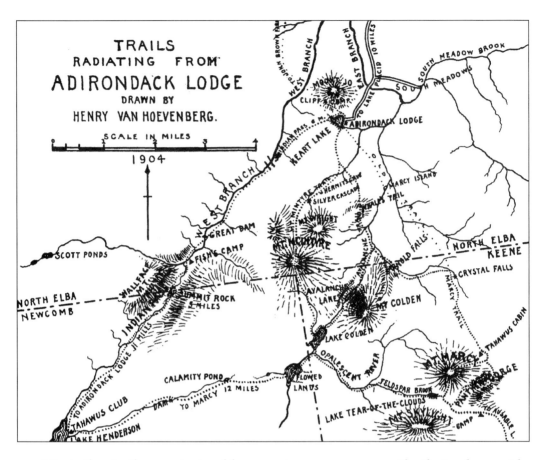

Most other trails were just ax blazes on trees or narrow paths that only a guide or experienced woodsman could follow, but Mr. Van's trails were cut wide and well cleared.[10] Thus, the ascent of Marcy could be made in four to five hours and the descent in two-and-a-half to three-and-a-half hours. But Baedeker's guidebook warned that the first half of the ascent is "generally very muddy and fatiguing."[11]

Parties guided by Mr. Van did not worry about fatigue. They could be energized by his unusual trail food. Why should hikers have to suffer with salt pork or hardtack? They needn't, preached Mr. Van. His hiking guests enjoyed fresh oranges, apples, hot coffee, and broiled steaks.

He encouraged women and children to enjoy the woods, too. And they did. They even climbed Mount Marcy. In 1894, 14-year-old George Roberts stayed at Adirondack Lodge and the next day climbed to Marcy Camp, the hut on the north slope. He recalled, "During the night we were wakened by a bear who invaded our larder, and while up on that cause were delighted with the aurora borealis."[12] Thus began his life-long love of the Adirondacks.

Evidently, Mr. Van was right: Show people the woods and the mountains. Give them good food and comfortable shelter. They will love Nature.

By the end of the 1880s, Van Hoevenberg had opened up fifty miles of hiking trails. "From a little-visited pond in the wilderness, Heart Lake became almost overnight a major center for Adirondack mountain recreation," wrote mountaineers Laura and Guy Waterman. "Van Hoevenberg must certainly be ranked as one of the major 'improvers' in this classic period of Northeastern trails history."[13]

Unfortunately, patent infringement lawsuits regarding Van Hoevenberg's inventions depleted his finances. In 1894, he sold Adirondack Lodge to cover his debts, but stayed on as caretaker. Eventually he left and went to work for Melvil Dewey at the Lake Placid Club. Soon thereafter, on September 12, 1900, the Lake Placid Club purchased the Adirondack Lodge and put Mr. Van in charge.

Through it all, the trampers kept going up Mount Marcy. Even the philosopher William James, who often vacationed in Keene Valley, stayed at Adirondack Lodge in July 1898. James came to the lodge to rest before heading to California for lecturing. Rest? He did no such thing.

"I have had an eventful 24 hours," he wrote to his wife, "and my hands are so stiff after it that my fingers can hardly hold the pen. I left, as I informed you by post-card, the Lodge at seven, and five hours of walking brought us to the top of Marcy—I carrying 18 pounds of weight in my pack."[14]

James met two friends on the mountaintop. Then he walked down to Panther Gorge camp, where he met other friends, "and two Bryn Mawr girls—the girls all dressed in boys' breeches, and cutaneously desecrated in the extreme."[15] James later apologized for his imprudent comment on their clothes. But one of the girls recalled feeling praised by his comment. She wrote, "I remember especially that he made us all feel in the van of progress," for wearing knickerbockers.[16]

That night, instead of sleeping, James "spent a good deal of it in the woods, where the streaming moonlight lit up things in a magical checkered play, and it seemed as if the Gods of all the nature-mythologies were holding an indescribable meeting in my breast with the moral Gods of the inner life. The two kinds of Gods have nothing in common."[17]

James was unable to explain in words the significance of this experience, but he wrote, "Doubtless in more ways than one, though, things in the Edinburgh lectures will be traceable to it." And, doubtless, many hikers have been impressed with great thoughts and emotions while embraced by the abyss of Panther Gorge.

At six in the morning, James shouldered his pack and climbed Marcy again. The group then "plunged down Marcy, and up Basin Mountain, led by C. [Charles] Goldmark, who had, with Mr. White, blazed a trail the year before; then down again, away down, and up the Gothics, not counting a third down-and-up over an intermediate spur [Saddleback Mountain]. It was the steepest sort of work, and, as one looked from the summits, seemed sheer impossible."[18]

James had gone into the woods in poor condition, suffering from fatigue and neuralgia in one foot. The two days of exertion not only worsened his condition but also caused heart damage, an irreparable valvular lesion. He was able to continue his normal activities but needed to avoid fatiguing himself.

Picnic on Mount Marcy, circa 1900. Man with white beard may be William White.
Courtesy of New York State Archives.

Unfortunately, he had not learned his lesson. The next year he returned and suffered yet another calamity. "Once a donkey, always a donkey;" he wrote, "at the Lodge in June, after some slow walks which seemed to do me no harm at all, I drifted one day up to the top of Marcy, and then. . .found myself in the Johns Brook Valley instead of on the Lodge trail back; and converted what would have been a three-hours' downward saunter into a seven-hours' scramble, emerging in Keene Valley at 10:15 P.M."[19] It was dark when he finally left the woods, having fainted twice along the way. James later realized the strain he had caused to his heart. "This did me no good," he wrote to a friend. "Anyhow I was an ass, and you ought to have been there to steer me straight."

William James never fully recovered his health. He died in 1910.

Another group of climbers came to Adirondack Lodge in 1903. William G. Distin, the son of a Saranac Lake photographer, and his friends Emmons, Hubbel and Dickinson planned a trip up Marcy via the lodge trail. How to travel the 20 miles from their homes in Saranac Lake to the lodge was a problem. They could hire a team, but that was too costly. They could walk, but that was too slow. Bicycles seemed to be the answer. "Later we regretted this decision as the roads were rough and sandy and we eventually had to walk most of the way anyhow and drag the bikes besides," wrote Distin.[20]

As they reached the lodge, they were met by "a strange looking little man dressed all in black leather—even to his bow tie." Of course, he was Henry Van Hoevenberg. He fed them dinner, gave them a lean-to for the night, and entertained them with mystery stories.

The next day they started up the Van Hoevenberg trail to Marcy. "The climb to the top was a strenuous one as we were soon floundering in ten or twelve inches of snow and, near the top, we encountered deep snow drifts," wrote Distin. "Our views from the top were very limited as that was the year of the big fires and we were facing heavy smoke clouds in every direction. But—we were standing on top of the state and our dream had come true!"

The Adirondack forest was highly flammable that spring. There was very little moisture on the ground because of light snowfall throughout the winter. Help did not come from spring rains; less than a quarter inch of rain fell between the middle of April and the end of May. Fires began breaking out and fire fighters fought to extinguish them, but many remained, smoldering in the dry duff.

The week after Distin's visit, wind stirred up the cinders and spread the fires. The lower half of the Van Hoevenberg trail was engulfed in flames and turned to charred rubble. The fire also destroyed Adirondack Lodge. Twenty-four years later, William G. Distin returned as the architect in charge of designing a new lodge.

Henry Van Hoevenberg with Emmons, Hubbel, Dickinson by Distin, 1903.

Johns Brook

The John's Brook trail, which for some time has been in what the politicians would call a state of "innocuous desuetude," has suddenly been cut into new life, which is perhaps the most notable event of the year in this part of the mountains.

NEWSPAPER CLIPPING, DECEMBER 1903

JOHNS BROOK VALLEY* was long ignored by seekers of Mount Marcy's summit. Not until 1903 was a practical trail cleared up the valley. And it took another twenty years for the route to become widely used.

Laura and Guy Waterman did extensive research on trail history for their book *Forest and Crag*, but found little information about the early history of the Johns Brook route. They determined that "the status of whatever Phelps put through Johns Brook valley is difficult to document."[1]

It is also difficult to determine exactly what other paths existed or who used them, but it is clear that the Johns Brook Valley had visitors—and even some semblance of a trail—long before 1903. As far back as 1847, the Tahawian Association proposed a trail through the High Peaks region "from Keene Flats, westward to the summit of Tahawus, estimated distance ten miles."[2] This clearly referred to a route up Johns Brook. Who knew about this route? Holt? Phelps? But Old Mountain Phelps didn't climb the peak until 1849 and he went by way of the Ausable Lakes.

The association's plan was scrapped. But perhaps it planted a seed because sometime within the next eight to fifteen years, Phelps found a route up Johns Brook. Exactly when is uncertain.

Dr. Walter Lowrie, a noted Alpinist who first visited Keene valley in 1887, wrote that Old Mountain Phelps had marked the route "thirty years before" (in 1857).[3] Other evidence shows that it existed by the summer of 1864. Visitor Lucia Pychowska wrote, "This John's Brook, by the way, is the shortest route up Mount Tahawus, the entire distance from the 'Flats' being only ten miles. As the greater number of visitors, however, desire to see the Au Sable Ponds *en passant*, no path has been 'bushed out,' and that mode of ascent is practicable only for hunters or woodsmen familiar with the region."[4]

Historian Russell Carson reported that Ed Phelps and Seth Dibble cut the Johns Brook trail in 1871. Their employer, Norman Dibble, a Keene Valley hotel-keeper, paid them twenty-five dollars for clearing the trail from the valley to the head of Panther Gorge. From there to the summit, the trail was never really laid out; it just developed.[5]

*The correct spelling of Johns Brook uses no apostrophe. This book will use that spelling, except in direct quotes.

The trail seemed to be readily embraced. In 1872, a guidebook said, "It [Mount Marcy] is perhaps more frequently ascended from Keene Flats, the nearest village to this mountain, by a path that follows the course of John's Brook S. W., intersecting with what is called the Panther Gorge Trail, which lies up the E. side. The distance by this route is 9 m and it passes within sight of Big Falls and Bushnell's Falls."[6]

Despite this glowing promotion, the trail had fallen out of use by the end of 1870s. According to hiker Walter Lowrie, no one had used the route to climb Marcy from 1877 to 1887.[7] Another hiker claimed that the trail was in such bad shape because "a hurricane had obliterated it."[8]

In 1886, Dr. Martin Bahler, a schoolteacher from New Jersey who established a summer school in Keene Valley, attempted to restore the trail. He led a group from the school up Phelps' old trail almost as far as the famous overhanging rock known as Slant Rock. "They failed to find the obscure blazes of the old trail just at the critical point where it turned and crossed the brook below Slant Rock," according to Lowrie. "Therefore in following up the left side of the brook they failed to notice that there was at that point a right branch, so they followed up the other, making a clear trail all the way, till they were well up between Basin and Haystack. When they discovered their mistake they were too much discouraged to try again, and this ill success confirmed the popular notion that it was impossible to find the way up Marcy from that side."[9]

It seems the guides and the visitors preferred the Ausable Lakes route anyway. And why not? There were permanent shanties, established trails, beautiful scenery, and plentiful game and fish. And according to Stoddard's 1878 guidebook, the owners of the lakes and the nearby mountain peaks, including Marcy, offered no objection to parties visiting.[10]

However, things changed in 1887, when the owners of the Ausable Lakes tract, Almon Thomas and Thomas Armstrong, lumbermen of Plattsburgh, decided to sell. The new owner was the Adirondack Mountain Reserve (AMR), an organization formed by people who loved the lakes and wanted to prevent clearcut lumbering in the area.

The AMR built cottages, completed a new wagon road to the Lower Ausable Lake, and recruited guides. These guides kept the trails in good condition and were assured work at the Upper Ausable Lake. Given such an easy task and good pay, they had no interest in maintaining trails outside the Reserve. They actually had an interest in discouraging use of the Johns Brook trail since it crossed Reserve property; they feared hikers might start fires or descend to the AMR's Ausable Lakes property.

The AMR had strict rules about cutting timber, making fires, and camping. They also had a "Rustic Gate" at the entrance to the reserve, and charged fees. In 1894, the toll for riding a saddle horse down the lake road was thirty cents. A guide was three dollars per day. Rental of a boat was a dollar per day and each day in camp was twenty-five cents per person. Nothing was sold or rented on Sundays.[11]

According to Walter Lowrie, who first came to Keene Valley in 1887, Mount Marcy had become an "aristocratic mountain." Reaching it from the AMR required a camping permit and a guide—a costly proposition. The other trail, the shortest trail, started at Adirondack Lodge. But it was almost impossible to get to the Lodge from Lake Placid and ascend Marcy in one day. Thus, the trip required climbers to spend the night at the expensive inn. As for the Upper Works route, it was a long distance from Keene Valley and also controlled by a private organization.

As a freshman at Princeton and a "callow youth," Lowrie looked for another way to climb Mount Marcy. He decided to take the Johns Brook trail. He tried to get a guide but the AMR guides "could hardly be coaxed to lead us to the mountain tops; and those who were not trappers could not be relied upon to find the way where there was no trail."[12]

Lowrie convinced his friend, Dr. Harry Catell, that they could do the climb without a guide. He had heard it was only nine miles to Marcy and then six miles to Adirondack Lodge. He estimated they could reach the Lodge in five hours, so they took only two soda biscuits, two boiled eggs, and an umbrella. Neither had any mountain climbing experience.

They started up the Johns Brook valley, following a fisherman's trail as far as Bushnell Falls. From there, they found a good trail. Unfortunately, it was the dead-end path cut by the Bahler party the year before.[13]

Lowrie and Catell reached the col between Haystack and Basin and stopped. It was late and it was raining. They ate what was left of their biscuit and spent the night camped under an umbrella. They had a good night's sleep, thanks to some of the doctor's opium pills, and returned to Keene Valley, hungry and tattered.

This sorrowful attempt did not deter Lowrie. He climbed Mount Marcy from Ausable Lakes and from Adirondack Lodge that summer. And the next year, he came back ready to try the Johns Brook trail again.[14]

Lowrie reasoned he had better hire a guide, so he chose an athletic-looking one. Partway up the trail, the guide said he had heard of wind slash in Panther Gorge that blocked their route. Lowrie suspected the story was a farce and that the guide simply did not know the way. They agreed to go toward Tabletop, find the Van Hoevenberg trail, and ascend Marcy from that trail.

However, once on the summit of Tabletop, the guide was unable to find the trail. They pressed on and eventually reached the summit of Mount Marcy. That night, the guide was too worn out to make a fire, cook supper, or prepare beds. "This was the last time I ever took a guide to show me the way in the Adirondacks," wrote Lowrie.[15]

Facing page: Slant Rock, circa 1920s. Courtesy of New York State Archives.

Author at Slant Rock, 2000, by William L. Weber, III.

The next year, 1889, Lowrie wanted to find the famous rock that was up Johns Brooks Valley. He visited Old Mountain Phelps and obtained a rough map of the location of Slant Rock, as Phelps had named it. Although the map was perfect, Lowrie had trouble finding the rock. "It might seem almost incredible now that Slant Rock was then a difficult thing to find," wrote Lowrie in 1928. "But *then* it was hidden by woods so dense that it could not be detected from the other side of the brook."[16]

Lowrie and a friend wound up on top of Haystack, "drenched by a prodigious rain." Across the gorge, they saw Marcy with an alpine waterfall flowing down its slope. After a difficult push through the thick balsams, they made it to the summit. On the descent, they found Slant Rock. It was quite conspicuous on the descent.[17]

Slant Rock served as Lowrie's base camp for many years. He covered the ends with logs and made a comfortable camp for up to six persons. He left his entire camping outfit there and even hauled up a large oven grate to put over the fire. He and his friends marked the trail up Marcy and tramped over it to get it into shape.

Having climbed Haystack, Basin, Saddleback, and Gothics, none of which had trails from the Johns Brook side, Lowrie decided to try a trip of the four peaks and Marcy in one day. At 5:00 a. m. on a July morning in 1892, he set out from Keene Valley with classmate Malcolm MacLaren. They reached the summit of Marcy at

10:00. They then proceeded to the other four summits, reaching Gothics at 3:40. They descended to the Ausable Lake road at 5:25 and rode a carriage, arriving home at 7:00 p. m.[18] Although it had been a fourteen-hour trip with ten hours and fifty minutes of walking, the two youths were not fatigued, according to Lowrie.

Lowrie did not encourage other hikers to use the Johns Brook trail. "I feel some shame in confessing that we did not make this trail accessible to the gener-

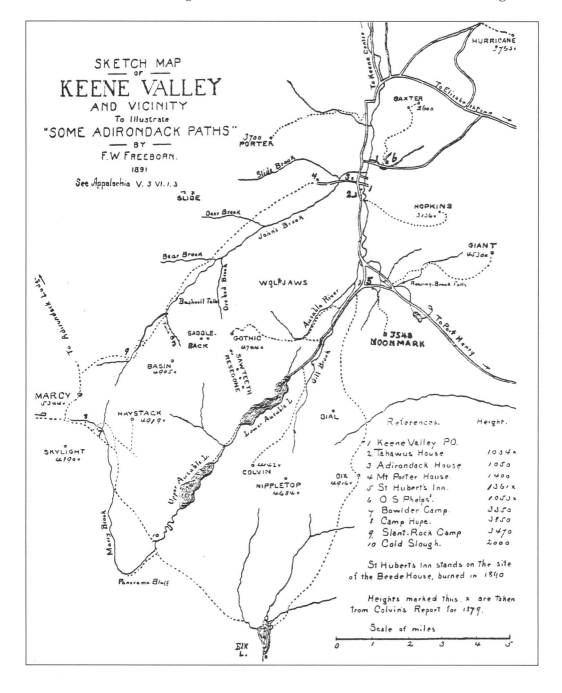

al public," wrote Lowrie, "but took pains to conceal the approach to Slant Rock at the one end and the entrance from the Lodge trail at the other."[19]

However, the route was general knowledge. Stoddard's map of 1879 showed the Johns Brook trail joining the Panther Gorge trail northeast of the summit. In 1891, *Appalachia* magazine printed an account and sketch map of the trail. Frank Freeborn's map showed the complete Johns Brook trail including the site of Slant Rock Camp. He said that the route was seldom used since "Many diverging trails marked by fishermen and exploring parties led into *culs-de-sac*."[20]

In 1895, *The New York Times* mentioned the Johns Brook trail up Mount Marcy, saying it was "almost impassable in places."[21] The *Times* also said there was a good grade up the valley and "an excellent trail could be opened." This proposed trail was quite elaborate. It consisted of an eight-mile bridle path from Keene Valley up the Johns Brook Valley and then a two-mile footpath to the top of Marcy. The estimated expense was two hundred and fifty dollars.

It seems that neither the state nor local authorities supported the plan. Thus, the Johns Brook Trail remained troublesome for several more years. No one took much interest in Johns Brook, with the exception of Lowrie—and Mel Hathaway.

Mel Hathaway was considered the best hunting and fishing guide in late nineteenth-century Keene Valley. For a while, Hathaway had a camp on the Upper Ausable. When the AMR acquired the land in 1887, they told the guides that they could keep their camps as long as they obeyed the rules, which included not shooting deer.

But Hathaway refused to stop killing deer and was ejected from AMR land. He decided to make his home in an abandoned lumber camp office in the Johns Brook Valley, on the present site of Johns Brook Lodge. He developed the clearing around his camp and raised vegetables and flowers. Visitors were greeted and shown the garden. He presented women with "bunches of nasturtiums and poppies."[22]

Mel raised honeybees that he had found in nearby hollow trees. He trapped in the winter for marten and other fur-bearers—and of course killed deer year-round to supply neighboring lumber camps with meat.

When Hathaway lived along Johns Brook, the trail was "in what the politicians would call a state of 'innocuous desuetude.'" In 1903, the Johns Brook trail was finally "cut into new life."[23] The route went right past Mel Hathaway's door.

"Mel took real delight in the trails," recalled one hiker. "He believed in them and did his share in trimming them up. He cautioned rollicking lads to be careful of fires and to clean up the shelters. The 'trail' was Broadway to him. It brought him company, admiring audiences, amusements and business. Without the trail to Marcy across his doorstep, Melvin Hathaway would have had little interest in life. Without Mel Hathaway and his clearing, the Johns Brook trail to Mount Marcy would be doubly toilsome."[24]

Billy Burger hiked the Johns Brook trail to Marcy in 1909 and called it "one of the finest bits of trail I've ever been on. . . . The forest is first growth, spruce and white birch, and is truly magnificent. The trail winds in and out through the great trees, and always up, once over a sharp hog back. Two impressions remain—openness and dampness. There is little underbrush and it is always wet."[25]

His party camped at Slant Rock, under the huge overhanging boulder on a bed of balsam boughs. "It is a most fascinating spot. . . . As I write, I can smell the balsam, look out over the edge of the blanket to the star be-studded sky above the sentinel-like spruce and listen to the flow of water but a few yards away. And as I turn over to go to sleep wonder if by any chance the rock might roll over on my mates and me while we're in slumberland."[26]

The four miles to the top of Marcy were hard work and Burger "laid out once. . . and wondered if I'd burst open." Then he went down the other side to Junction Camp (now Four Corners). "Our grub was getting low," Burger recalled. "So low in fact, and we were so hungry that when a careless member of the party kicked over an open can of clam chowder, we all joined in eating the scraps of potatoes and clams right off the ground. I have a mental picture of a particularly finicky member of the party gathering up and eating bits of chowder without even blowing off the dirt. So quickly does the veneer of civilization rub off when we are removed from social sanction and taboo—and when we're hungry!"[27]

Writer Georgia Pangborn also hiked along the Johns Brook trail in the early 1900s, and found her veneer removed. When writing nature articles, she found the pen always rose to a high childish chant and an outdoor ecstasy came upon her. Yet she noticed that the guide loved the mountains in a better way. "There is no occasion for *him* to be sentimental," wrote Pangborn, "any more than a baby is sentimental about its mother. I, the chance visitor, the intruder, I can be sentimental."[28]

She was allowed to be scared, too. "We are alone, with our unskillful ears," she wrote, "and no weapon but an ax, a hunting-knife, two hat-pins, a camera, a pair of scissors, and a fountain pen." What if a bear came by? What would he care for a hat-pin? "Didn't I see by his tracks up there on Crow that he carries some five or six hat-pins at the end of each of his hatefully human paws?"[29]

Pangborn "pottered about the brook" for several days. Mount Marcy did not call her, but "at last we too felt we must climb Marcy or be forever shamed." So she went up for "mucky and stony miles" and found some reward for the climb. At the top, she perceived what the world was like before "it was made stale by that problematical creation of the sixth day."

She wrote, "It is only mountains that can preach in this manner; to hear them, boldly take them by the beard and go up through all their discouragements. Then, when you have fought through the stunted, sharp-fingered trees, you will find a quite bare space at the top, where it is proper to raise an alter to an unknown god. And straightaway come down again, with nothing whatever to show for a foolish adventure except the right to brag ever afterward to other climbers: 'Well, I've done Marcy,' or this or that other mountain."[30]

Some of the younger generation wanted more than to brag they had made the climb. They competed for the bragging rights to the fastest climb. "Bushnell Cheney rushed up Marcy and down in five hours and a half," recalled Lowrie, "only to see his record beaten by Will Glover (or perhaps it was the other way round)—at any rate both suffered a nervous collapse which broke off their studies at Yale."[31]

Despite the occasional detriment, the thrill of climbing Mount Marcy attracted more hikers, including a young "Jimmy" Goodwin.

> I first climbed Marcy in the summer of 1919 when I was 9 years old. Our family had rented a cottage for the summer at Interbrook Lodge, located a short distance below the site of the present Garden parking lot in Keene Valley. A group of adults had planned to climb Marcy and because my father was one of them, I managed to be included. We followed the tote road that was part of what is today's South Side trail to the hermitage of Mel Hathaway. Beyond this, we continued on the Phelps Trail (which had been abandoned for some years to this point because of lumbering) over land then belonging to the Adirondack Mountain Reserve and reached Slant Rock in time for lunch.
>
> Leaving our packs at the rock, we set out for the top of Marcy. I'll never forget that first view of the summit just above the junction of the Phelps and Van Hoevenberg trails. At last I was seeing a perfect mountain—what my parents had been describing to me so many times. It was a mind picture I carried for the rest of my life. The top was even more exciting. Though I knew that my father and mother had climbed Marcy, I doubted that many others had, and looking at the sea of mountains to the west, I decided that certainly no one had ever gone into that great wilderness beyond.
>
> Significantly, though this was a clear day in August, our party met no one else throughout the day. We descended to Slant Rock where I slept my first night in the open in a place where in a few years, I would be serving as the "boy guide."[32]

James Goodwin has climbed Mount Marcy 196 times. Although he has climbed higher mountains in other parts of the world, Mount Marcy is his favorite mountain. He has a life-long association with it. From the time he was 12, he has climbed it professionally as a guide or as a good friend of his friends and acquaintances. He kept climbing into his eighties.

"I look back especially to my days as the 'boy guide,'" he says, "camping with my followers at Slant Rock, enjoying the good fellowship and listening to their conversations—including their convictions and doubts about life's problems. . . . Also, before I knew enough about rock climbing, but thanks to the good Lord, I roped two boys up the highest cliffs of Panther Gorge. There are countless other memories."[33]

Another reason for his fondness for Mount Marcy was "the matter of [Phelps's] Heaven up-h'isted-ness." He read and re-read the chapter about Old Mountain Phelps in Warner's *In the Wilderness*. "For Phelps, an ascent of Marcy

Summit of Mount Marcy, 1923. Gertrude Anderson, Jo Humphrey, and Jim Goodwin, boy guide. Courtesy of The Keene Valley Library, Archives Collection.

was a beautiful, spirited experience. Growing up with this background," says Goodwin, "I continued to think of Marcy as more than a mere highest peak in the state of New York."[34]

And he relied on that spirit during hard times. "With the 10th Mountain Division, I served on the front lines in Italy," he says, "perhaps playfully imagining that Old Mountain Phelps was taking care of me. Discharged from the Army and returning to Keene Valley, to my Interbrook Road cottage below the Garden parking lot, I left at dawn to run to the top of Marcy. To my surprise, I made the top in an hour and forty minutes—returning safely to the spot I loved best."

Mud Pond or Elk Lake

Elk Lake is extremely picturesque. Its shores are skirted with majestic mountains interspersed with inviting glens and shady nooks; and as the eye is impressed with its beauty and grandeur, the whole mind is filled with a sensation of ecstasy.   LUCY BOHRMANN, 1896

KEENE VALLEY had paths to Mount Marcy via the Ausable Lakes and Johns Brook. Lake Placid had the popular Van Hoevenberg trail or the longer routes via Indian Pass or Avalanche Pass. The Opalescent route brought trampers from the southwest. But what about the southeast?

The possibility of a route up Mount Marcy from Mud Pond (now Elk Lake) had been discovered in 1837. When the first ascent party headed toward the McIntyre Iron Works, they stopped along the way at Johnson's at Clear Pond, three miles south of Mud Pond. "The position of the High Peak of Essex [Mount Marcy] was now known to be but a few miles distant," wrote Redfield, "and Johnson informed us that the snow remained on a peak [Mount Marcy] which is visible from near his residence, till the 17th of July of the present year. We obtained a fine view of this peak the next morning."[1]

Toward the end of the report, Redfield wrote that Mount Marcy could be "most conveniently reached from Johnson's, at Clear Pond, by a course N. 20° W." Apparently no one had an interest in trying to follow that northwest line. They chose other routes—until August 1849. That month, Old Mountain Phelps and two men from Schroon, Almeron Oliver and George Estey, made a descent from Mount Marcy to the "south", presumably to Mud Pond. The exact course of their descent is uncertain.

Throughout the 1850s and 1860s, the paths cut around the Mud Pond area were not for hiking, but for lumbering. In fact, so many woods roads existed in 1865 that author Alfred Billings Street and his two guides couldn't find their way from Clear Pond to Mud Pond, a distance of only three miles. They searched everywhere for the path, finding instead "etchings of roads" that led to "some chopping, and then ceased."[2]

The party returned to Clear Pond and camped for the night. The next day they determined to reach Mud Pond by marching through the woods. "We fought the forest hand to hand up the acclivity," wrote Street, "to find but a rough path at best, leading us through blinding thickets, until at last the welcome gleam of water broke from far below." It was Mud Pond and "blue as heaven it shone."[3]

Street did not attempt to climb Marcy from Mud Pond; he went around to North Elba. But sometime in the 1860s, Old Mountain Phelps cut a trail from Mud Pond to the inlet of Upper Ausable Lake, which was known as the Cold Slough. Soon afterwards, hotel proprietors from Schroon paid guides to cut a trail over the

View from Clear Pond by Emmons. Courtesy of New York State Library.

west side of Bartlett Ridge to the foot of Panther Gorge. This trail was completed sometime before the summer of 1871.

It seems Mud Pond then started to flourish. Phelps proclaimed the Mud Pond trail to be "as feasible a way to Mount Marcy as any one, except from Keene Flats."[4] Guidebook author E. R. Wallace declared Clear Pond and Mud Pond to be "among the loveliest of the Adirondack waters—indeed almost peerless in their majestic surroundings." And Mrs. Moore and her husband, John, operated a "charming sylvan resort" at Mud Pond. They offered lodging for 12 or 15 in a log house, "which is humble and rustic of course, but clean and wholesome as can be made."[5]

The Schroon Lake hotel operators tried to take advantage of the Mud Pond charm, too. In Stoddard's 1874 guidebook, an ad for Wickham House said, "Schroon Lake is upon the most direct and desirable route to the great Northern Wilderness, and distant but 23 miles ride from the summit of Mount Marcy." Of course, they were stretching the truth a little; the horse trail ended four miles past Moore's.[6] Still, it was the only route by which tourists could ride to the foot of the mountain.

In 1875, Phelps made the trip even easier. He cut a mile-long trail from Panther Gorge up to the newly discovered notch between Skylight and Marcy. From there, he cut a side trail that led almost directly north to the summit of Mount Marcy. Trips from the southeast could now be started at Elk Lake or at the Cold Slough. Other routes to Marcy from the Ausable Lakes area fell out of use. The Cold Slough trail became the preferred trail.

A party of three, including a 10-year-old boy, took the trail in 1879. From their camp on Upper Ausable Lake, they rowed three and a half miles up the lake to the slough. The first four miles through the woods were at a very easy grade and they soon arrived in Panther Gorge. One of the trampers wrote, "Here in this gloomy mountain fastness we were startled by an unexpected sight—a large, muscular woman! Our fears soon subsided and we passed on unharmed!"[7]

The party continued up the trail to the summit, and the boy was surely one of the first, if not *the* first, 10-year-olds to stand atop Mount Marcy.

In 1894, a party of sixteen ladies and gentlemen chose to ascend Marcy along the same trail. The large group spent a rainy night at Upper Ausable Lake. In the morning, a thick gray mist hung about the camp. The party debated whether it would clear. "The party of hope finally triumphed over the 'calamity howlers' and the lazy guides, and after a hurried breakfast, the start was made," wrote Mr. Going, a member of the party.[8]

They departed from the Cold Slough. What was the condition of this trail? True to its name—it was swampy. "First a tract of evergreen wood, full of mud-holes after the rain and carpeted with the leaves and white flowers of the false violet. Then a peat bog, crossed by a frail track of spruce poles laid on the ground, and woe to him who strays off them, unless friendly aid be at hand, he will 'settle down in the country' and stay there, and the monument over him will be purple pitcher-plants and the little orchids—ladies' tresses and rattlesnake plantain—which fringe the path."[9]

After another bog, the real climb began. As the party struggled up the steep slope, the sun came out and made climbing steamy work. The "Lady from Washington" hung her jacket and hat on a tree. She figured there would be no one along *this* path to carry them off.

Finally, four miles up the trail, the party caught a glimpse of Marcy and Skylight. "Here is where the ladies generally turns back," said the guide, hoping to end his tramp.

But these ladies were "not of that stamp." They said, "Oh, how glorious! Let's hurry on," and proceeded up the path.

By now the sky was mostly blue and "the bet on the weather is triumphantly decided against the 'calamity howlers.'" The trampers got up another steep mile. The guide again hinted that the ladies might wish to stop, but the suggestion was "disdainfully ignored." The party moved on, without looking up, for fear of spoiling the grand effect.

They fought through the short balsam and came out onto bare rock, with a full view of the summit. They stopped, "breathless and appalled." Then they climbed the rocky cone to the summit.

"And the view!" wrote Going. "Marcy is indeed a king, looking down on the highest peaks around. The summit seems so small, that there is an instinctive desire to clutch something and hold on until one grows accustomed to the elevation. . . .The air is marvelously clear, and only the curve of the world limits the outlook." One boy in the party said, "It is like a big geography all spread out."[10]

In a cairn, they found a sealed brass cylinder left by the Appalachian Mountain Club.* The party wrote their names on a register inside the cylinder. Then it was time to descend.

"It is a scramble, a slip, a hurried jumping, and clutching at staying shrubs and trees," wrote Going. "The constant descent makes our hold-back muscles ache and cry out in rebellion: and shoes, being soaked in the wet trail, become unpleasantly soft and pervious to sharp stones in the way. The miles lengthen out and distances passed in the morning seem doubled by afternoon, till the Lady from Washington announces her intention of 'giving it up and going back.' Revived by the thought of a bear wearing off her good hat, we strike on again."[11]

Finally, they reached familiar landmarks, including the hat and jacket, and arrived at Cold Slough. "Marcy is only a memory," wrote Going, "but a glad and glorious memory which no one can take away."[12]

Two years later, another large party attempted the Cold Slough trail. They started at Mud Pond, which had been renamed Elk Lake for "it was once the common haunt of the North American Elk, or Moose." But more than the name had changed. The lake was no longer the "loveliest of the Adirondacks waters." It had become "dismally fringed with dead trees" and the path was no longer suitable for horses.[13]

Despite these circumstances, "six jolly careless trampers" set off for Marcy on September 3, 1896. Lucy Bohrman of Schroon Lake was the recorder of the trip.[14] Professor John W. Wiseman from Solon, Ohio, was also in the party, bringing along his baked beans and other useful articles: rubber blankets, mackintoshes, woolen blankets, shawls, bottles of Jamaica ginger, and cases of needles and thread.

The party boated across Elk Lake, removing a stump along the way. Then they walked like tightrope walkers on a log across Ausable River. At last they reached Panther Gorge Brook. "Such pebbles as were in the bed of that stream," wrote Bohrman. "Sister Haydon lamented that she could not take a few of them with her as momentoes [*sic*] of the 'Brook,' but as they weighed several tons each, she decided to leave them."[15]

Up and up they went—climbing, puffing and wheezing all the way. They reached Panther Gorge camp, ate ham sandwiches, and were soon "sleeping the sleep of the just."

In the morning, the trampers walked to the cold stream and "washed their smoked faces, rinsed the cinders of their eyes, then sat down on an old moss-covered log and pulled the tangles out of their hair." By eight o'clock, the party sat atop Mount Marcy's summit. They stayed for an hour and a half, chatting merrily and chattering their teeth. Finally, before they were frozen, they descended to

---

*Records from an 1890 meeting of the Appalachian Mountain Club indicate that the club had placed "Record Cylinders" on three Adirondack mountaintops: Marcy, Dix and Haystack.

Lake Tear of the Clouds. They found it an enchanting spot and recalled the writer who said, "Great things have small beginnings."

After a few minutes, the party started down the trail toward Lake Colden. Like Going's party, they soon discovered that walking down a mountain tosses a hiker as many troubles as going up. Bohrman wrote, "They did march down, down, down, over a trail so very crooked that a cat with a knot tied in its tail would have had great difficulty in getting through it. Then again it reminded of the darning process, for it was, over a log, and under a log, over a log and under a log."[16]

Luncheon was served atop a flat rock in the Opalescent River. It consisted of the Prof's baked beans, bread and butter, deviled ham, pickles, fig cakes, cookies, and coffee. Then the tramp began again.

At Lake Colden, they decided to return via Upper Works and Indian Pass. After spending a rainy night in a make-shift tent along the trail, the wet and bedraggled crew set off through Indian Pass.

After a while, Sister Finch sat down on a large rock and demanded a jack knife. Professor Wiseman, not knowing what she might be tempted to do, paused a few moments before handing over the weapon. She seized the knife and "with the practiced hand of one used to doing horrible things, she began to cut and slash with a ruthless hand. When she had finished, her dress was at least ten inches shorter than when she began. The remains of that dress were tenderly wound around a huge rock in the middle of the stream and left, a mute witness of the struggles which she had passed through while wearing her dress 'en traine.' "[17]

Sister Finch then led the way down the path. Bohrman lagged behind and finally sat on a large log. Finch knew just what to do—she seized the jack knife and "began an operation, which made the dress which Lady Bohrman wore, about a foot shorter than it was." This time the scraps were wrapped around a stump.

The party made slow progress and was forced to spend the night in the pass. They spent most of the evening wringing water from what was left of their garments. Thus, they named the spot "Camp Wringer."

The next day they arrived safely at the Grand View Hotel in Lake Placid. There was some difference between the elegant hotel rooms and the previous night's accommodations of "a balsam twig for a bed and a rubber shoe for a pillow."[18]

Kate Field, an international journalist, author, actress, and reformer, encouraged more women to be like Sister Finch, Lucy Bohrman, and the Lady from Washington. She encouraged those women "willing to be tanned, freckled, and even made to resemble antique statuary," to try the wilderness. She said, "Helter skelter, off with silks, kid gloves, and linen collars, on with bloomer, stout boots, and felt hat, and we helpless women are transformed into helpful human beings."[19]

Social change was in the air and fabric of the alterations was strewn along the trail down Mount Marcy.

Some hikers wished they had found some of that warm cloth to wrap around themselves. Howard Goodwin, Joe Twichell, and Dick Cole could have used it in the summer of 1901. The three friends set off from Elk Lake for their first climb of Mount Marcy. They were told that there were plenty of blankets, cooking utensils, and other supplies at Skylight Camp, a lean-to between Panther Gorge and Four Corners. They took some food and an axe and set off without even taking a coat. When they arrived at the camp, there was nothing there.

"It was so cold that our breath steamed even before sunset," recalled Goodwin. "That was a mighty cold night. We tried to sleep with our hands in our pockets, and of course, we stoked the fire all night. We were very glad to get some breakfast and to start climbing next morning."[20]

Winter Ascents

[We] could enjoy now the exhilarating purity of the air,
the frosty aroma of the balsam. The immaculate beauty of
the snow itself and its many wonderful forms; the hushed
silence; the many records of the feet of passing animals
and birds; the sweet notes of the friendly chick-a-dees; the
varied colors and textures of tree trunks and sumptuous
richness of the evergreens, and the air that is like new life;
all these rejoice the eye and the heart.
C. GRANT LaFARGE, FEBRUARY 1899

MOUNT MARCY is impressive at any time of year but in winter it can be frightfully glorious. Of course, on the summit, winter conditions can come every month of the year. The first climbers back in 1837 found half an inch of ice on the summit in August. Verplanck Colvin and his guides coped with snowstorms and icy ledges in October of 1875 as they tried to measure Marcy.

In the fall of 1883, Colvin's assistant, Mills Blake, spent thirty-seven days on Marcy in snow and ice storms.[1] While measuring angles for the Adirondack Survey, Blake tented on the top of Mount Marcy from September 10 to October 17. A violent storm on September 25 drove Blake and his crew from the top, but the next day they were back, repairing the damage done by the wind, drying out their blankets and the contents of the tent, and continuing their work. The long sojourn was an arduous experience. It was also striking proof of the devotion to duty that inspired Colvin and his aides.

Blake's diary noted that they had visits from four parties of tourists. One party arrived on October 4. Scott D. M. Goodwin of Albany, W. Scott Brown of Elizabethtown (later superintendent of the AMR), and Henry Tracey of Keeseville had left Elizabethtown to do some exploring, but quickly found themselves overtaken by a snowstorm that dropped over six inches of snow. Goodwin knew of Blake's mountaintop campsite, and so the men sought it out for shelter. They stayed overnight, making eight on the summit that night and taxing the little tent and the supply chest to the limit.[2]

Brown later wrote of the experience: "We surely had a warm reception in a decidedly cold spot. . . . [T]he snow had drifted so much that the tent was practically drifted in except in the front flap-entrance. The wind howled and the snow hurtled all night long. . . the hospitality shown to us three trampers on the occasion named above, was unbounded. It had the true cheer-ring of the Adirondacks which I had never before, nor have I since seen, so clearly and freely manifested."[3]

Blake, Colvin, and their associates braved winter conditions, but there are no accounts of them attempting to climb Mount Marcy in the official winter season.

Finally, near the end of the nine-teenth century, two local men gave it a try. J. Wesley Otis, forester and game warden for the Adirondack Mountain Reserve (AMR), and Benjamin Pond, also employed by the AMR, joked about climbing Marcy on the next clear day. The next morning, March 18, 1893, dawned clear and cold, eighteen degrees below zero. After a hearty breakfast, they set off from Otis' camp on Upper Ausable Lake with little hope of reaching the summit. They took no food with them.

At the head of Panther Gorge, they estimated the snow was ten to twelve feet deep. "The snow here was crusted and frozen so hard

John Wesley Otis. First Winter Ascent of Mount Marcy, March 18, 1893, by Benjamin Pond. Note ax for chopping ice. Courtesy of Adirondack Collection, Saranac Lake Free Library.

that snow shoes were not needed and the climb to the timber line was comparatively easy," wrote Pond. "From there on not a bush or rock could be seen. All were covered with a thick coating of glistening ice and climbing was exceedingly difficult and hazardous. But by carefully picking our way and pecking footholds here and there we made the last quarter mile and reached the top about noon. There was not a cloud to be seen and there was absolutely no wind. It was bright but cold and after taking a few pictures of scenes about the summit we started on our way down, taking a haphazard course." Otis and Pond reached camp after dusk, tired and hungry. But according to Pond, they were "none the worse for our experience, and claiming the distinction of being the first to climb Mount Marcy in winter."[4]

Thus the winter adventures on Mount Marcy were begun without ceremony by two local men. The notion that Marcy was an easy winter climb was, however, quickly dispelled. In February 1899, a winter ascent was attempted by two prominent visitors, Gifford Pinchot, chief of the United States Forestry Division and later governor of Pennsylvania, and C. Grant LaFarge, a wealthy Boston architect. They spent a week at a camp on Lake Colden, where the idea of climbing Marcy was tossed around. It was decided "it might be pleasanter to let it wait, say until June."[5] After a time, however, the notion gained a firm hold on them. Despite cold temperatures and raging winds, they set off with two guides toward Mount Marcy.

After snowshoeing all morning, they reached Lake Tear of the Clouds at noon and ate lunch.

Gifford Pinchot, 1909, by Pirie MacDonald (ADK President and Advocate for the Summit Hut on Mount Marcy in 1928). Courtesy of Library of Congress.

LaFarge thought it would be no great task to go to the top, so off they went. As the day wore on, the guides stopped; one said his snowshoes were too long and the other said his leg had gone numb. Pinchot and LaFarge pushed on.

"The wind was no more to be faced than a battery of charging razors," wrote LaFarge, "and to stand upright in it was more than we cared to attempt."[6] Pinchot estimated the temperature was between minus twenty-five and minus forty degrees Fahrenheit. It became unbearable for LaFarge. Just two hundred feet below the summit, he turned around and crawled down the slope. He stomped in the snow, trying to return circulation to his frozen feet.

Pinchot kept going. "I crawled on, over glare ice, holding by rocks that stuck through," he wrote in his diary. "Got to top. Foolish."[7]

Acres and acres of forest were beneath the chief of the U. S. Forestry Division, but the view was hidden in fog; he saw nothing but snow and ice.

The men returned to the safety of the forest. They looked at each other and burst into laughter when they saw their peculiar appearances. "Icicles hung even upon our eyelashes," LaFarge wrote, "and Pinchot's beard was coated so solidly with ice that he looked like nothing I can think of, unless, perhaps, a walrus."[8]

It happens that Pinchot had made the second winter ascent during the Blizzard of 1899, the "Storm King." Arctic temperatures and great snowfalls lasted four days, paralyzing the eastern states from the Gulf of Mexico to New England.

Four years later, when a group from Keene Valley announced they intended to ascend Mount Marcy, people said "the cold, the snow, and a limitation of the winter supply of grit, would defend them from such rashness." However, a newspaper article reported, "they went, came back alive and unfrozen, and declare that the world has not yet found out what this season is good for, which according to them is climbing Marcy in the winter."[9]

The news article about the trip was pasted into a scrapbook and marked December 1903. Was it the official winter season? Perhaps.

The trip members were Mel E. Luck and Raymond Edmunds, of Keene Valley, and a Mr. Swift, who had spent the fall there. They made the climb up the new Johns Brook trail. "The deer seem to prefer the trail to sleep upon," the newspaper reported, "for their beds of the night before were here and there, and at one point a large congregation of them had gathered for morning service—for it was Sunday—but the meeting seemed to have broken up suddenly, for nothing remained but a mass of tracks."[10]

The last two or three miles of trail were beautiful, as the snow had settled upon the boughs of the balsams, giving every tree a wonderful pure white form of its own. "When the summit is reached there is almost a sense of terror in the grandeur of the situation," according to the article. "One is in the centre of a howling snow storm with nothing else visible or audible, but the feeling of immensity and of nature's awful forces is overwhelming. Every form at that altitude is clad in heavy frost so that every stub is beautiful and the cactuses extend their arms like white sign-posts."[11]

The men returned to Keene Valley to complete their day's walk of twenty-one miles.

The next winter ascent party did not follow the Keene Valley route or Pinchot's Lake Colden route or Otis' Ausable Lakes route. This party, a group of Appalachian Mountain Club snowshoers, including several ladies, took the northern approach from Lake Placid.

The *Lake Placid Club Notes* reported (in simplified spelling): "They came, saw and conquerd. They askt for all sorts of weather and a good time, and had both."[12]

At 8:40 a. m. on January 14, 1908, they set out from the Lake Placid Club for the summit of Mount Marcy. They rode horse-drawn sleighs for twelve miles to Strock's lumber camp. The first group arrived at 10:50 and soon began walking up the lumber road under the lead of Mr. Strock. After about a mile, they donned their snowshoes and headed into the forest. After about twenty minutes of difficult progress, they were on the Van Hoevenberg trail and Mr. Strock left them.

A group of six men started off swiftly and the other twenty or so followed behind. The snow became deeper and deeper until it was three feet high and covering the trail blazes. They lost the trail but pushed on through the hard wind in the best direction. At treeline, the thermometer read seven degrees below zero and the wind grew stronger. Four of the leading men turned back.

Lewis Wells, of Hyde Park, and D. A. Harrington, of Boston, removed their snowshoes, donned ice-creepers, and pushed on. The rocks and ledges were covered with hard snow and ice, but they slowly made progress up the northerly ridge. Then, surprisingly, two climbers from the other party, Alec Newhall and Laura Banfield, appeared on the southeast slope and overtook the leading men.

At 4:10 p. m. Laura Banfield, of Worcester, Mass., stepped onto the summit. She was "The first woman on record to ascend Mount Marcy in winter, the first member of our party to arrive, and the only lady in it who ventured above the tree-line," wrote Lewis Wells. "Mr. Newhall of Jamaica Plain arrived immediately after, and Mr. Harrington and myself, after a futile attempt to ascend by way of the ridge, followed their route up the steep incline and reached the top at 4:15."[13]

The view was magnificent but the bitter wind made it impossible to linger. At 4:25 they descended the steep slopes, running and sliding most of the way. A magnificent sunset followed by a nearly full moon made the walk through the snowy woods "weird and fantastic." They arrived at South Meadow at 8:15 p. m., after nine hours in the woods. Sleighs returned them to the Lake Placid Club, "with no one the worse for the trip."

The Alpine Zone

The luxurious cit will cool his champagne amid the snows of Mount Marcy; and his botanizing daughter, who has read in Michaux's American Sylva, of pines more than two hundred feet in height, will wonder to pluck full-grown trees of the same genus, which she can put into her reticule.   CHARLES HOFFMAN, 1837

HIKING UP MOUNT MARCY requires a passage through four vegetation zones. From the northern hardwood forest of beech, sugar maple, and yellow and paper birch, you ascend to the dark green forest of balsam fir and red spruce. Above 3,000 feet, you enter the sub-alpine zone where the hundred-year-old spruce and fir trees are short and gnarly. Above 4,000 feet, there are few trees, and bare rocks intersperse with patches of vegetation. You have entered the alpine zone. It comprises only about forty acres on Mount Marcy, but it is of great interest.

Since botanist John Torrey first stepped onto Marcy's summit in 1837, botanists, naturalists, and outdoor enthusiasts have marveled at the Arctic-like environment and the plants that live there. Torrey wrote, "On the fifth of August we found plenty of ice near the summit—and in the shade, the water was freezing in the middle of the day. I found many interesting alpine plants never before seen in the United States, except on the White Hills of NH."[1] He noted the presence of sandwort, goldenrod, crowberry, rush, sedge, meadow grass, and club moss.

Ebenezer Emmons and James Hall, geologists who climbed with Torrey, also noted the ice and alpine characteristics. "The summit is a naked rock and for many feet below the vegetation is moss and lichens with a few stinted spruces and alpine plants," wrote Hall.[2] No other mountain range in the state was known to be of such great elevation as to hold alpine features. This was a great boon for the scientists and the Natural History Survey.

The very next month, author and poet Charles Hoffman visited the area and predicted this alpine summit would become a botany playground where the "luxurious" city gentleman would cool champagne in the snows and his daughter would pluck dwarf pines.[3] The prediction did not materialize, but the alpine habitat did attract attention.

Botanist Charles Christopher Parry began his plant collections in northern New York, climbing Mount Marcy in the early 1840s.[4] He earned a medical degree at Columbia College, where he studied medical botany under Dr. John Torrey.[5] Parry later became a noted western botanist and is best remembered for his discovery of the Torrey Pine. Unfortunately, records of his Mount Marcy explorations have not been located.

Summit of Mount Marcy from south, 2000.

Scientist Farrand Benedict did record his findings. He wrote, "In the highest Alpine regions are, of plants, the Alpine willow-herb and bilberry, the Lapland diapensia, and others peculiar to the clime, reindeer-moss and lichens."[6]

In 1870 an anonymous female botanist came. Along the trail she noted the sundew plant, dwarf cornel, Linnaea, creeping snowberry, sheep laurel, and red peat moss in two varieties (Sphagnum acutifolia and Sphagnum sedoides). On the summit, she found mountain sandwort, mountain cranberry, "curious" lichens and a few mosses.[7] Another visitor picked "a perfect, though diminutive, blossom of the harebell" within three feet of the highest point of the summit in September 1872.[8]

About 1873, Old Mountain Phelps described the overall appearance of the alpine zone. He wrote, "[The summit] is comparatively level for 6 rods north and south, and 15 rods east and west. A few loose boulders lie about promiscuously. . . . It is bare and clear the fartherest down the southwest side. The west side of this mountain has more the appearance of a pasture hillside than a mountain above vegetation. Its partial covering of alpine grasses and other alpine plants and shrubs give it a domestic and agricultural appearance. The whole south side is covered with bristly balsam up within a few rods of the top."[9]

State Botanist Charles H. Peck made more detailed observations during his visits to Mount Marcy. By 1867, he had found several rare mosses, including two, Dicranum polycarpum and Aulacomnion turgidum, which had not been found elsewhere in the state. On another trip in 1871, Peck collected alpine plants, mushrooms, fungus, and "everything of interest to his department."[10]

It was an exciting time to be a botanist, a chance to discover new flora on mountain summits. "We might suppose that we had been suddenly transported to some boreal region, for here we have many of the characteristic plants of Labrador and other frozen climes," wrote Peck's colleague. "Hence we have a rich and peculiar field of research."[11]

In his report of 1879, Peck presented an extensive list of the species found on Mount Marcy, and described the tundra-like environment:

> The summits of the high peaks of the Adirondack Mountains are destitute of the forest trees that clothe their slopes. A few of the hardy species do spring up in these elevated places, but they do not attain the stature of trees. They are dwarfed into mere shrubs, and are sometimes so transformed in appearances that they are not readily recognized by those who are unaccustomed to close observation. These open summits are inhabited by various species of plants that do not grow on those mountains whose tops are covered by trees. . . . As Mount Marcy surpasses its neighbors in altitude and extent of open summit, so it also surpasses them in the number of its species of plants. With few exceptions a list of plants of its summit would include the species found on any of the high peaks of this region. On the other hand, several species occur on the summit of Mount Marcy that have not been found on any of the neighboring mountains.[12]

But Peck feared that these plants might be disappearing.

> About forty years ago the little Moss plant, *Cassiope hypoides*, was found by Dr. Parry growing in a sheltered depression on the summit of Mount Marcy, but it does not appear to have been found there since. Some years ago Prof. Lesquereux found a rare Moss, *Tetraplodon mnioides*, near the summit, but in my subsequent visits to the mountain I failed to rediscover it. Other plants, such as Rhododendron lapponicum, Betula glandulosa, Juncus trifidus, Aulacomnion turgidum, Myurella julacea, and Hypnum sarmentosum are in such small quantities that they are in danger of being exhausted from the locality if taken too freely by botanists and other visitors.[13]

Of course, the summit vegetation was no longer in its pristine state. Visitors had made cairns, burned moss and spruce, built a stone hut, trampled vegetation, and taken vegetation samples. But these early accounts, in company with early sketches and carvings, provide the best picture of what the alpine zone looked like before masses of people arrived on the summit.

One recurring observation is of the naked rock at the upper summit. It seems the summit was not completely covered in luxuriant vegetation. What surprised Peck was that the summit imitated the conditions of marshes. The abundance of marshy sphagnum moss caused the botanist "a feeling of surprise in his mind when beholding it for the first time."[14] This observation is startling, but astute; Mount Marcy's summit is a bog-type ecosystem. As scientist Edwin Ketchledge explained in 1970, "The summit may be visualized as a thin veneer of sphagnum bog arching over the summit rock like a giant, upside-down bowl, a concave cap of bog environment sitting inverted on a mountain top, of all places!"[15]

Other scientists studied other aspects of Mount Marcy. Professor J. A. Lintner, state entomologist, spent time in the area in 1869.[16] His list of insects appeared in an Appendix to Colvin's 1879 report. The same report contained an account about the winter fauna of Mount Marcy, prepared by Verplanck Colvin in 1876. He called them "winter fauna" because he identified many of them by their footprints in the snow. But as he noted, the summit is often whitened "as late as the beginning of July, and the first of September rarely passes without a premonitory, though temporary, covering of the crest with snow."[17]

Colvin reported the following habitants on Mount Marcy: panther, Canada lynx, fisher, sable, varying hare, rabbit, red squirrel, deer mice, raven, grouse, snowbirds, bald eagle, hawk, owl, Canada jay, woodpecker. On the other hand, he was surprised to find no signs of deer, bear, moose, raccoon, fox, or wolf.

During the summer of 1905, Elon Howard Eaton, professor of biology and ornithology at Hobart and William Smith Colleges, made an exhaustive study of the bird life about the Ausable lakes and Mount Marcy. With the help of his assistants, he found that at least one hundred species of birds were nesting within ten miles of Mount Marcy.[18]

On August 26, 1914, John W. Harshberger, of the University of Pennsylvania, climbed to the summit of Mount Marcy to look at the plants and, more important, the bare rocks and soil. He concluded that several acres of the summit were a fell-field, "a rocky flat, or plateau, situated in arctic or subarctic regions or on the alpine summits of mountains in northern as well as southern latitudes."[19]

The soil of a fell-field is broken up by stones, rocks, boulders, rocky slabs, or outcropping ledges. Thus the surface of the fell-field is never completely covered with plants. In regard to the fell-field on Mount Marcy, Harshberger wrote, "Here is a relatively flat surface covered with large angular blocks of crystalline rocks which have resisted the action of the elements of ages. The open summit, just below which is a rock ledge behind which the writer's party took shelter from the icy blast, may be compared to an ellipse whose axis lies in a northeast and southwest direction but whose circumference is irregular."

Alpine vegetation among rocks, 2000.

Harshberger noted that the spaces between the tufts of mosses were filled with dust and sand, apparently composed of particles of disintegrated rock. In the bigger spaces between the boulders and in the rock pockets, there were particles of disintegrated rock, soil, and sand mingled with the stems and leaves of the mosses and other alpine plants. This provided sufficient soil for the growth of the few low shrubs, prostrate balsams, and other characteristic species that grew on the summit.

Then, he pointed out the importance of the summit boulders: "The boulders serve to protect the growing plants from the dry winds and icy blasts which blow across the mountain dome. The soil in most places is but a few inches deep, but as the rock crannies are filled with it and with loose rock fragments, the roots of the alpine plants can descend to considerable depths without opposition to their growth."[20]

Harshberger succinctly articulated the role of moss, sand, rock particles, and boulders in the growth of alpine plants. Unfortunately, his report must not have reached the public or was ignored. Fourteen years later, summit rocks were used to build a stone shelter atop Mount Marcy.

In 1919, Charles C. Adams, George P. Burns, T. L. Hankinson, Barrington Moore, and Norman Taylor made a comprehensive study of the plants and animals of Mount Marcy. Their findings were published in three parts in *Ecology* magazine in 1920. They examined two localities in detail: the dwarf birch meadow at 5,250 feet (sometimes called the snowbowl or cirque) and the meadow on the southeast side at 5,100 feet.

The surprising finding in the dwarf birch meadow was that a good percentage of lowland species were inhabitants of this upland site. Under these elevated conditions, the species assumed different characteristics from their usual lowland ones. They were stunted and discolored and made only poor, shriveled fruits, but they persisted. "Their gradual, slow encroachment of this mountain top is sure and likely to end in the curtailment or disappearance of true alpine plants," Taylor said during a lecture. But he also recognized that "this process must be very slow; centuries long even at its swiftest."[21]

This spot, protected from winds, was also favorable to animals from lower altitudes. Spiders, beetles, bugs, grasshoppers, butterflies, and ants were observed.

The meadow on the southeast side contained a number of lowland species, too. "Nowhere is the elevation great enough nor conditions unfavorable enough so that there is not this encroachment of lowland species up through the timber line and quite over the summit," the scientists wrote.[22] Contrariwise, the alpine species were not found invading the lower elevations.

Another important finding of the study was that the vegetation was constantly subject to destruction, not only by climate, but also by sliding boulders and slabs of rock. Something as mundane as a spring thaw could send an ancient clump of plants sliding down a steep slope.

The scientists concluded that the vegetation was in a constant state of flux, and "it might be difficult or impossible to describe or conjecture what the ultimate type of vegetation would be, nor the steps that lead to that fulfillment." In some less steep places, the alpine vegetation had reached a climax state but it was doubtful that the vegetation would ever cover the whole mountain.[23]

The findings of Peck, Harshberger, Adams, and the other scientists were of vital importance to the preservation of the summit of Mount Marcy. They paved the way for more recent scientists such as Orra Phelps, H. E. Woodin, and Ed Ketchledge, and they confirmed that this high peak was more than a place of recreation and aesthetic appeal—it was a rare and fragile ecosystem.

Roosevelt's Ride

Vice-President Roosevelt started at 6 o'clock yesterday morning from the Tahawus Club with guides on a hunting trip through the forests. On receipt of the dispatches stating that President McKinley's condition was critical, men were immediately started in search of him. Up to 5 o'clock last evening it was impossible to locate him, but he was finally found on the top of Mount Marcy.

THE NEW YORK TIMES, SEPTEMBER 14, 1901

THEODORE ROOSEVELT'S affinity for the Adirondacks began when he was a boy. At Lake George, he played with a salamander and observed a hamster mouse and a bald eagle. Then he tried to ascend a mountain but the climbing was so hard that he was "dead beat" before he came to the top. Near the Lower St. Regis, he was allowed to go "in the bush." He pitched tents, caught trout, and listened to his father read *The Last of the Mohicans* by the light of the campfire. At Lake Placid, he helped collect a hundred species of lichens and fungi from a peninsula on the lake.[1]

In 1877, at the age of eighteen, Roosevelt and Henry Minot, a Harvard classmate, published *The Summer Birds of the Adirondacks in Franklin County, N.Y.* Besides listing ninety-seven species, the book provided a glimpse of Roosevelt's intense interest in nature and the Adirondack wilderness.

Roosevelt moved on to political appointments, big game hunting in the West, and rough-riding up San Juan Hill. Yet it seems fitting that the Adirondacks—and the tallest mountain among them—provided the setting for one of the most exciting events in his life.

The story starts on September 6, 1901, with Vice President Roosevelt on an island in Lake Champlain, a stop on his way to the Adirondacks. He was speaking at an outing of the Vermont Fish and Game League at Isle la Motte when a telephone call came from the wife of the manager of the New England Telephone Company. She said that a story was coming in over the wires that President William McKinley had been shot at the Pan American Exposition in Buffalo.

Roosevelt boarded the yacht of Dr. W. Seward Webb and headed to Burlington. His friends warned him to avoid Buffalo because as heir to the Presidency he might be in danger. Or he might appear ambitious and opportunistic. But not to go might appear insensitive. Roosevelt decided to do what seemed natural to him. He boarded a special train for Buffalo.

In Buffalo, he learned that the President's recovery was almost certain. He remained near the President, conferred with Cabinet members, and talked to the press. On Tuesday, September 10, after three days in Buffalo, Roosevelt

President William McKinley and Vice-President Theodore Roosevelt, 1900.
Courtesy of Library of Congress.

announced to the press: "You may say that I am absolutely sure that the President will recover, so sure, in fact, that I leave here tonight."[2]

Roosevelt and his private secretary, William Loeb Jr., left Buffalo. Loeb stayed in Albany to await further news while Roosevelt went to the Adirondacks to join his family. Roosevelt's travel itinerary was kept quiet for fear there was a plot against his life.

On Wednesday, he arrived unannounced at the North Creek railroad station. The next twenty-five miles were over rutted country roads in an open buckboard. As if that was not enough, it started to rain. A drenched Roosevelt arrived at the Lower Works, the headquarters of the Tahawus Club (formed in 1897 as a successor to the Adirondack Club). Mrs. Edith Roosevelt met him and together they rode another ten miles to a cottage at the Upper Works.

No doubt Mr. Roosevelt asked about the health of Alice and Quentin, who had both been in the hospital recently. And Mrs. Roosevelt told him the exciting news: Theodore Jr. had just shot his first deer.

At the cottage, Alice, Theodore Jr., Kermit, Archie, Ethel, and Quentin greeted their father. He probably added his wet clothes to the "shoes and stockings and little trousers and skirts, hung on lines in front of the fire to dry." As Mrs. Roosevelt put it, "The Adirondacks is probably the wettest place in the world."[3]

MacNaughton Cottage in 1999 where Roosevelt family stayed in 1901.

Perhaps it is, but her children were only steps from the banks of the Hudson River and as she said, "they did nothing but play there." Nothing, except sliding down the sloping roof of the cottage. Thankfully, she didn't know about that.[4]

It seems that Roosevelt and the family had planned to leave the mountains on Friday or Saturday, but since the roads were bad from the storm, they decided to stay for several days. Besides, Roosevelt, the renowned woodsman, declared that he wanted to climb Mount Marcy. He probably needed to escape the scrutiny and political pressure. And the criticism from some who said he seemed like a vulture at McKinley's bedside.

Apparently, Loeb was never informed of the change in plans. Of course, communications from Upper Works were not easy. The telegraph line came only to North Creek, thirty-five miles away. Telephone service was still quite rare in 1901. There were fewer than two million phones in the country. Yet a single-wire grounded telephone circuit connected North Creek with Lower Works. That telephone was still ten miles away—ten muddy, rutty, wretched miles away.[5]

On Thursday afternoon, word reached Roosevelt that the President was in "splendid" condition. So the whole family, except four-year-old Quentin, set off for the woods. Miss Young, the governess; James MacNaughton, president of the Tahawus Club; two Harvard law students, Beverley and Herman Robinson; guide Noah LaCasse; and several guides came along, too.

The large group walked five miles up the Calamity Brook trail to Flowed Land and then went by canoe to the western end of Lake Colden. They stayed overnight at two cabins, where they had "miserable little cots," slept on "balsam boughs," and rowed across the lakes to get to breakfast, according to Mrs. Roosevelt.[6]

She may have had an uncomfortable night but at least she was far from newsmen and assassins. Far from trains and phones. Far from the trouble in Buffalo. During the night, President McKinley's condition worsened. He was in great danger of dying. Earlier reports had favorably construed his condition. The truth was that President McKinley "never had one chance to recover from the assassin's bullet." The surgeons had used all of the resources of their science and their skill, but complications were beyond their control. They could not have detected the gangrenous infection.[7]

Vice President Roosevelt had to be summoned quickly.

A telegram was sent to North Creek. It was relayed by telephone to the Lower Works and written down on a piece of paper. The paper was carried by buckboard and delivered to David Hunter at the Upper Works a little after ten o'clock in the morning. Hunter called to the guides sitting around the fire at the clubhouse. "There is bad news from the President. Who will carry the message to Mr. Roosevelt?"[8]

Tall, thin, 53-year-old Harrison Hall was chosen. He quickly set off on the trail to Lake Colden. Along the way, he met Mrs. Roosevelt and the children returning to the cottage. Hall pushed on toward Mount Marcy and Roosevelt. But it was not easy.

"From the club to Lake Colden the path was plain and clear. Beyond there it had been rarely used, and the fallen deadwood clogged every step," reported the *New York Herald*. "Still, with the same sure, catlike stride, too wise to hurry, too eager to slacken speed, he pushed on through the black tangle of primeval forest. Many strange sights had those huge old gray pines beheld, many tragedies of hunter and hunted, but this spectacle of the silent messenger, with the fateful slips of yellow paper in his hand, was new to them. New also to the world, for never before had so strange a courier borne notice to a man of destiny that his time of ruling was at hand."[9]

Roosevelt and his companions were far ahead of the messenger. They had left Lake Colden at nine o'clock that morning and arrived at the summit about noon. Clouds loomed over the scene; it was not a good day for views. It was not a good day, period. It was Friday the 13th.

Eventually the sky cleared and they could see far and wide. "Beautiful country, beautiful country!" Roosevelt said over and over.[10] Then the sky darkened and heavy clouds rolled in. They quickly descended a thousand feet to Lake Tear of the Clouds and stopped for lunch.

Roosevelt started eating from a tin of ox tongue. "I was perfectly happy until I saw a runner some distance away," he later told a friend. "I had had a bully tramp and was looking forward to dinner with the interest only an appetite worked up in the woods gives you. When I saw the runner, I instinctively knew he had bad news, the worst news in the world."[11]

Exactly what bad news was delivered and how Roosevelt reacted is unclear.

In his autobiography, Roosevelt said, "He handed me a telegram saying that the President's condition was much worse and that I must come to Buffalo immediately."[12]

Two accounts said that Hall handed the Vice President a slip of paper that read, "The President appears to be dying and members of the cabinet think you should lose no time in coming."[13] Another account said the message read, "Cortelyou wires President's condition causes gravest apprehension. Ansley Wilcox telephoned 6 a.m. slight improvement. Advise your coming here immediately. Will meet you if necessary. Will send special engine to bring you in case you miss the 10:20 train this morning."[14] Roosevelt is reported to have said, "Complicated, complicated, it cannot be. I must return to the club at once."[15]

Norman Hall presents a different version. "What happened next angered my grandfather, Harrison Hall. He had hurried as fast as the wet, slippery, foggy trail would permit any guide to travel. He knew the message he bore was urgent, and he had not even taken time to tell Mrs. Roosevelt about it when they met on the trail below. The Vice President took the message, read it, said nothing but calmly turned and finished his lunch. My grandfather never had much to say about that moment. It left him flabbergasted."[16]

Regardless of what was said, or not said, the party started down the mountain. Roosevelt reached the house about 5:30 and immediately asked if there were any further messages. No further word had come.

He decided he would not go to Buffalo right away. He sent a messenger to Lower Works to arrange for a relay of horses in case he needed them and to pick up any later messages. Mrs. Roosevelt reported that her husband told her "I'm not going unless I am really needed. I have been there once and that shows how I feel. But I will not go to stand beside those people who are suffering and anxious. I'm going to wait here."[17]

Surely Roosevelt must have been tense wondering about the condition of the President. Of course, the entire country was tense, but for a different reason. They knew the President's condition; they knew he was dying. But they did not know the exact whereabouts of Vice President Roosevelt, and that was troublesome. They might have been even more troubled had they known that New York City detectives had just arrested a man who declared he was on his way to kill Roosevelt.[18]

Throughout the afternoon and evening, Mike Breen at Lower Works took down various messages telephoned from North Creek—from McKinley's secretary, who reported on the poor condition of the President; from secretary Loeb, who was on his way from Albany to North Creek with a special train; from various newspaper men requesting to accompany Roosevelt to Buffalo. Some of these messages were relayed to Roosevelt between ten and eleven o'clock that night. One of the messages stated that Roosevelt should come at once. Another said, "The President is dying."

Roosevelt threw on his clothes and jumped into a waiting buckboard. His friends argued that he should wait until morning; it was dangerous to go over dark mountain roads. He is reputed to have said that if they would not provide a rig he would go on foot.[19]

Dave Hunter hitched up a horse and wagon. "It had been raining a lot during the last few days and the road was in terrible shape," he recalled. "So we started out down through the mud—plunk, plunk, plunk."[20] Amused by later news reports of breakneck speed, Guide Ira Proctor said, "It was Jimmy Lindsay's big bay—must have weighed over 1,400 pounds. Of course he didn't poke along any, but he hardly broke a record."[21]

At one o'clock, Hunter pulled the buckboard into the Lower Works. Roosevelt immediately went to the telephone. He called Loeb to say that he was on his way. Loeb told him the President was in a coma.[22]

Plaque commemorating Roosevelt's Ride from the Tahawus Club to North Creek.

Roosevelt drank a cup of hot coffee and jumped into another wagon for the next nine-mile ride. Orrin Kellogg drove this leg of the relay through drizzle and rain. He gave Roosevelt his old raincoat to protect himself from the mud splashing from the wheels. Unknown to either man, about halfway through the ride, McKinley died and Roosevelt became President.

Down the road at Aiden Lair hotel, Mike Cronin waited and prepared to drive the next leg of the trip. Shortly before Roosevelt's arrival, a telegram from North Creek was telephoned to Cronin. The message said, "The President died at 2:15 this morning."

The people at Aiden Lair now knew they were waiting for the President of the United States. But Cronin asked them to keep the news a secret from Roosevelt. Why? "The astute driver thought it best not to increase his impatience or further try his nerves," reported the *New York Herald*.[23]

When Roosevelt's wagon finally arrived at Aiden Lair at 3:15 a. m., very little was said. Roosevelt was urged to wait. He was told there were some bad spots in the road and it would be light in only a few hours. But Roosevelt wanted to push on. For him, it was still a race against death.[24]

Cronin agreed to speed along the dark road, "keeping as tight a grip on his secret as he did on his reins." Cronin recalled, "At one place, while we were going down a slippery hill, one of the horses stumbled. It was a ticklish bit of road and I was beginning to get somewhat uneasy and began holding the team back, but Mr. Roosevelt said, 'Oh, that don't matter. Push ahead!'"[25]

About two miles from North Creek, they halted. Roosevelt got out, stretched his legs, and straightened his clothes. "To Mike Cronin, this was a treasured pause, as he watched his friend the President of the United States 'spruce up' for the occasion. Besides, those fleeting moments gave the horses the chance they needed 'to blow' before the last dash."[26]

At dawn, the horses drew up beside the waiting train at North Creek. Cronin had covered the sixteen miles in one hour and forty-one minutes. He beat his own speed record by a quarter of an hour.[27]

The excitement of Roosevelt's arrival was mixed with the graveness of the news that needed to be delivered. Cronin handed Loeb the slip of paper with the notice of McKinley's death. Loeb passed it to Roosevelt. Then the two men climbed aboard the train.

"As soon as Mr. Roosevelt was aboard, the engineer, with instructions to make the run of his life to Albany, pulled the throttle open and the train sprang out of the dawn into a stretch of track 104 miles long." However, the track was not clear. Two men on a handcar were on the track just north of Albany. Fortunately, the men jumped just a minute before the speeding train knocked the handcar off the track. Without further mishap, the train reached Albany shortly after eight o'clock. They changed engines and sped toward Buffalo, reaching there at 1:38 P.M. and "having broken every record for a run between Albany and that city."[28]

Just past 3:30 that afternoon, Roosevelt took the oath of office as the nation's twenty-sixth President. In one fast and furious gallop, he went from the summit of Mount Marcy to the highest office in the country. "It is a dreadful thing to come into the Presidency this way;" he wrote to a friend, "but it would be a far worse thing to be morbid about it. Here is the task, and I have got to do it to the best of my ability; and that is all there is about it."[29]

According to guide Noah LaCasse, the story does not end there. In a news interview, he said, "The man [Mike Cronin] that drove the last team of the three was also the proprietor of a resort hotel, where the rich and fashionable of the East gather yearly. And a half dozen times each year he has brought out a pair of horse shoes to show his guests, claiming that they were the original shoes on his team on that memorable occasion.

"The guests immediately suggest an auction and according to Mr. LaCasse, the driver has since disposed of 25 pair of horse shoes at $25 a pair—all of which were the one and only 'originals.'"[30]

Obviously, this was a tall tale, which grew taller with time. In 1960, author William Chapman White said there were four hundred genuine shoes.[31]

The truth is that Cronin never sold horseshoes to anyone. But his wife says he did like a good story and perhaps had a hand in starting this tall tale.[32]

Guide Noah LaCasse with Frying Pan Clock given to him by President Roosevelt.

Horseshoes are no longer required along the route from Upper Works to North Creek. The lower part is now Route 28N and designated the Roosevelt-Marcy Memorial Highway. A marker beside the macadam road marks the spot Roosevelt passed at 2:15 on the morning of September 14, 1901—the moment McKinley died.

In July 1999, a more permanent "marker" was designated in honor of Theodore Roosevelt. A 3,821-foot mountain located about two-and-a-half miles north of Mount Marcy was officially named TR Mountain.

A New Century

We had never seen anything like it. For mile after mile, there was nothing but charred blackness. Every bit of the Marcy trail was burned away, as was the forest floor covering of leaves, duff and everything else.
HOWARD GOODWIN, JULY 1903

AT THE TURN OF THE CENTURY, thirteen-year-old William Glover went up Mount Marcy with Walter Lowrie, Ed Isham, and a boy named John. The foursome went up from the Ausable Lakes, crossed Marcy Brook on a "stringer," and climbed to Panther Gorge lean-to. At camp, Isham told the boys, "Now fellows, here's the batter and here's the frying pan, and if you two can't toss your own pancakes, you don't eat, that's all!"[1]

For young Glover, the joy of flipping his own pancakes overshadowed the entire trip, even the view of the "seemingly infinite universe of peaks" from Marcy's summit. But perhaps he would have felt differently if the life of President McKinley had not ended so tragically. It happened that Glover's party was on top of Mount Marcy in September 1901, on or near the same day that Vice President Roosevelt was there. Glover may have met the Vice President if Roosevelt hadn't been called to Buffalo to take the oath as President.

Roosevelt's race through the woods focused the world's attention on Mount Marcy. Two years later, the mountain attracted attention again. What was racing through the woods this time? Fire.

The fire of 1903 caused no loss of human life but it scorched over 600,000 acres of timberland in northern New York.[2] Cascade and Porter Mountains burned. From South Meadow to Indian Pass, and over the shoulder of Algonquin. Burned. The sides of Phelps Mountain and Big Slide. Burned.[3]

Along its path, the fire destroyed one major structure: the Adirondack Lodge. And it obliterated the Van Hoevenberg trail to Marcy. Howard Goodwin described the scene a month later:

We [Goodwin and Joe Twichell] arranged for a guide, a man by the name of Burt Hines [Bert Hinds], to take us through the burned forest. Driving to the ruins of the lodge, we started off through the blackened woods. We had never seen anything like it. For mile after mile, there was nothing but charred blackness. Every bit of the Marcy trail was burned away, as was the forest floor covering of leaves, duff and everything else. It was a cool, cloudy day, and those woods certainly looked dark. Hines was a good guide and led us to the edge of the burned forest right where the unburned Van Hoevenberg trail came down to what is now called Phelps Brook.[4]

Goodwin and Twichell said good-bye to Hinds and went up to the summit of Marcy. They came down the other side via the Elk Lake trail.

Although forests had burned and trails been altered, the summit of Mount Marcy was still intact and still charming hikers. Seneca Ray Stoddard dedicated the entire May 1906 issue of his *Northern Monthly* magazine to Mount Marcy. "Pen can convey but little of the scene, pencil can not suggest its blended strength and delicacy," he wrote. "The rude laugh is hushed, the boisterous shout dies out on reverential lips, the body shrinks down feeling its own little-ness while the soul expanding rises to claim kinship with the Creator, questioning not His existence."[5]

Unlike his nineteenth-century peers, Stoddard did not think

Top: South Meadow, with Mount Jo in background, 1911. Note the charred trees.
Above: Summit of Mount Marcy from south, 1916/17.
Courtesy of Adirondack Research Library.

Marcy was a mountain of wild grandeur. Instead, he felt it was a place of restfulness and harmony and peace. "Does it pay to climb the Mountain?" he asked. "A thousand times yes! In return will come back a flood of memories when the weariness is forgotten, lifting the soul a little higher and making one better for having stood on a summit above the common world."[6]

But he warned novice hikers about those notorious Adirondack miles. "One day suffices for those who have strength and some experience on mountain trails, but at best the distance will seem three times its actual length."[7]

The warning did not scare Governor (later Chief Justice) Charles Evans Hughes. But of course, he took three days to climb Mount Marcy. In August 1908, he went through Indian Pass and spent one night at the Tahawus Club. He camped the next night at Lake Colden and then ascended Marcy. The governor wished no reporter or photographer to accompany him. But L. E. Shattuck, of the *New York Tribune*, followed him into the woods anyway.

The day of the Governor's hike dawned dark and gloomy and promised rain but the governor refused to postpone his plans. He left the Stevens House in Lake Placid at 5:30 a. m. After a ten-mile buggy ride to Heart Lake, the party set off toward Indian Pass.

Reporter Shattuck and his guide, Pierce, followed some distance behind, trying not to be detected by the Governor's party. Pierce was unfamiliar with the route through the pass, but he easily followed the footprints in the soft, muddy trail. Still, it was not an easy walk. Shattuck wrote,

> Quivering in every muscle under the sustained exertion, sweating at every pore, covered with mud from top to toe, soaked with rain water and about ready to abandon the trip in disgust, we pulled ourselves up over the last ledge of rock, where the trail swings to the left at the top of Indian Pass, and there we found not only the "height o' land," but what we had come all the long, dreary, rain soaked, mud spattered nine miles from Adirondack Lodge to find—Governor Hughes and his party, just about to eat luncheon beneath a little hemlock lean-to erected on Summit Rock.[8]

The governor had no choice but to let the newsman join him for lunch.

The rain came down in torrents as they resumed the hike. When they reached the clubhouse of the Tahawus Club, the governor was given a hot bath, brisk rubdown, and dry clothes. The newsman was given warnings: the trail up Marcy was a bad one and there was no boat to carry him across Lake Colden.

Shattuck refused to give up. The next day he proceeded with the Governor's party seven miles to the camp at Lake Colden. The governor proved to be a great fly fisherman, hooking one trout after the other. Thus the party enjoyed a supper of trout, bacon, flapjacks, and tea.

After supper, everyone agreed to pose for a picture. Someone suggested that the governor seat himself on the stump beside the fireplace. "No, thanks," replied

Governor Charles Evans Hughes.
Courtesy of
New York State Library.

the Governor. "I've been on the stump before. I think I prefer a chair."[9]

The next morning they started for the top of Marcy. Spirits were high. They sang and laughed and shouted until a glimpse of the summit came into view. "Why, that mountain is a long way off yet," complained the governor. Evidently he didn't know about Marcy's reputation for tricking hikers into thinking they must be near the summit when in reality they have only reached a little bump. "Fourteen-top mountain" was its nickname.

The governor and his party kept climbing the steep bumps. Just as they reached the open rock, the clouds opened to reveal a view of Panther Gorge and a panorama of mountains. Then the clouds closed in again.

The first member to reach the top was Limit, a little spaniel. When Governor Hughes reached the top, some women who had climbed from the other side greeted him. They were delightfully surprised at meeting the Governor atop the highest mountain in the state and graciously presented him with a handful of blueberries they had picked along their way.

What the Governor wanted most was to see the famed view, but the defiant clouds would not lift. Eventually the Governor bid adieu to the summit and started down the northern trail toward South Meadow. The trip back was uneventful except for the "customary rain."

At last they reached the awaiting automobile. Shattuck observed, "Whisked away to the hotel at top speed, refreshed by a hot bath, arrayed in dry clothing, and with 'Bob' Fuller, his secretary, by his side, the man who had been the jolly, happy-go-lucky fellow up the trail to Mount Marcy was once more that august personage, the Governor of New York."[10]

In 1910, Governor Hughes called for "larger outlays than annual appropriations" for the purchase of forestlands. I suspect that he was greatly influenced by that three-day trip up Marcy and the fire and lumbering damage he saw in the forest.

Lumbering, in some form, had been going on in the region for a long time. Early settlers cut trees to build houses and barns. They used wood for heating and cooking. They cleared and burned fields for farming. Some supplied wood to charcoal manufacturers. Some ran sawmills.

It wasn't long before lumbering became a major industry. Most of the labor was done in the winter with axes, handsaws, and horse-drawn sleds. Generally, lumbermen cut only the most saleable trees, the softwoods, which could be floated down rivers to mills. Some hardwoods were cut for sawlogs.

Evidence of these lumbering operations was observed on all sides of Marcy. In 1851, artist Jervis McEntee noticed that most of the pines between Newcomb and the Adirondack Iron Works had been cut. A great number of logs were lying along the Hudson. And several shanties stood waiting for winter and the return of the lumbermen.[11]

On the outlet of Lower Ausable Lake, in 1854, David Hale helped build a dam. Nearby, he built a sawmill. He cut wood, selectively, taking hemlock and white pines from along the river. When Plattsburgh lumbermen bought the property in 1866, they allowed Hale's cutting and sawing operations to continue.[12]

In 1865, as author Alfred Billings Street walked south from Scott's farmhouse in North Elba, he found a lumber road through the forest. Here and there were cleared spaces and a decayed log hut.[13] When he visited Mud Pond and Clear Pond, he found abundant evidence of lumbering there, too.

As lumbering operations expanded, more people joined the call for preservation of the Adirondack woods and mountains. After descending Mount Marcy in 1879, one tramper hoped that the State would have "consummated the project of the Adirondack Park and rescued at least thirty miles square of this wilderness from the relentless grasp of business speculation. . . .There is no reason why Adirondack Park may not be made to attain not only a national but world wide reputation."[14]

In 1892, the Adirondack Park was established. It contained 2.8 million acres, of which about one quarter was Forest Preserve land and three quarters was private land. The park boundary was shown on a map as a blue line. Thus, the phrase "inside the blue line" came to refer to the land inside the Adirondack Park. The blue line has been expanded several times and now encompasses almost six million acres, of which almost half is state-owned Forest Preserve land.

In 1894, preserve land received legal protection from timber cutting and development. The passage of Section 7, Article VII (now Article XIV) of the State Constitution made it "forever wild." Of course, lumbering continued on privately owned lands in the region.

In the late nineteenth and early twentieth centuries, great quantities of pulpwood were lumbered and floated down the rivers in the High Peaks region. The increased demand for newspaper raised the price for pulpwood and made it profitable to go deeper in the woods and higher on the mountain slopes.

Lumbering in areas adjacent to Heart Lake began in 1892, and was most extensive in the South Meadow-Klondike and Indian Pass sections. It was so extensive at South Meadow that a little village, complete with schoolhouse,

sprang up for the loggers and their families. A large logging camp known as the Hennessy camp was also established in the Indian Pass region, where only spruce was cut. Timber was drawn out to the west branch of the Ausable, cut into four-foot lengths and floated down the river. An extensive logging road was constructed from South Meadow to Keene Valley.[15]

The great fire of 1903 brought this large lumbering operation to an end. It burned several buildings at South Meadow and scorched the surrounding forests.

In order to salvage usable timber, logging roads were built from South Meadow up the Marcy Brook valley. Lumber camps sprang up and tote roads were improved to allow wagons and

Pulp Wood Logs on the high slopes on Mount Marcy, circa 1919.
Below: Marcy Dam, early 1900s.
Courtesy of New York State Archives.

sleds to service the camps. The roads were gradually extended above the fire zone, eventually reaching Indian Falls, where live timber was harvested.

Other lumber roads led up Phelps Mountain and Tabletop, nearly to their summits. The flanks of Mount Colden above Avalanche Pass were logged, too. It was too steep for roads so dry chutes dropped the logs down to horse sleds, which hauled the logs down to the newly built Marcy Dam. Piles of pulp logs accumulated throughout the winter at Marcy Dam. In spring, water released from the dam helped carry the logs down the river to the mills in Ausable Forks.[16]

Hikers going up Marcy could follow lumber roads from South Meadow to Marcy Dam and then up to Avalanche camps and Indian Falls. Then, the old Van Hoevenberg Trail could be traced to the top of Marcy. This is the route Governor Hughes took down in 1908, and the route a group of young hikers from Camp Pok-O-Moonshine went up in 1914. One of the campers recalled that there was an "active lumber camp at Marcy Dam where the lean-tos are now located, although personnel during the summer months consisted in only a cook and caretaker."[17] Logging operations at Marcy Dam ended in 1922.[18]

Other hikers left from the old Adirondack Lodge site. They followed a tote road over the "Whale's Tail" of Algonquin Peak and down to Hunter's lumber camp, just north of Avalanche Pass. From there they followed Marcy Brook east to Indian Falls and the old Van Hoevenberg trail.[19]

For hikers, if there was a lumber road going your way, hiking was easy. If not, it took hours of climbing under and over "slash," the piles of discarded tree limbs left rotting in the woods.

Efforts to improve the trails led to the formation of trail crews. In 1910, Henry Van Hoevenberg became the first president of the Adirondack Camp and Trail Club (AC&TC), which was affiliated with the Lake Placid Club. "Many parts of the Adirondacks are still practically inaccessible to all save the strongest and most hardy," wrote Van Hoevenberg. "Beautiful waterfalls, sublime mountain passes, grand ravines and the exquisite scenery of numerous points in this our country remain closed to nearly all who would appreciate them most, because of want of the small amount of attention the labor necessary to make them easily available involves. This work so ably and thoroughly done in the White Mountains by the Appalachian Club, has been totally neglected in the Adirondacks. It is to cover this deficiency that the Adirondack Camp and Trail Club has been organized."[20]

The goals of the AC&TC included cutting new trails, clearing out fallen trees and other debris each spring, building new camps, marking trails, organizing and conducting parties into the woods, arranging lectures on conservation, and teaching camp craft to young people and adults.[21] The Adirondack Mountain Club would adopt many of these goals in the 1920s.

The first item on Van Hoevenberg's list of projects was to re-open the old trails that used to radiate from the Adirondack Lodge. Sometime between 1915 and 1919, Henry Baldwin, working for the AC&TC, constructed a trail from the old lodge site to Marcy Dam and from there to Indian Falls, paralleling the route of the original trail. His crews also greatly improved the trail above the falls.[22]

On the southern approach, Tahawus Club guides and wardens maintained the trails. Of course, accommodations at the clubhouse and Colden Camp were available only to Tahawus Club members and their guests. Without a place to spend the night, the climb to Marcy was almost impossible from the south.

This area was also alive with lumbering operations. As early as 1892, there was a lumber road from Upper Works to Calamity Pond.[23] Later, the Tahawus Club leased land to Finch, Pruyn and Company. Their operations were based at Buckley's lumber camp, a group of at least seven or eight buildings located at the junction of Uphill Brook with the Opalescent River. One road to the camp actually bridged the Opalescent Flume.

Cuttings went high on the shoulder of Mount Marcy: as far as half a mile up Feldspar Brook toward Lake Tear of the Clouds and nearly a mile up the Opalescent River. Areas around the base of Cliff and Redfield Mountains were also cut. The logs were drawn by sleigh to just below Lake Colden, then floated down Calamity Brook to the Hudson River, aided by the flooding from Flowed Lands.[24]

Buckley's lumber camp was still in operation in 1919. A hiker recalled, "The trail was bordered at places by piles of pulpwood, the product of lumbering operations which were seriously marring the forest scenery."[25]

There was lumbering to the east of Marcy, too. Selective cutting had always been a practice around the Ausable Lakes area. But not clear-cutting. In order to prevent clear-cutting, the Adirondack Mountain Reserve (AMR) was formed, and purchased the land in 1887.

But the AMR had taxes and other expenses. To pay their bills, they sold timber. "Few people realize that the Adirondack Mountain Reserve only protected forests in the valley of the Ausable Lakes," wrote mountaineer Jim Goodwin. "They leased land to lumber companies for clear-cutting spruce for pulp in many other areas, including the Indian Falls and Lake Arnold area. The 1903 fire had not burned this area. Here, live spruce and balsam were cut."[26] They also sold cutting rights near the Stillwater below Panther Gorge and in the Elk Lake watershed.[27]

The hiking trails on the AMR property and on the approaches to mountains, including Marcy, were maintained by a group called the Adirondack Trail Improvement Society (ATIS). William A. White, a New York City furrier, served as the first president. White was a great walker, climbing Marcy every year for fifty-four consecutive years.[28]

Despite the efforts of White and the ATIS, the trails had their bad spots. From the lower end of Panther Gorge to Four Corners was called Hell's Half Mile. Yet, according to hiker John Lowe, "it is to be remembered that in those days there were no trail markers and there was no such regularity of visits that showed the best root holds or which side to go round a particular rock. There was then some option to hiking!"[29]

Given the restricted access to the AMR lands and the destruction of the Van Hoevenberg trail, the Johns Brook approach became more popular. Improvements made to the Johns Brook trail in 1903 made it an easy, unrestricted, free approach to Mount Marcy. Mel Hathaway's camp and Slant Rock offered some shelter.

But lumbering found its way into the Johns Brook Valley, too. Jim Goodwin visited those lumbering operations in the winter of 1921. Shorty Luck and Goodwin, age 11, walked up the tote road and then hopped aboard the empty pulp rig drawn by horses and driven by Alan (Bob) Washbond. In 1936, Washbond won the Olympic gold medal in two-man bobsledding. But that day in 1921, he simply drove his rig up the valley toward Mount Marcy.[30]

In the Big Flume area, lumberjacks had moved rocks and covered them with dirt to make a smooth road. The road was constructed so as to avoid even the slightest uphill grade because the horses could move the great loads only downhill or on the level. Steep descents could be a problem, too. Sometimes chains were put under the sled runners or ashes were thrown on the road to slow down the sled.[31]

Experienced drivers knew how to handle all that. So when guide Homer Brown climbed on top of a loaded rig and told Goodwin and Luck to climb on the end dragging in the snow, they did.

On his ninetieth birthday, mountaineer Jim Goodwin wrote, "Living through most of the 20th Century, I did have the unusual opportunity to have climbed Adirondack High Peaks and ridden down parts of them on lumber sleds when they were privately owned."[32]

In 1916, those "larger outlays" of funds that Governor Hughes wanted for purchasing state lands finally came. New York State voters approved a bond issue. Starting in 1919, large tracts of private lands were purchased and added to the Forest Preserve. These purchases, as well as the sudden drop in pulp prices in 1921, curtailed lumber operations.

Nearly all lumbering on the high slopes around Mount Marcy ceased by 1925, but lumbering operations on the lower lands to the south continued for years.

Logs in Hudson, 1931. Courtesy of Adirondack Research Library.

Victory Mountain Park

To commemorate the Victory of the United States and Allied Nations in the European War, the Victory Mountain Committee, formed under the auspices of the Association for the Protection of the Adirondacks and other public-spirited organizations, proposes to acquire by popular subscription, for the public benefit, the summit and adjacent territory of the highest mountain in New York State, Mount Marcy, in the heart of the Adirondacks, and to call this great tract Victory Mountain Park.

VICTORY MOUNTAIN PARK BOOKLET, 1919

ABOUT TWO MONTHS after the end of World War I, the Association for the Protection of the Adirondacks held a meeting to consider creating a memorial park in the Adirondacks. After various options were discussed, state Conservation Commissioner George D. Pratt asked, "why not buy the summit of Mt. Marcy and call it Victory Mountain?"[1] The idea caught on and not since Roosevelt's descent from Lake Tear to the presidency had Mount Marcy attracted so much attention.

A committee was formed and money gathered to print an attractive booklet about the project. The Victory Mountain Park booklet said, "What nobler monument, what more beautiful testimony of thanksgiving could there be than this—a monument not made by hands; a mountain sculptured only by the Creator himself; a tract of God's earth in all its pristine beauty; a majestic monolith, literally begemmed with opalescents, garnets, carnelians, sapphires, amethysts, jasper, chalcedony, celestine and calcite, which light up the ancient rocks with their brilliant iridescence."[2]

The monument would serve three purposes. First, it would express gratitude for sacrifices and show a sense of indebtedness to the soldiers. It would promote patriotism toward military efforts and encourage good citizenship. Lastly, the monument would be beautiful and expressive, as well as useful because, according to the booklet, "These men, returning from the front and home camps, will never be content hereafter without more open-air recreation than they had before the war. . . .Thus the park, both as a memorial and by actual use, will keep alive the epic of individual and national participation in the great war for human liberty."[3]

Another major objective of the Victory Mountain Park drive was to stop the lumbering on the slopes near Marcy. This could only be accomplished by bringing Mount Marcy out of private hands and into the state Forest Preserve.

The 1919 appeal sparked some attention. Mountaineer Jim Goodwin recalls, "I made my first contribution for a worthy cause to the Victory Mountain Park fund."[4]

Author and climber T. Morris Longstreth attempted to attract more contributors by writing an account of what the mountain meant to him, but concluded that "Many of the thousands who have contributed their dollar in memory of some dead or wounded hero-relative will never reach the top of Tahawus. Nor can the camera bring it to them. Nor will my mouthing over the map, pointing out my particular pleasures, help very much to convey the sense of space, the smell of ozone in the air. But Mr. Alfred L. Donaldson, a neighbor of Marcy's, has written a poem that is well to engrave beneath the picture of Tahawus that each must paint for himself in his imagination."[5]

The Song of Tahawus
by Alfred Lee Donaldson

I am the tallest of the mountains where many mountains rise—
I am Cleaver of the Cloudland and the Splitter of the Skies—
I am keeper of the caverns where the God of Thunder sleeps—
I am older than the waters that once hid me in their deeps.

For the eyes I hold the visions of the things that make men whole—
Of the woodlands and the waters that can whisper to the soul.
In the winter robed in whiteness, in the summer garbed in green,
I am warden of the wonders of an ever shifting scene.

I am guardian of the goblet that is filled with hopes of life
For the weary and the broken, and the wounded in the strife;
And I offer them the freedom of my great cathedral shrine,
With its sanctity of silence and its fragrance of the pine.

For I crave to be the symbol of the strength that won the fight—
Of the spirit of the heroes who fell battling for the right.
For those dead, who died to save us, let me say eternal mass,
And be God's volcanic voicing of the words: "They shall not pass!"

The Victory Mountain Park drive encountered two problems: There was great competition from other war memorial campaigns, and the proposed name struck a nerve. The idea of replacing "Mount Marcy" with "Victory Mountain" disturbed many people, including the editors of *The Sun*, who printed an editorial titled "Hands Off Mount Marcy!" Edward Hagaman Hall, secretary of the Association for the Protection of the Adirondacks, responded that the name was intended only as a "local designation for a mountain park, which may contain several other mountains besides Marcy."[6]

That did not appease the protestors. Dr. John Bassett Moore responded with a lengthy letter deploring the designation of the "commonplace and unimaginative title 'Mount Victory.'" He detested the idea that the name and fame of William Marcy, "one of the finest products of the great American democratic ideal," should be forgotten.[7]

After collecting only $2,636, the Victory Mountain Park drive was postponed. However, the goal did not go unrealized. The state decided to pursue the acquisition of Mount Marcy, largely thanks to the efforts of Conservation Commissioner Pratt. "Pratt probably did more to shape the form of the Forest Preserve in the High Peaks region than any other person," says Jim Goodwin. "He focused on promoting use of the park by the public as well as saving the land from future lumbering operations. He lobbied in the Legislature for the 1916 bond act with which to purchase more land."[8]

New York state voters approved the 1916 bond issue, the first bond issue used to acquire lands for the Forest Preserve. Seven and a half million dollars were provided. The Conservation Commission stated that their first goal was to "acquire land on the high mountain slopes where the danger of denudation following lumbering and forest fires is the greatest. These are the sections that should forever be maintained as protection areas and upon which no lumbering should ever be permitted."[9]

Land determined to be valuable for Forest Preserve purposes would be appraised and a purchase price negotiated with the owner. However, if a price could not be agreed upon, and the land seemed sufficiently valuable for the Forest Preserve, a recommendation would be made that the land be appropriated. And that did happen.

The state was interested in acquiring the area known as the Gore around Lake Colden. The McIntyre Iron Company owned this area, but the Tahawus Club had leased parts of it for a private preserve and timber rights had been sold on parts of it. Extensive cutting on the sides of Mounts Marcy, Colden, Cliff, and Redfield threatened the forest, so the Conservation Commission recommended to the land office commissioners that the tract be appropriated.[10]

Although the iron company and the Tahawus Club protested it, the Gore around Lake Colden was appropriated by the state in October 1920. The five-thousand-acre tract included all of Lake Colden, Avalanche Lake, Flowed Lands, Mount Colden, Calamity Mountain, and Cliff Mountain. It also included parts of Indian Pass, Mount Marcy, Redfield, and Wallface.

The state was also interested in purchasing the summit of Mount Marcy, but there was a problem. No one really knew who owned it.

For century upon century, the mountain summit had no owner. Perhaps early hunters claimed territories. Perhaps they even battled about the lower slopes. But it is doubtful anyone cared to claim title to any land in the Dismal Wilderness.

Then the colonists arrived. About 1772, the Crown allowed Joseph Totten and Stephen Crossfield, who were Loyalists, to attempt to obtain from the Indians title to a tract of land containing over one million acres. However, it was actually Ebenezer Jessup, an enterprising businessman, who was chiefly engaged in the enterprise. Title was obtained but, as was customary, passed directly to the Crown, which promised to issue patents to various individuals interested in the land.

Meanwhile, Jessup divided the property into townships of about 24,000 acres each. He then contracted Archibald Campbell to explore and survey the lands. Campbell grew tired of the difficult work and went home without running all the boundary lines.

Mount Marcy turned out to be near the intersection of several boundary lines. It was within the Totten and Crossfield Purchase, near its boundary with the other two great land patents: Old Military Tract and Macomb's Tract. Marcy's summit was nearly on the border between Townships 45 and 48 of the Totten and Crossfield Purchase.

The Crown never got around to fulfilling its promise to issue patents; the Revolutionary War intervened. Consequently, after the war, ownership of the tract passed directly to the State of New York. The state then proceeded to dispose of these perceived wastelands but would issue patents only to those who had supported the cause of the Revolution. Lumber companies, charcoal makers, railroad builders, tanners, and others bought or used the land.

In 1786, Zephaniah Platt of Poughkeepsie, after whom Plattsburgh is named, bought Township 45. After several owners, it was sold to the Adirondack Iron and Steel Company, which later became the McIntyre Iron Company, which eventually owned more than 100,000 acres in the area. It leased the property to the Adirondack Club (precursor to the Tahawus Club) and sold lumbering rights to Finch, Pruyn and Company.[11]

In 1791, Platt became owner of Township 48. Later, Sylvanus Wells, New York State Canal Commissioner, bought a total of about 40,000 acres in the area as a logging investment. The tract stretched from Lake Arnold and Indian Falls over Marcy to the flanks of Dix onto Round Mountain and back over to Wolf Jaws and Tabletop.

About 1866, Almon Thomas and Thomas Armstrong, lumbermen of Plattsburgh, bought Township 48. It was thought that their land holdings included Mount Marcy. Kate Field, a famous journalist, actress, and reformer, even tried to purchase the summit of Mount Marcy from them in 1870. Mr. Thomas told her that "he could only sell it to her on condition that she would make it a permanent residence, which she declining to do the trade fell through."[12]

Maps of this era indicated that the summit of Mount Marcy was in Township 48. David H. Burr's 1839 *Atlas of the State of New York*, the first map to show "Mt. Marcy," clearly placed it in Township 48. So did French's 1858 map. But with what certainty?

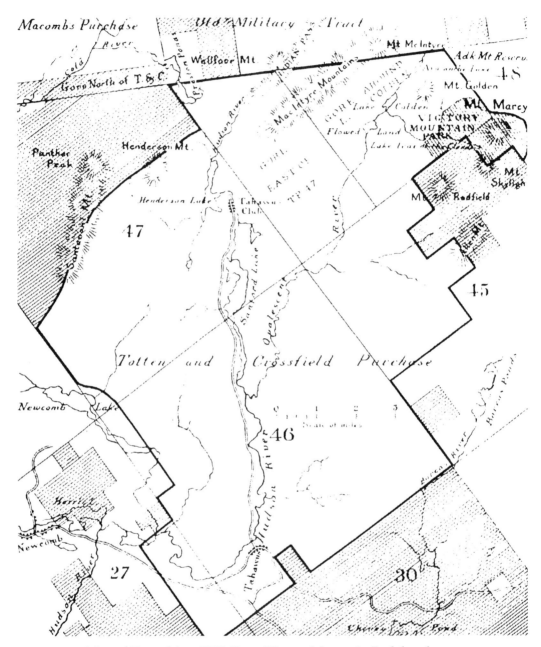

Map of Townships, 1919. From Victory Mountain Park brochure.
Courtesy of Adirondack Research Library.

In 1823 surveyors believed that an important intersection came in the middle of an inaccessible slide on Dix. "So they set the point 'by guess and by gorry,'" according to Harold Weston, "and this crucial spot happened to be the crossing of latitude 44°05' with the boundary of the townships of Keene and of North Hudson and of the original Township 48."[13] Thus the southern boundary of

Township 48 was set inaccurately, as was the western one, which passed over Mount Marcy.

In 1872, surveyor Verplanck Colvin reported that the position of Marcy was never established—"the place of that great mountain landmark upon the maps being miles distant from its real location." As for the boundary lines, he wrote, "The investigations relative to the old patent lines, had shown no systematic survey of them had been made since New York was a colony of Britain." The land lines were "obscure" and it would be "culpable and improper to represent such lines upon the new maps."[14]

In 1886, Thomas and Armstrong decided to sell their land to a lumber company that planned to clear-cut the mountainsides for spruce pulp. Upon hearing this, two Ausable Lake campers, William Neilson and William Alderson, bought most of Township 48, which included the Ausable Lakes. They persuaded other people who loved the Ausable Lakes to join them in forming an organization to be known as the Adirondack Mountain Reserve (AMR), which took ownership of the lands. However, their ownership of Mount Marcy was short-lived. Arnold's land survey of 1893 indicated that Marcy was in Township 45, and not part of the AMR property.

Although the boundary lines were still in dispute in 1919, the state went ahead and purchased some tracts of land in Township 45. They also pursued a purchase of the other side of the mountain from the AMR. Problems with the titles regarding the AMR land initially caused the commission to approve the appropriation of these lands. But, issues with the outstanding titles were resolved and an agreement of sale was worked out with the AMR.[15]

In 1922, A. S. Hopkins was assigned to survey the land that the AMR proposed to sell to the state. This proved to be quite a job, but finally settled the boundary disputes.

When Hopkins checked the lines, he discovered that the intersection of the towns of Keene and North Hudson was too far north. He also discovered that the western boundary of Township 48 was too far east. These two changes meant that the AMR owned a few thousand more acres, including the summit of Mount Marcy. The boundary line was fifteen chains (990 feet) west of the summit.

A deed dated November 28, 1922 records the sale of the parcel of Township 48 that Hopkins determined included Mount Marcy's summit.[16] This purchase also included valuable timberlands in the Johns Brook and Elk Lake watersheds and the headwaters of the Boreas River. For these lands, the state paid $550,000, of which $2,636 was contributed by the Victory Mountain Park Committee.

Other purchases in the Mount Marcy area were soon completed, as were purchases of other high peaks. On February 21, 1923, *The New York Times* declared, "The ownership of all or part of practically every high peak in the Adirondack region is now secured to the state." Dial and Sawteeth were excluded.[17]

These purchases signaled a new movement. First of all, many of the high mountain areas remained non-lumbered, unlike many of the denuded lands previously purchased by the state. Second, many of these forests resided along the watersheds of important streams. Perhaps most significant, the purchase of the actual summit of Mount Marcy was clearly made to create a recreational opportunity and to preserve an aesthetic scene.

The state could now improve those recreational opportunities, too. A 1919 court opinion supported limited cutting to provide for public recreation. This permitted the construction of trails, bridges, and lean-tos as an acceptable way of making the "forever wild" lands a little less wild. So the Conservation Commission built trails, mostly along old logging roads. It put up a system of trail markers. It erected the first state lean-to at Four Corners and the next at the junction of Feldspar Brook and the Opalescent River.

Almost ninety years after its discovery, it was time for public ownership and enjoyment of the highest land in the state.

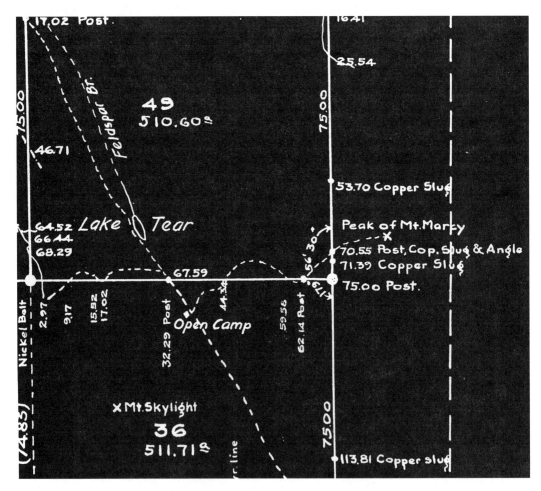

Blue Print of Boundary Lines. From Essex County Deed Book 172, dated November 28, 1922. Long dashed line on far right is the old boundary line. The solid line to the left of the peak of Mount Marcy is the line run and marked in 1921.

The 1920s

Mount Marcy (Tahawus) 5,344 feet; Rating 9. This is the highest, most famous, and possibly most often climbed of the Adirondack peaks.

ROBERT MARSHALL, 1922

A T THE AGE OF SEVENTEEN, Robert "Bob" Marshall climbed his first Adirondack high peak, Whiteface Mountain. Later that summer of 1918, he stood atop Mount Marcy for the first time, with his brother George and guide Herb Clark.

"During that season a sort of spell came over them, a binding enchantment known by those who venture into high, remote, and wild places," wrote Marshall's biographer.[1] Over the next few years, the three men climbed all 46 peaks in the Adirondacks thought to be over 4,000 feet high. They became the first "Forty-Sixers."

Marshall filled his little book, *High Peaks of the Adirondacks*, with observations and hiking tips about each of the peaks. "The view from Marcy is not so fine as from several lower peaks," he wrote, "yet it is beautiful enough to suit the most exacting. The view I like the best is over the Lake Tear Notch toward those three magnificently wooded mountains, Allen, Skylight and Redfield."

Others, like Russell Carson, were drawn in by these writings. Carson recalled that Marshall's book "obsessed me with the Adirondacks." The product of Carson's obsession was *Peaks and People of the Adirondacks*—"the definitive work on the history of the Adirondack high peaks."[2]

Writer T. Morris Longstreth added to the wealth of Adirondack literature, too. In his popular book, *The Adirondacks*, he wrote, "From Marcy you have a view of a stupendous jumble. It is like being on top of the biggest bubble in a boiling cauldron."[3]

Marcy was one of Longstreth's favorite subjects. In an article, he wrote, "Mt. Marcy's greatest gift to the climber is isolation—a difficult commodity to achieve these days. The gods rejoice in stillness, and for a man to emerge from the racket of cities into the mile-high quiet of Tahawus' top is the greatest luxury procurable."[4]

A new generation was looking for a romantic wilderness and once again Marcy was their masterpiece. Longstreth rediscovered Marcy, using words similar to those used eighty years earlier. "The supreme surprise of the view from Marcy peak is the infinity of wilderness. The chief features of the Marcy view are its great range of vision and the singular freedom from the evidence of man," he wrote. "Dimly to the north can be seen the Lake Placid settlement 15 miles away, and 2 houses show in Keene Valley to the E. Otherwise no habitation; all the rest is wilderness, chiefly forest, 1600 square mi. of blue undulation from the Mohawk

Robert Marshall, Herb Clark, and George Marshall
on Mount Marcy, about 1920.
Courtesy of The Adirondack Museum.

to the St. Lawrence and from the White Mountains to New York's western counties. But this intrigues the imagination rather more than the eye. There is, however, one tremendous feature—Panther Gorge, the splendid abyss separating Marcy from Haystack."[5]

Like Lossing in 1859, Longstreth struggled with whether the view was better from on top or from below. "The first-timer on Tahawus spends himself gazing vaguely over into Vermont or Canada, mesmerized by distance, and a little disappointed, I think, that there are no more heights to conquer. For he who is on the roof must look down; that is the price of domination."[6]

Maybe the view was better from above, in an airplane. A 1921 guidebook said, "There remains the airplane trips, popular each season in machines which, guided by experienced pilots, circle the summits of Marcy and Whiteface and do tail spins and nose dives over Mirror Lake and Lake Placid."[7]

The early 1920s were momentous years for Mount Marcy. It had a new owner and new literature. It had new growth—raspberry bushes and birch trees were springing up everywhere, "as if they were trying to cover the ugly stumps and scars left by the axe."[8] And new visitors arrived in airplanes and automobiles.

Automobiles made weekend visits easy. A mountain vacation no longer required wealth or a week's stay.

A group of Scouts came from Vermont via a ferry and truck. The Scouts went up the Slant Rock (Phelps) trail, pulling themselves over mossy boulders, edging along cliffs, and maneuvering around fallen trees. "Truly, this trail, like the pathway of life, is varied and complex at every step," wrote H. S. Douglas, the leader.[9] They continued up and up until they reached the far-famed and ill-famed "Marcy bog." They waded through and scaled the summit rocks, but Douglas did not attempt to describe the view for fear that he would "bankrupt the dictionary."

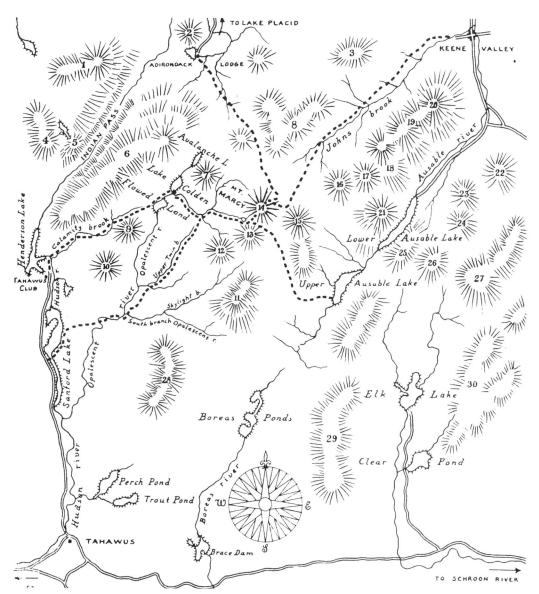

Trails to Mount Marcy, 1920. 1. Street. 2. Jo. 3. Big Slide. 4. MacNaughton. 5. Wallface. 6. MacIntyre. 7. Colden. 8. Table Top. 9. Calamity. 10. Adams. 11. Allen. 12. Redfield. 13. Skylight. 14. MARCY. 15. Haystack. 16. Saddleback. 17. Gothic. 18. Armstrong. 19. Wolf Jaws. 20. Hedge Hog. 21. Saw Teeth. 22. Noonmark. 23. Bear Den. 24. Dial. 25. Covin. 26. Nipple Top. 27. Dix. 28. North River. 29. Boreas. 30. McComb. From the American Scenic and Historic Preservation Society magazine.

The Scouts might have found the trip easier if they had taken the new, drier Hopkins trail.[10] It branched from the Slant Rock trail just beyond Bushnell Falls and kept to the north side of Johns Brook before eventually joining the Van Hoevenberg trail. One hiker claimed, "the so-called Hopkins Trail to Marcy, being both shorter and better, is preferred by almost all."[11]

For a longer trek to Marcy, the Great Range trail offered "one of the greatest mountain walks in the Northeast," according to mountaineers Laura and Guy Waterman. Ed Phelps, Ed Isham, and Charlie Beede first cut the trail, which went from Gothics to Saddleback, Basin, and Marcy, in 1905.[12] The route was sometimes extended to include Haystack, Lower Wolf Jaw, Upper Wolf Jaw, and Armstrong Mountains. The state promoted the trail as "the most scenic as well as the most difficult of all trails in the neighborhood of Mt. Marcy."[13]

Several members of the Blair County Branch of the Pennsylvania Alpine Club selected this trail precisely on account of those two features: scenery and difficulty. One member of the party, Harry P. Hays, wrote, "The state made this trail, leading through places that require experience in mountain climbing, a steady nerve, sure-footedness, agility and well-developed muscles, without which it would be impossible to negotiate it."[14]

The alpine club's trek started on a warm sunny September day in 1922 in Saint Huberts. They followed the Ausable River for a while and then went up Armstrong Mountain. Next was Gothics. It was a long, hard grind, but they made it up through the timber to the top and the panorama "held them spellbound."

That night they camped at a shelter at the base of Gothics, and feasted on a supper of bacon, coffee, potatoes, soup, "and other substantial viands." Hays wrote, "We seemed to be in a little world of our own, as great mountains rose all around us as if to the very skies, cooping us in a narrow slit at the base where the silence of the forest was awe-inspiring, the bright fire cleaving a circle of light in the dense blackness, while the stars twinkled brightly from the blue dome on high. Here all Nature was as silent as the tomb, as not the slightest breeze stirred through the trees, or silvery ripple from the brook."[15]

In the morning, they climbed Saddleback, which was "not a very hard climb," and Basin, which was "very difficult." At one point on Basin, they were confronted with a wall of rock that was almost perpendicular. "There is no way round," wrote Hays, "and one must grasp a dangling rope attached to a root at the top of the slide and walk up the cliff, going hand over hand on the rope."[16]

At the foot of Haystack, they stopped for the night at a shelter. In the morning, "we performed our ablutions at the brook, partook of an appetizing breakfast, and were soon ready for the day's journey." They went up and down Haystack, and then west around the top of Panther Gorge toward Mount Marcy. This peak, "that towers 5,344 feet into the blue ozone," was the last one they climbed.

As they stood atop Mount Marcy, they thought, "The human being who stands on the top of a lofty mountain and gazes over the wonderful panorama, enjoys the delightful sensation of being high above the sordid, in another realm, where all is pure and good, and feels fully that he is only a grain of dust in this vast sphere, the splendid handiwork of the Master Artisan."[17]

Well, all was pure and good except the gnats that swarmed about their heads, "making a clear, singing noise, of a much higher pitch than mosquitoes." Despite the pesky gnats, the group looked around the summit and found a lone bluet, "the humble little blue flower looking very much out of place on that great pyramid of stone."

They also found a copper box with the inscription: "In grateful memory this mountain finder is dedicated to Alexander MacBride of Brooklyn, N.Y., killed in action in France, 1918." In the box was a map of the Adirondacks and a registry book in which they wrote their names as members of the Blair County Alpine Club.

The group went down the south side of Marcy toward Lake Colden. "At one place [along Avalanche Lake], we disappeared beneath a huge boulder as if entering a cave, and wormed our way over a broken, rocky surface for some distance," wrote Hays. "The trail also passes through a place known as the Lemon Squeeze. There are two immense rocks, fixed at a slant, with a narrow space between, through which we crawled with great difficulty, emerging at the top of a slanting wall, flanking the lake, down which it was necessary to clamber."

With the aid of flashlights, they reached the site of the old Adirondack Lodge at nine o'clock and were filled with "deepest pleasure over our wonderful tramp through one of the most impressive and scenic mountainous sections of this mundane sphere, and fully rewarded for all the discomforts and dangers we encountered."[18]

One more reward was to come their way. Later that same year, on October 2, U. S. Senator George Wharton Pepper, of Philadelphia, climbed Mount Marcy with his son. He was very pleased to find the names of his fellow Pennsylvanians in the registry. He wrote a letter to the club's chief guide, saying he would like to meet with them some time to compare notes about the trail. Pepper was immediately elected to honorary membership in the Pennsylvania and the Blair County Alpine Clubs.[19]

The Adirondacks finally saw its own version of an Alpine Club that year. Under the guidance of former Conservation Commissioner George D. Pratt, a new trails and recreation organization was formed—the Adirondack Mountain Club, ADK (the initials "AMC" having already been claimed by Appalachian Mountain Club). Among its charter members were T. Morris Longstreth and Bob Marshall. Pratt was the first president.

Shortly after ADK formed, the J. & J. Rogers Company gave the club a parcel of land in Johns Brook Valley. In 1924, ADK authorized a $15,000 mortgage to build Johns Brook Lodge. One hitch in the project was Mel Hathaway. His shack sat on the site of the proposed lodge. Mel had to go.

Jim Goodwin recalls:

Mel, of course, was a squatter and after painful deliberations with ADK officials and members of the Conservation Commission, Mel agreed to leave his homestead and live with a daughter in Syracuse. I met Mel as I was returning from

Marcy with a group. He had tears in his eyes: "Jimmy, they are going to burn down my cabin and take me away."

I was naturally very sorry for my old friend, but at the time, of course, didn't grasp the significance. Mel had lived too long. The old-time life involving lumbering operations and freedom to hunt where and when one wished to were passing. Soon there would be well-marked trails that no longer required guides, public lean-tos and even a lodge in the middle of the wilderness,—all publicized by Conservation Commission pamphlets and ADK guidebooks. The woods would soon be full of hikers, instead of lumberjacks.

The last story of Mel Hathaway may be apocryphal. Soon after getting established in his daughter's Syracuse house, he decided to go out and explore the city. Taking an axe, he proceeded to blaze (cut) telephone poles so that he would know his way back. He was soon arrested and taken to a police station by policemen who probably didn't know what a blaze was.[20]

Johns Brook Lodge (JBL) opened on July 4, 1925, and was an immediate success. Over three hundred guests came the first year. The woods were indeed full of hikers instead of lumberjacks. And the strategic location of JBL made it the hub of mountain climbing and trail building. The new trails emanating from the Johns Brook Valley linked trails in the Heart Lake area with trails in the Ausable Lakes area. The Adirondacks became a united hiking region—with Mount Marcy at its center.

New York State, the proud new owner of Marcy, tried to draw even more attention to Marcy. The Conservation Commission printed a recreation circular titled *The Trails To Marcy*. Page five stated, "It is hoped that this guide book will be the means of disseminating much information not generally known relating to the accessibility of Mt. Marcy, and will be the inspiration leading many to make the trip for the first time."[21]

But there was one hitch in the "accessibility" of Mount Marcy: state ownership of the mountain did not give people free access to it. The access to the Johns Brook trail was across the "Wells' Garden," a plot of land owned by the Alfred B. Wells family and used as a garden—"never very successful"—for a few years.[22] Huge private preserves surrounded other approaches to Mount Marcy. The Lake Placid Club owned the northern trailhead, the Adirondack Mountain Reserve owned the Ausable Lakes, and the Tahawus Club controlled the southwestern approach. These private owners could, at their whim, prohibit hikers from traveling over the popular trails to Mount Marcy or restrict lodging and camping on their property.

In 1927, Harry Hicks, a charter member of ADK and secretary of the Lake Placid Club, conceived the idea to replace the burned lodge at Heart Lake. The new "Adirondak Loj," which owes its odd spelling to the influence of Melvil Dewey and his passion for simplified spelling, welcomed its first guests on December 26, 1927. But of course, those "guests" had to be Lake Placid Club members or "invited" visitors.

The new Loj meant good things for the old Van Hoevenberg trail. Just a few years earlier, Bob Marshall had described it as "very muddy and running mostly through slash." Now the trail was a gradual climb and "in no place difficult."

The southern approaches to Marcy were not doing so well. The Elk Lake trail was seldom used because it was long and passed over private land where camping was not permitted. The original trail from the southwest was cut off. The Tahawus Club did not welcome the public going through their private preserve to the Colden-Marcy area via Calamity Brook. The more popular route in the 1920s was the so-called Upper Twin Brook approach that started at a tote road near the present-day bridge that leads to National Mine Company offices.

As for lodging at the club-house at the old iron works, "That's no good any more," said one hiker. "It's a strictly private club, with no food for sale and no beds for rent and no warm welcome, either. The adventurer into the pass from this south end does well to load up with bread and bacon, chocolate, beans, and sardines, way back at North Creek, where a branch of the railroad ends, and be beguiled by the

Above: Johns Brook Lodge, 2000. *Top:* Mel Hathaway, age 83, on left, and Jed Rosman, age 58, circa 1920. Courtesy of The Adirondack Museum.

tiny dot on the map (which usually means a real village) that is marked 'Tahawus,' and is the dot closest to the opening of Indian Pass."[23]

"Tahawus is only a post office," he continued, "and the postmaster has the distrust of a Scotchman in his keen, gray eyes as he informs the traveler with a pack on his back that 'We don't make a practice of selling anything to strangers.' Present yourself as a starving man, just arrived destitute from Indian Pass, and he relents and cuts out a pound of bacon and a loaf of bread. Give him a $1 bill and he shouts, in seeming wrath, 'Eighty cents! eighty cents!' for he doesn't care to make change. Manage to buy apples from him and he insists that you take the rotten one with the rest, crying out, 'Hit a bear in the nose with it, if you don't want to eat it.'"[24]

Of course, past the postmaster, at Lake Colden, the land and shelters were now owned by the state and open to the enjoyment of all.

One day in the summer of 1922, Alice Jones, of Minerva, decided to get together a group of twenty or so friends to visit Lake Colden and climb Mount Marcy. It was an arduous three-day journey, but that didn't dampen spirits. People came from Saratoga Springs, Stony Creek, Thurston, Horicon, and other places to Jones' home on August 1. A local girl, Grace Leach (now Hudowalski), was invited, too.

The fifteen-year-old Leach begged her father to let her join the group of mostly college students. Her father consented but told her to do her share and more, and to do it with good cheer. He also told her to walk softly and reverently. "The last pull up Marcy is tough," he said. "Whether or not you make it, and how, is important."[25]

So young Grace Leach went off to climb Mount Marcy. The travelers filled packbaskets and then packed into one of the four cars taken on the trip. They arrived at the Tahawus Club in mid-afternoon and set off down the trail toward Flowed Lands. "The woods were lovely!" wrote Grace.

Clinton West, the fire ranger, met them at the water's edge and rowed them and their gear across the lake. They reached the camp on Lake Colden just before sunset. The men shared a large lean-to and the young women slept in the fire ranger's cabin.

Despite a cloudy sky in the morning, the group left at eight o'clock for Mount Marcy. A drizzling rain soon began to fall. "The trail was very rough, leading over huge boulders, and giant tree roots with scarce a level stretch, very steep in places and made slippery and dangerous by the wet weather," wrote Gertrude Carragan, one of the hikers.[26]

From Feldspar Lean-to to Lake Tear of the Clouds was a tough stretch for young Grace. "My legs ached: if only I could sit down!" she wrote. "Perspiration ran down my face and black flies tormented me. . . . Between catching breaths I asked myself, 'Why did I ever come?'"[27]

At Four Corners lean-to, several of the party turned back. Grace had three choices: she could wait in the cold at Four Corners, she could turn back down the

Grace Hudowalski, seated on
Mount Marcy, 1922.
Courtesy of L. John Van Norden.

mountain, or she could go on. She chose to push on toward the top.

"'Can't' never did anything," has always been her mantra. It is a lesson she learned in second grade. Her older sister Nora had told her she wouldn't pass, and she didn't. Grace learned never to tell anyone they can't do something. They can do it if they try.

That August day, Grace never gave up. She reached the summit on all fours, crawling like a dog, feeling her way through the soupy fog. "Everything else was forgotten but the fact I had reached the summit," she said. Atop Marcy, the fog lifted for one shining moment. She saw Lake Tear of the Clouds and, "That was all. It was enough!"[28]

Grace Leach took a hiatus from climbing until she moved to Troy and met her eventual husband, Ed Hudowalski, an engineering student at Rensselaer Polytechnic Institute. The couple began their love affair with the High Peaks in earnest in the mid-1930s. Grace Leach Hudowalski completed her forty-sixth peak, Mount Esther, on August 26, 1937. She was the first woman to become a Forty-Sixer.

Orra Phelps was another exceptional young woman who would attain fame among Adirondack climbers. Before becoming a doctor and botanist, Orra came to ascend Mount Marcy in July 1924. Orra, her mother, her brother Leon, and her roommate, Lee Miller, drove to Lake Sanford and set off into the woods via the Upper Twin Brook route. They carried knapsacks, blanket rolls, camera, botany can, canteens, and citronella-drenched kerchiefs.

That night, they camped under a tent, cooked soup and hash over a fire, and then tried to sleep despite a thunderstorm. Orra Phelps' recollections of the trip are filled with descriptions of the soil, trees, birds, flowers, and views. "One can walk miles in the woods without seeing the mountains," she wrote, "but at the top of this grade, we looked back through the narrow trail opening to view the rolling expanse of green forest and distant mountain peaks rising out of a sea of clouds, our first view of the mountains since leaving the car."[29]

As they climbed toward Buckley's Clearing, the abandoned logging center, Orra noted the bunchberry, goldthread, and wood sorrel beside the trail. "Our feet made no noise on the soft carpet of needles, nor did we speak, but marched on under the great spruces, thrilled by the beauty, the silence, the majesty—and we gave thanks."[30]

Eventually they reached an old-growth forest of spruce, balsam, and white cedar, including the largest white cedar Orra had ever seen. Then they came to Lake Tear and examined the early spring flowers—violets, false Solomon's seal, and goldthread—that were still in bloom.

While Lee rested below, Orra and her mother and brother clambered up the high slope of Mount Marcy. Orra wrote, "The keen wind made scrambling over that rock surface, with only cracks for handholds seem like a steeplejack's stunt. The top at last! Bare of vegetation, strewn with rocks, it had weathered many storms. . . . Just over the edge, in every protected crevice, the sturdy alpine plants flourished. Though rocks crumbled, the winds and rains would not let any soil accumulate on top."

Eventually, the three botanists lifted their eyes from the ground and looked at the distant scene. They were unimpressed. "The view from Marcy is by no means the finest in the state but it is immense," Orra wrote.[31]

They ate their lunch of bread, cheese, and chocolate "in the highest and most exclusive dining room in the state." After eating, they reluctantly packed their bags and left the summit.

Orra Phelps climbed Mount Marcy again in 1925. This time she hiked from the Deserted Village up the Calamity Brook Trail. Her party camped below Flowed Lands that night. When they reached Lake Tear the next day, it was covered in clouds. There was no grand view of Marcy this time. Yet, the party stayed in good spirits. Phelps recalled that "they laughed when they recalled Lawrence's story of his scouts spitting across Lake Tear's outlet so that when they returned to Brooklyn they could say that had spit across the Hudson River."[32]

Although Orra chose to climb from the southwest, others were looking for new routes. Hikers, such as Edward Everett Hale, Union College professor and charter member of ADK, had been exploring the possibility of a trail up Marcy from Lake Arnold or the north peak of Mount Colden. In 1923, Norman Marshall descended Colden to the Opalescent, and ascended Marcy by way of the north end of Gray Peak. In 1924 and 1925, Hale descended the spur of Colden to Lake Arnold and went up some distance on the ridge leading to Marcy, but both times bad weather prevented the final ascent.[33] He must have made it the next year, because in 1927 the Conservation Department trail guide showed a trail from the north spur of Mount Colden directly southeast up Mount Marcy.

Even with all these trails, there was still plenty of room for adventure on Mount Marcy. On August 5, 1927, the ninetieth anniversary of the first ascent, George Marshall and Russell Carson climbed Mount Marcy by the original route of the Emmons party. Carson brought along a copy of Redfield's account and followed the route along the upper Opalescent to the ridge and the little mountain meadow.

"This was a great day for Russ, combining as it did his historic and his mountain enthusiasms," wrote George Marshall. "It was also a delightful day for me."[34]

Although lots of hikers now tramped through the woods without a guide, and some, like Marshall, even went off-trail, a few still hired guides. Jed Rosman (1870-1937) was a favorite guide in the Heart Lake area.[35] In 1921, Jed became the regular caretaker at the Heart Lake property, then owned by the Lake Placid Club. He took good care of the folks who came to stay in the open shelters. He particularly had a rapport with the city folks.

One "city fellar" arrived after dark for his first sleep in an open shanty. He asked Jed if there were any wild animals in the area. Jed told the fellow that once he found "two bears in one trap and 8 sitting on their haunches waiting patiently to get into the trap." The fellow went to his shelter where he spent a sleepless night.[36]

Jed enjoyed poking fun at the city folks, but "there never was a sting in his joke or story, and by his humor he won many a close friend."[37] Author T. Morris Longstreth was one such friend. In 1930, Longstreth wrote a poem, "The Guide," in which Jed Rosman told another story about a city fellow that he guided up Mount Marcy.[38]

Jed and the chap spent the whole afternoon on the top. Jed smoked his pipe while the chap just lay on his back. When the chap was done, he nodded to Jed and they walked down the mountain. Jed couldn't figure why the chap had hired him. So when they got back, Jed said to him, "I hadn't much call to go up there with you; I don't like takin' money when I'm no use."

The man laughed and said, "No use? What is the use, Jed, if someone isn't near? I don't like standing on the brink of heaven unless I have a friendly hand to hold to." Then he shook Jed's hand and pressed a gold piece in it.

Unfortunately not all of the throngs of new hikers were as sensitive as that chap. Author and historian Russell Carson remarked that on mountaintops "we have met people who it is a real pleasure to run into and we have met muckers who have made us wish that no trail had ever been cut."[39]

Carson strongly favored, and promoted, the recreational use of the mountains. Yet, by 1928, even he was becoming concerned with conservation. He wrote, "In all our thinking about recreational development, we ought constantly to remember that wilderness and natural beauty are the real charm of the Adirondacks, and that preservation is as much our objective as helping more people to share our joy in them."[40]

The struggle between recreation and conservation would soon focus on Mount Marcy. The issue: Was a summit hut a help to people or a blemish on the natural beauty of Marcy?

Built On High

And if thou wilt make me an altar of stone, thou shalt not
build it of hewn stone; for if thou lift up thy tool upon it,
thou hast polluted it.   EXODUS, 20:25

WHAT did early climbers do when they reached Mount Marcy's summit? Some carved their names in rock. Others fired pistols and listened to the silence. Some built a fire of moss and dwarf spruce. And others erected a stone hut.

In August 1858, Frederick S. Perkins, Mary Cook, Fanny M. Newton, and Old Mountain Phelps constructed a stone hut in a nook on the southwestern end of the summit. It was made of loose stones gathered from the summit and covered with moss.

Author Benson Lossing's party arrived the next year and found the hut. From a sketch made by Lossing, the hut appears to have been about five feet high and nine feet long. The walls were stacks of five, six, or seven big rocks. The roof was made of moss with the roots and branches of spruce protruding at odd angles.

Who else used the hut? On a paper that Lossing found, four men recorded visits in August 1859. Did no one else visit from August 1858 to August 1859? And did no one else see the hut after Lossing? No further mention of it has been found.

Remnants of the hut must have been gone by the time Verplanck Colvin began his survey work in the 1870s. He surely would have noticed the structure and made use of it. In 1873, he even suggested building such a hut. He wrote, "I cannot too strongly urge the erection by the State of a small stone hut or hospice, near the summit of Mt. Marcy, to afford shelter, from sudden, severe and dangerous storms, to scientific observers. . . . The knowledge that such a protection against storm existed, would induce more tourists to visit the summit and well repay the small expenditure, by bringing thousands of dollars into the State annually."[1]

Colvin's hut idea did not win support. However, in 1877, he was given funds to replace his lighter, movable signal towers with more substantial ones. The new towers would be left in place, with the pillars secured by iron ringbolts leaded into holes in the rock. To take a reading, the theodolite was simply positioned beneath the tower.[2]

On August 2, Colvin's party climbed to their old Lake Tear lean-to in preparation for erecting the Marcy signal tower. The next day, Sunday, a reverend friend who was in the party held religious services. With logs for seats, a bright sky for a roof, and rich mosses and rare ferns for carpeting, the party gave thanks for all the blessings they had received.

The next day the guides began cutting timber for the tower pillars. Since the trees near the summit were short and small, timber had to be cut a thousand feet below. Then it had to be carried "along the tortuous trail, up through the dense dwarf forest, up over ledges and the open rock of the peak."[3] Sometimes it took a day's work for three powerful guides to bring a single timber to the summit.

The worst part of the job was yet to come. The holes for the iron ringbolts were drilled on August 8 and the men began to pour melted lead around the iron bolts. Then boom! An explosion. The melted lead was blown with such force that one of the men was nearly blinded.

Original sketch of Hospice on the Summit of Tahawus, August 30, 1859, by Lossing. Reproduced by permission of *The Huntington Library, San Marino, California.*

With only minor troubles, the remaining bolts were secured. Before nightfall, the crew raised the frame and plumbed the center. The next day, the work was completed. The highest signal on the highest mountain of New York was done.

Two years later, Colvin reported, "Bolted, ironed and spiked, it has now withstood one earthquake, a dozen tornadoes, and the frosts of two winters, and is still fixed and firm upon the summit mountain of New York."[4]

Unfortunately, more than wind, rain and snow hacked at the tower. Firewood was so scarce near the summit that visitors chopped away at the wooden pillars and crossbars. Tourists were using parts of the tower "to boil tea with."[5] A party who ascended Marcy on a cold September day in 1896 reported enjoying a "brisk little fire made of the pieces of bark and chips from the new signal station that had just been erected."[6]

Somehow, the new tower managed to survive, at least until February 1899 when forester Gifford Pinchot completed his winter ascent of Mount Marcy. Pinchot crawled over glare ice to the summit tower and brought back a souvenir—a fragment of wood.[7]

From time to time, the idea of a stone shelter atop Mount Marcy was resurrected. In 1922, T. Morris Longstreth wrote that the Camp and Trail Club planned to erect a stone shelter on the summit of Marcy, as soon as funds would permit. The estimated expense was $1,000.[8] Evidently, the funds did not appear.

One October day in 1924, the shelter idea stirred in the mind of Pirie MacDonald, New York photographer and later president of the Adirondack Mountain Club. "A couple of nice girls came up and climbed up to Marcy peak," he recalled. "They were

Signal on the summit of
Mount Marcy, 1877, by Colvin.

clothed in thin summer dresses." He feared for their safety because he had read of two girls and a man who climbed some mountain on a nice fall day and ended up in a snowstorm and died.[9]

MacDonald watched the two girls on Marcy and waited until they were safely off the peak. "Poor dears, their dresses were so transparent that I could see the contour of their legs as they walked away from me—suppose they had been caught by the snow!"

MacDonald began planning a hospice. He studied exposure, winds, light, and location. Then he arranged with an architect friend to design the hut. The architect later boasted that he designed "the highest building in the State of New York!"[10]

Early in 1925 MacDonald proposed the idea to the Conservation Department. "The Mount Marcy project is precisely a hospice, not a summer resort," he explained. "The saving of life is the object. . . . Three or four times in recent years, unexpected blizzards at the top of the mountain have resulted in a serious situation for climbers." MacDonald said that the state "should not wait until there is a fatality to move for protection."[11]

MacDonald hut, 1946. Joan Emerson, age 14, standing, and her mother, Mildred Emerson. Courtesy of Joan Sleinkofer.

The state accepted the shelter proposal, with some conditions. The hut had to be erected against the high perpendicular ledge near the summit and have doors, but no locks. It had to be built of rock from the summit and made to look natural. The rocks could not be blasted; they had to be loose rocks and boulders.[12]

Several builders studied the project and told MacDonald that it couldn't be done. Others gave absurd prices. Finally in the fall of 1927, Abe Fuller of Newman said, "I kin."

MacDonald paid him $2,500 for his services. The Conservation Department furnished the materials at a cost of $115. Most of the materials were brought to the top in December 1927. A pile of lumber, iron, sandbags, window frames, and a gasoline drum sat atop Marcy for months. Then construction of the stone hut began.

"They had an abused looking horse on the summit to drag a stone boat for carrying stone to the building," recalls Jim Goodwin. "They had dug out a spring a few yards west of the summit to furnish water for horse and cement mix."[13]

The shelter had two rooms with a concrete wall separating them. Each room was about six feet by eight feet and included a window, chimney, small cast iron stove, and two wooden bunks, which were later replaced by iron frame ones. Steel doors covered the entryways.[14]

Some conservationists were not happy about the shelter. New York lawyer Louis Marshall, Theodore Dreier of Schenectady, and John Apperson of the Association for the Protection of the Adirondacks opposed the building of such a shelter in the state Forest Preserve. Mr. Dreier said that the proposed structure appeared to be wholly unnecessary since there were two shelters very near the summit. He also pointed out, "Of course, the structure is entirely at variance with Article 7, Section 7 [the "forever wild" article of the State Constitution]. . . . Somewhere the line must be drawn."[15]

In a letter to the *New York Herald Tribune*, Dreier explained further that it was absurd to spoil a wild mountaintop simply because some tenderfoot might some time get caught in a blizzard. He also pointed out that this was not to be a mere shelter. "It is to be a closed two-room house of stone and reinforced concrete, having a door and windows," he wrote. "There will be trips up to it, and people will spend the night in the house." And, he feared that a larger house would soon be required. Eventually a road and hotel might inhabit the summit.[16]

The *Tribune* editors took a different view: "Such protests as the one against building a small stone shelter near the summit of Mount Marcy, for the convenience and safety of mountain climbers in case of storm, are no help to sane conservation. . . . The shelter is to be built on rock, in harmony with the background, and placed inconspicuously on a ledge against a cliff below the mountain's crown. . . . If the State Conservation Department cannot permit reasonable provisions for comfort and safety to be established, the forest preserve, might as well be closed to recreation entirely. If one did not know the admirable motives of these too hasty conservationists one might imagine that they were driving at just that. In this case, they have certainly made a mountain out of a molehill."[17]

Apperson responded, "Such a structure would encourage people to linger on the mountain when they should, if the weather is threatening, be on their way back to the timber line. . . . If we attempt to make our mountains entirely safe for foolish people we ruin them for every one else, and those who are seriously interested in preserving the charm of the wild forest land are very properly alarmed at any encroachment of this character."[18]

The hospice, which Apperson later called a "wart on the bare dome of Marcy,"[19] was completed on July 28, 1928. This was the first time since the establishment of the Forest Preserve in 1885 that anything other than a three-sided lean-to had been erected on public land. Others argued it was a "legal lean-to" because the fourth wall was the face of the summit rock.[20]

The debate over the Marcy summit hut was part of a new dance between recreation and conservation. The state bought the land so people could enjoy recreational opportunities. State officials thought a shelter was the logical way to help do this. Meanwhile, conservationists feared the state was headed toward development of these new lands.

Conservationists had just fought against the construction of Whiteface Memorial Highway, and lost. They also feared a repeat of the shelter expansion that occurred in the White Mountains. Because of a recent death on Mount Washington, an "emergency" hut was built on the summit. The hut was used as a regular camping spot and within one year was abused and damaged. A more substantial facility, Lakes-of-the-Clouds Hut, was then built lower on the ridge.[21]

Ironically, when Pirie MacDonald was elected president of ADK in 1928, his concern was conservation. He felt it should be the number one priority of the club. Apparently, he did not see the hut as contradictory to his principles.

On the summit hut issue, history proved both sides to be right, and wrong. There was no further encroachment; no road or hotel was built. However, Dreier's concern that "There will be trips up to it" proved legitimate.

The very first New Year's Day after the hut was built, three college students camped in it. "Until this year [1929], no man had yet enjoyed the experience of a midwinter sunset and sunrise from this glorious eminence," wrote Terris Moore.[22] Among his later mountaineering feats, Moore made the first ascent (and first ski ascent) of the Mount Sanford volcano in Alaska—skiable vertical more than 10,000 feet.

On January 1, Moore, Lewis Thorne, and D. Little left from Adirondak Loj with the hope of spending the night in the new summit shelter. They carried two sleeping bags, three spoons, small pot, hatchet, motion picture camera, Kodak camera, Vaseline, extra clothes, and food. Moore wore an experimental parka made from a buckskin shirt, trimmed with long fringe and rigged with a hood and drawstrings to pull it close to the face.

The men found the first part of the climb easy. But when they passed Plateau Camp, conditions changed. "Rifts in the flying clouds revealed glimpses of icy slopes and swirling snow. The cold wind was penetrating," wrote Moore. The transition to open slope was even more abrupt. "A moment before we had been laboring and climbing through deep snow and actually perspiring in the comparatively quiet, cold air. Here by merely climbing around a few rocks we were hammered by a perfectly steady and relentless blast. It was staggering. The first impression was that of being blown off one's feet."

Their faces, thickly smeared with Vaseline, fought the wind and driving snow. Nothing was visible. When they reached the top, they were unable to find the shelter. With darkness approaching in half an hour, the three searched frantically. Moore happened to glance back toward the summit and see a window. They were soon inside, sitting beside a small fire. Yet, the granite walls were covered with frost.

That night, the two sharing one sleeping bag fared well. But the lone individual "had lots of time to hear the black night winds seize the chill little hut and drum on the door with icy fingers during the long night."

At dawn, they rose and stood—"three awe-struck boys on the highest frosty pinnacle watching the lower clouds dissolve and reveal in turn Whiteface, Colden, MacIntyre, and finally the whole Santanoni range to the west."[23] After breakfast, the three young men descended through soft cottony snow.

The hut quickly became a regular place to camp in winter and summer. This was the norm of the times, as seen in the White Mountains, too. But the MacDonald shelter was not a cozy camp for long. The very first year it was damaged by ice and frost and "subject to considerable vandalism."[24]

The shelter was repaired and restored to good condition for a few years. "It was in good shape when I left for the war," recalls Jim Goodwin, "but during the war it was apparently struck by lightning. After the war, nothing was done to repair the damage and it became a popular latrine."[25]

When George Marshall saw it in 1952, he said it had been "transformed into a garbage dump!"[26] In 1956, it failed to prevent the first recorded fatality on

Above: MacDonald hut. Courtesy of Adirondack Research Library. *Facing page:* Summit area after Shelter removed, 2000. *Below:* Scree wall along revegetation area, 2000.

Mount Marcy. Eventually, the state decided to remove the hut since it did not conform to the concept of wilderness surroundings. On October 23, 1967, Forest Rangers Gary Hodgson and David Ames, with Spencer Cram, the caretaker at the Johns Brook ranger station, removed the stone hut.[27]

That's not the end of the story. The hut had a big impact on the Marcy trail and on the summit environment. During the spring of 1928, several improvements were made to the Marcy trail. Bridges were built and corduroy was put in muddy spots along the trail to Marcy Dam. From Marcy Dam to Indian Falls, the trail was widened, and up on the Plateau, some clearing was done. The Conservation Commission maintained that these activities had nothing to do with the hut. They claimed the improvements were made

to address numerous complaints from hikers and for fire protection purposes. But conservationist John Apperson believed the trail had been improved to haul more material for the hut or for a local horse-riding club.[28]

During its construction, no one considered what the hut would do to the alpine environment. The state actually encouraged MacDonald to use rock from the summit to build the stone shelter. As Harshberger's study in 1914 showed, those rocks and boulders were valuable resources—prime real estate for alpine vegetation. They created windbreaks, held the snow pack, and provided rock debris for the production of soil. The rocks also served as natural barriers that directed footsteps along pathways and away from fragile plants.

Today, people carry rocks up to the summit. They aren't building huts; they are building scree walls. The loose rows of rocks help to reduce erosion by holding soil in place and serve as that "natural" barrier to direct footsteps along the hiking path.

The 1930s

In a mountain's life a century is less than the trembling of a leaf, yet it is fitting that the first recorded ascent of Mount Marcy by white men. . . should be fittingly celebrated. THE NEW YORK TIMES, JULY 31, 1937

But the best of it is that when all the hot-dogs are eaten, the words spoken and the guests gone home, Mount Marcy will be there unmoved.

T. MORRIS LONGSTRETH,
THE NEW YORK TIMES, AUGUST 1, 1937

NEARLY a hundred years after the first ascent, Mount Marcy still averted climbers with June snowfalls and rugged miles. Yet by 1930 it also had marked hiking trails, a summit shelter, and many lean-tos: Four Corners, Lake Colden, Feldspar, Uphill, Sno-Bird, Marcy Dam, Indian Falls, and Plateau. And in 1932, Marcy Dam had more than 1,700 visitors.

Among the visitors that year was a group of Saranac Lake girls. A June snowfall canceled their original trip, but they didn't give up. They tried again two days later. On June 23, sisters Mary Dittmar and Helen Menz and their friends left Heart Lake for a trip up Marcy. They found that the trails were muddy, the streams high, and their shoes awful. But they made it to the top of Marcy and could not believe the wonderful views. "We knew the name of not a single mountain that we were looking at, but it didn't matter," wrote Menz. "We rested, ate, and looked; we were hooked on mountain climbing then and there."[1]

The girls explored inside the stone hut. "It smelled musty because cracks in the walls let moisture in," wrote Menz. "We wondered how many people had had to use it."

They retreated to the Four Corners Lean-to. Evidently, that shelter was not too impressive either. Menz wrote, "It 'leaned to' so much that it was propped up with two stout logs. The stream from which we scooped water almost ran through it, and the fireplace was but a pile of rocks."[2]

The girls slept that night "packed into the lean-to like sardines." The next morning they walked down to Lake Colden and out through Avalanche Pass to Heart Lake. As they reached the end of the trail, they started singing; no one would see a Saranac girl acting tired from a hike up Mount Marcy.

Mary Dittmar and Helen Menz both went on to climb all forty-six high peaks, becoming Adirondack Forty-Sixers number 29 and 42, respectively.

A guy from Saranac Lake climbed Mount Marcy a few weeks after the girls. But it was no ordinary hike. The hike was really a mountain marathon, and the guy was Bob Marshall, Forty-Sixer number 1.

After spending thirteen months in the Alaskan Brooks Range, Marshall came back to visit the Adirondacks. Never content to sit still, Marshall set out to improve Herbert L. Malcolm's record of climbing eleven peaks in one day. At 3:30 a. m. on July 15, he began his hike.

Purely by chance, conservationist Paul Schaefer chose the same day to carry a movie camera up Mount Marcy. Schaefer feared encroachments were being made on the wilderness character of the mountains. He intended to film the beauty and the destruction of the Adirondack Park.

When Schaefer arrived on Marcy's summit, he met the famous guide Herb Clark. Schaefer learned that Clark was carrying a lunch for Bob Marshall, who was soon expected to bound up the mountainside.

Marshall arrived about one o'clock, dressed in baggy blue denims, high-topped sneakers, and an old plaid shirt. He greeted Clark and then introduced himself to Schaefer. "His eyes reflected a great joy for living," recalled Schaefer, "and his face was deeply tanned and ruddy with health."[3]

Schaefer and his companion, Bob Cromi, looked equally hardy—heavy with beard, unkempt, and blackened with the char of a forest fire. Schaefer told Marshall about a proposal to build cabins on state land, the stripping of virgin spruce from Mount Adams, and a crown fire along the Opalescent. Marshall ate his lunch, listening to Schaefer and admiring the views.

"Marcy has always impressed me with the breadth of vision," Marshall wrote later, "encompassing as it does in its panorama practically the entire expanse of the Adirondacks. . . and being the only mountain from which all 46 of the 4,000 foot peaks are visible. But if this familiar delight was pleasant, it was exceedingly disconcerting to find the nearby slope of Mount Adams all scarred by logging operations, which I had supposed were ended in the high mountain region."[4]

Marshall paced on the summit rocks. He had seen these same kinds of infringements and intrusions in other wilderness areas in Montana, Colorado, Washington, and Oregon. "We simply must band together," he said to Schaefer, "all of us who love the wilderness. We must fight together—wherever and whenever wilderness is attacked. We must mobilize all of our resources, all of our energies, all of our devotion to the wilderness. To fail to do this is to permit the American wilderness to be destroyed. That must not happen!"[5]

Many environmentalists feel this was the moment Bob Marshall realized that there was an urgent need for an organization dedicated to fighting for wilderness protection *nationwide*. This was the moment he conceived of the Wilderness Society.

Marshall shook Schaefer's hand and then ran down the side of Mount Marcy. He finished his "day" hike on the summit of Mount Jo at 10:00 p. m. having ascended fourteen peaks and a total of 13,600 feet in elevation.

Marshall wrote that his accomplishment "would fit perfectly in a class with flagpole sitting and marathon dancing as an entirely useless type of record, made only to be broken, were it not that I had such a glorious time out of the entire day."[6] Of course, among that "glorious time" must be included that short conversation atop Mount Marcy.

As for Schaefer, he was "acutely conscious of having met a dynamic personality that day. . . . There was about him [Marshall] the essence of a wild freedom and an utter determination to preserve wilderness for generations to come."[7]

Group at centennial celebration, 1937. Courtesy of New York State Archives.

On August 5, 1937, more than two hundred people, including William L. Wessels, chairman of the Mount Marcy Centennial Commission, and Lithgow Osbourne, Conservation Commissioner, walked to the summit of Mount Marcy. They gathered to observe the hundred-year anniversary of the first ascent. In 1837, all twelve climbers had been men, but now women were almost as numerous as men were. One woman, Dr. Orra Phelps, even climbed the circuitous trail taken one hundred years earlier.

Grace and Ed Hudowalski were there, too, with a group of friends. "We always packed the car with people when we went hiking," said Grace. This time they brought Bill Lance, Grace's sister, and a lady and her niece from their church. The lady was not a hiker; she wore a dress instead of hiking attire.

The group couldn't get a room at the Loj so they stayed in the "cow shed." In the morning, Grace went on ahead up the trail while the lady and an experienced hiker walked slowly behind. At the top, Grace waited anxiously for the slower hikers.

"I shall never forget with what joy we greeted the older members of our party and how unsuppressed tears of happiness rolled down our cheeks to see that one woman—housewife—literally crawling up!" wrote Grace. "A lot of things about that climb stand out in my mind, but paramount is the daring and courage of that unsuspecting woman."[8]

Sisters Mary Dittmar and Helen Menz and a friend, Alice Waterhouse, also attended the celebration. They were almost late—held up by a slow city fellow. The women set out from Elk Lake with a photographer from the New York *Daily News*. They soon realized that if they stayed with the man they would miss the summit festivities. The women went off at a fast pace and made it to the top just in time.

After almost everyone had gone home, the photographer reached the top. "He never looked to the right or left," Dittmar said. "The guy just went right over the top of the mountain and right on down."[9]

The most amazing feat of the day was the radio broadcast from the summit. The General Electric Company proclaimed the fifteen-minute broadcast to be one of the hardest and most difficult broadcasts ever made. The act of hauling 500 pounds of equipment, including a 350-pound gasoline-driven generator, up seven and one-half miles of narrow, wet, and steep mountain trails was unequaled.

The crew started up the trail with the heavy generator packed on a logging sled pulled by two horses. They went a mile

Horse with sled, 1937. Courtesy of Adirondack Research Library.

through mud, over broken branches, and up steep rocks before the ropes to the sleds broke. "We had to carry the equipment the rest of the way on our backs," recalled Seaver Fay, one of the hauling crew. "It just took brute strength and ignorance."[10]

After bringing the equipment to the peak, Fay hiked back to Lake Placid. "I had a date," he said, "so I went back down and kept it."

The next morning, C. D. Wagoner, the man who had arranged the program, set out for Marcy's summit. He caught up with one of the horses and it looked quite tired. He expected to find the other horse dead. Instead, he saw the other horse perched atop a knoll of Marcy. "It was one of the queerest sights I have ever seen," he recalled, "a horse standing like a deer or some wild animal alone high up on a mountain side."[11]

Eventually the heavy generator was pushed, pulled, and shoved to the summit. Despite the rough handling it had received, it started on the second attempt.

At 12:15 p. m., just forty-five minutes before the start of the broadcast, the signal tested satisfactorily. The broadcast began on schedule.

Conservation Commissioner Osbourne unveiled a plaque, engraved with the names of those thought to be the first climbers. "It is a hundred years ago today that white men looked from this same peak," he said. "It is significant that the view which met their gaze is substantially that which meets ours. To be sure some of the mountain slopes have been burned, while others have been lumbered and have only come back into a second growth of hard wood. Nevertheless it was a wilderness upon which they looked, as it is a wilderness upon which we look."[12]

Osborne told the people of New York that it was their land and that the constitution guaranteed its wilderness character. "There is no prospect, present or future, that the lands within the Forest Preserve will be needed for economic or commercial uses. They should be kept free from any taint of such uses. These woods and lakes and streams must be preserved. And the work of preservation includes in first line the majestic profiles of all these peaks we see before us."[13]

When the ceremony ended, hikers quickly descended. But it was late the next afternoon before the horses and the equipment were off the mountain. The hauling crew discovered Lucy Bohrman's lament: the coming down is practically as difficult as the going up.

Although media reports claimed the broadcast was a success, others told a different story. A listener of station WGY in Schenectady reported that she heard the beginning of the program and then the broadcast went dead.[14] As Grace Hudowalski put it, "all that work and the broadcast didn't work."[15]

While the main event of the day centered on the summit, other activities took place at Adirondak Loj. Among the many speeches was an extraordinary one by Russell Carson that reflected on the conflicting views of recreation and preservation and what ADK stood for. Carson said, "The Adirondack Mountain Club stands for recreational use of the preserve for the health and pleasure of the people in a manner, not inconsistent with its wild forest character, but nevertheless is most sympathetic towards the 'protection' idea sponsored by the Association [for the Protection of the Adirondacks]. Between these two ideas there is a medium which if found and carried out, will enable the forest preserve to afford its widest and wisest benefits to man. To have a part in finding this medium is the true function of the Adirondack Mountain Club."[16]

Finding that medium was soon put on hold. A second World War erupted. And 220 acres of the Forest Preserve were about to serve an unforeseen purpose—neither recreation nor preservation.

The U. S. government became concerned that foreign supplies of titanium would be cut off during the war. Titanium was desperately needed for the manufacture of white paints and enamels for warships, tanks, and planes. For example, Allied planes were painted with wide white stripes to reduce hits by friendly fire.

The old McIntyre Iron Works were rich in titanium. In 1941, the new owner, the National Lead Company, began extracting what had once been viewed as an impurity in the iron ore. A village sprang up near the mines at Lake Sanford and took the name Tahawus. Over 325 men worked at the mines, digging in open pits with power shovels and driving truckloads of ore to the concentrator. At first, trucks hauled the concentrates from Tahawus to the railroad at North Creek. Then the old idea of a railroad was reborn.

But how would it be possible to put railroad tracks across state land that was protected as forever wild? The titanium was deemed "strategic materials," and thus, under the National Emergency Act, the federal government took a temporary easement on 220 acres of Forest Preserve land. The thirteen-mile railroad was complete in 1943.

As some people had feared, the "temporary" easment opened the way to "forever." In 1946, the

Conservation Commissioner Lithgow Osborne broadcasting from top of Mount Marcy, August 5, 1937. Courtesy of New York State Archives.

federal government extended the easement through 1967. Then, in 1962, it used its power of eminent domain and condemned the land for a one-hundred-year easement.[17]

But the prosperity at Tahawus would eventually come to an end. Titanium mining halted in 1982, and once again, Tahawus became a ghost town.

There Ain't No Road Up Marcy!
by Orville N. Cobane

Marcy is a majestic mountain;
I'll admit its crown is bleak!
Many people like to climb it
Because it's New York's highest peak.
I have climbed it many times
And I give this reason why:
I *walk* up that grand old mountain
Just because I cannot fly!
...Fer there ain't no road up Marcy!

Many times I've climbed that mountain,
Used the trails from every side,
And when asked just why I did it,
Ofttimes this I did reply:
...Fer there ain't no road up Marcy!

I have climbed it from Heart Lake
On my well-waxed hickory skis;
The wind on top was howling
And my nose did nearly freeze—
...Oh, there ain't no road up Marcy!

I have climbed it from John's Brook,
Up through mud and roots and rocks,
And when I reached the summit
Found I'd worn out both my socks—
...Fer there ain't no road up Marcy!

Someday you may climb Mt. Marcy,
And while you climb this grand old mound,
I would like to have you ponder
On your problems coming down—
...Fer there ain't no road down Marcy!

Sitting up on top this mountain,
There your pride would fairly glow:
For the view is like an eagle's
And at last you'll surely know—
Why we want no road up Marcy!

Winter Adventures

*Here is relaxed skiing in the smooth corn of the bowl and
Panther Gorge—long, lazy swings down the wide slope;
effortless turns made on a thought, with no edge worries.
Below timberline, there is trail skiing for those who like
to feel the trees near their elbows. . . . Marcy remains one
of the finest ski trips on the continent.*
WILLIAM IRVING, SKI MAGAZINE, FEBRUARY 15, 1950

BY THE 1930S AND 1940S, ski ascents of Mount Marcy were becoming commonplace, but in the early 1900s they were still extremely rare. Skiing anywhere was rare. "Untaught, you strike out on skis and find what it is to be unable either to stand up, sit down, move ahead or turn round," reported the *Boston Transcript*. Skiers did not roam far in those days. There were no such things as ski poles or steel-edged skis. There were only wooden skis, which were long and probably very heavy. If you wanted to go into the woods and climb a mountain, you wore snowshoes.[1]

All of the nineteenth-century winter and near-winter ascents of Mount Marcy were made on snowshoes. But on February 18, 1910, a party of four men on snowshoes was joined by a man "so fortunate as to have become proficient in the use of the Norwegian skees."[2] The group started at Upper Ausable Lake and climbed over Bartlett Ridge. When they reached Skylight Camp, it was entirely buried in snow. The "skee-runner's stick" measured five feet of snow on the roof. The group successfully climbed to the summit of Marcy and returned, without any further mention of the one on "skees."

The very next year John S. Apperson led a ski trip up Mount Marcy. It had been thought that this was the first ascent of Marcy on skis but the previous account contradicts that claim. It is doubtful that even the 1910 ski ascent was the first.[3]

Apperson's ascent has been pieced together from old glass plate slides and photos preserved at the Adirondack Research Library in Schenectady.[4] No written account of the trip has been found. It was originally thought that Irving Langmuir, a Nobel Prize winner in chemistry, was one of the party since he had introduced Apperson to skis. However, only the names Apperson, Canivet, and Paskey(sp.?) are written on an envelope containing trip photos.

The skiers' route had been reported to be up the Van Hoevenberg trail, but closer inspection of the photos shows the route was from South Meadow to Lake Colden and then up past Lake Tear to the summit. A letter from Apperson, stating that he had "come in from the way of Colden and Avalanche Lake," confirms the latter route.[5]

Apperson ski party, 1911. *Top:* At the summit. *Above, left:* At Lake Tear. *Right:* Looking toward Skylight. Courtesy of Adirondack Research Library.

It wasn't long before the tracks of Langmuir, Apperson, Canivet, and Paskey were followed by expert Norwegian skier Hermann Smith-Johannsen, later known as "Jackrabbit." While others continued to use snowshoes, Johannsen insisted that skis could go anywhere. And he took them on exploits that were amazing, considering the equipment and the steep, narrow trails at the time. He supposedly skied up Mount Marcy via the Opalescent route in 1915 and skied it via the Upper Ausable Lake route another year.[6] On January 6, 1923, Johannsen joined two ski professionals from the Lake Placid Club for another climb. It was eighteen degrees below zero Fahrenheit when they started from Heart Lake at 7:30 in the morning. By 2:00 they had reached the summit of Mount Marcy. They made the seven-and-a-half mile return in less than four hours.[7]

At the time of the 1932 Winter Olympics, Johannsen was living in Montreal and thus was selected as co-coach of the Canadian Olympic ski team. When the team came to Lake Placid for the games, Johannsen wanted to give them a feel for the Adirondacks. He took them up Marcy. "It will be good for their legs!" he said.[8]

The team skied out of Lake Placid following Johannsen. They went through South Meadow, then up assorted brooks to the summit. According to his daughter, "They came down the 'summer' trail, dodging trees, clinging to branches, schussing the pitches. When the trail became too steep, they zigzagged through the woods. They reached the bottom in pitch black, and skied ten miles back to the village, 35 miles in all, 'during which Jackrabbit had led, or had kept up with, the best ski-runners Canada could produce at that time. None of them would ever forget it.' He was age 55."[9]

Besides racing and coaching, Johannsen designed ski courses. He liked to make cross-country courses tough, like the courses in Norway. According to ski racer Harry Pangman, "he would usually include a few sections of bushwhacking (literally 'to strike bushes with a loud resounding blow'). It was this ability of his to bounce around from tree to tree that earned him the title 'Jackrabbit'."[10]

Johannsen had a different explanation. In a 1980 interview, he said, "We had hare and hound races and I was the hare, the jackrabbit. They tried to catch me. They haven't caught me yet." That was at age 104. At age 106, he was living in Montreal, and still skiing. He died in 1987, at the age of 112.[11]

Johannsen, Apperson, and others helped to make Mount Marcy a popular winter destination. Others followed their lead. The Sno-Birds of the Lake Placid Club became active in the 1920s. Fay Loope, Schenectady YMCA Executive and Forty-Sixer number 4, regularly led ski groups up Mount Marcy, sometimes starting in the middle of the night so as to view the winter sunrise on top. On January 1, 1929, three college students started what became a minor tradition of camping overnight in the MacDonald summit shelter. (See "Built on High" chapter.)

But the most fantastic feat was accomplished in 1933 by a group of General Electric scientists from Schenectady: Dr. C. Guy Suits, Larry Shaw, and Dr. Klaus Sixtus. They came to ski the summit snowfields and take weather observations. Their goal was to stay on top of Mount Marcy and experience arctic conditions for a full week. Could it be done?

The summit hut was helpful, but firewood was scarce. They decided to carry firewood, food, and other supplies to the summit in November. They packed the food in rodent-resistant coffee cans and buried it under rocks on the east side of the hut. Next they covered it with firewood carried from below. How much wood was needed? "We did not have a handy 'Marcy Summit Woodstove Slide Rule' for the purpose," wrote Suits.[12] Sadly, their calculation would be too low.

Along their way from Adirondak Loj to the summit on Sunday, February 5, the group met Vincent Schaefer, another Schenectady scientist, and Charles F. Flurscheim, who had skied up Marcy from Upper Ausable Lake. Schaefer made the trip with eighteen inches broken off the tail of one of his skis. He later wrote, "My broken ski actually was an advantage in skiing down the narrow Marcy trail, and I was able to make excellent time without any falls. What fun!"[13]

After the two groups exchanged greetings at timberline, Suits, Shaw, and Sixtus headed toward the summit dome. They found that skiing was impossible due to the glare ice on the rocks and the strong wind. They cached their skis below the tree line and walked on crampons to the hut.

Their firewood was intact but rodents had tampered with some of the food. No matter, they faced a bigger problem; the doors were coated with five inches of ice. After half an hour of chopping, they finally opened one of the doors and went inside. Since the window seemed too small for an exit, they had to leave the door propped open so it wouldn't freeze shut and trap them inside.

The door problem hampered the Schenectady group as they tried to live on top of Mount Marcy in temperatures that fell to forty below at night. Because of the draft, the fire burned more wood, yet provided little warmth. Suits said, "We soon found that cooking on the stove was a lost cause. It never got hot enough. In fact, in the morning we took turns sitting on the stove to get warm."

The first chore every morning was melting enough snow and getting it hot enough for coffee. "Hardly anyone took a morning shower," noted Suits. "Shaving in the morning was another item that fell by the wayside."[14]

After the morning chores were done, the party went skiing and "loved every minute of it." This routine lasted for four days and nights. They were forced to leave on Thursday because they were running out of firewood. No matter. They concluded that their stay "was adequate to prove whatever it was that we were trying to prove, which was that we could manage a skiing vacation on Marcy in mid February."[15]

Mountaineer Jim Goodwin proved he could manage a Christmas Eve on top of Mount Marcy. He had made his first ski ascent of Mount Marcy on Christmas Eve of 1930, but in 1935 he and a friend decided to spend the night. They slept in llama wool sleeping bags in the stone shelter while the outdoor temperature dropped near minus twenty degrees Fahrenheit. They awoke to a sea of clouds. Jim said it looked as though "someone could paddle a canoe to the neighboring 'islands' of Haystack, Nippletop and Dix."[16] Of all of his many adventures in the Adirondacks, including his 196 climbs of Mount Marcy, this was Jim Goodwin's most memorable moment.[17]

Winter climbers didn't really have to stay overnight on the summit. The new Adirondak Loj opened for the winter of 1928. And Johns Brook Lodge (JBL) was open, too. A group came to JBL in 1928 during a severe cold snap and never attempted Marcy. But they learned that JBL was a cold place in the winter. The next year they stayed at Homer Brown's camp across the brook from JBL. Shortly thereafter, the warm little camp was bought by ADK as its Winter Camp. Despite the warmer lodging, the climbers were once again prevented from reaching the summit of Marcy. The problem this time was deep soft snow.

In the winter of 1930, an ADK party finally reached the summit of Mount Marcy. Russell Carson, George I. Davis, Lawrence Kenney, Robert C. Carter, Harry McIntyre, and Thomas Gilchrist stayed at Winter Camp and started for the summit at 7:00 a. m. on Saturday, February 22. Davis and Kenney made the ascent on skis in five hours; the others, on snowshoes, took six hours.[18]

It was the first time any of the men had reached the summit in winter. The flat top was almost bare of ice and snow because of the warm weather preceding the climb. "This day was so warm," wrote Carson, "that one of the party warmed his bare feet in the sun while his wet socks were spread on a rock drying."[19]

Why did all these people come in the winter? Most days were not warm. Most days the temperatures were below zero and strong westerly gales whipped the exposed upper slopes above tree line. The snows were deep. The climb was long. The days were short.

Snow-covered Mount Marcy, looking toward Haystack Mountain.
Courtesy of New York State Archives.

But there was also the hushed silence, the crisp air that awakens droopy lungs, and the wonderful and weird forms of wind-whipped snow. A. T. Shorey wrote, "Defects of every sort are obliterated. Practically no evidence of man is found. Even the trail markers are buried. That priceless gift of nature, solitude and silence, reigns supreme. The bark of the fox, or twitter of the chick-a-dee and, toward evening, the hoot of the great horned owl, only occasionally breaks the heavenly silence of which the constant sighing of the wind thru the spruces is a part."[20]

One early March weekend in 1939, Shorey, Grace and Ed Hudowalski, Herbert Lance, and Louise Goark went up Johns Brook Valley. Night was falling and a full moon rising. "The stream itself, in imagination, was an Alpine glacier with deep crevasses and dark holes. The snow, blue in the moonlight, lay deep and smooth," wrote Shorey. "After mushing two hours thru this wonderland, the party slid down off a snow bank, ducked under the roof and landed on the porch of the winter camp."

At 8:15 the next morning, they put on their snowshoes and went toward Marcy. At Bushnell Falls lean-to, they rested on the roof, which was about the only part visible. The deep, wet snow made the going hard and slow.

It was already 3:00 p. m. when they reached the Range Trail junction. They decided to turn back at 4:00 p. m., regardless. "And at 4:00 p.m. near the Van Hoevenberg junction the sun came out, the icy dome of Marcy beckoned like a siren, but stern judgment called a halt," recalled Shorey. "Returning, the route down Slant Rock brook was possible and great fun. All the party except Grace sat on their snowshoes and slid down the snow-covered frozen cascades, but Grace spread her wings and sailed down erect —a picture of poise and 'grace'!"[21]

Hiking trails were great for sailing on snowshoes. But skiing was becoming more popular. Many skiers were not content with gliding on flat trails and roads; they wanted to ski on mountains. But Adirondack hiking trails were not really suitable for skiing, so skiers went to New England to find down-mountain runs.

The Adirondack region needed ski trails. Skiers lobbied for the widening of some foot trails to make them more suitable for skiing, especially on the curves. Of course this necessitated cutting some trees. But the "forever wild" provision prohibited the cutting of any trees. Did this literally mean none?

In March 1930, Judge Frederick C. Crane ruled on the building of a bobsled run on Forest Preserve land. He decided that trees might be cut to protect forests from fire and other hazards, and that facilities might be provided for public use, as long as they did not call for the removal of timber "to any material degree." But Crane ruled that trees could not be destroyed to make space for bobsledding; thus the bobsled run was built on private lands.

So how many trees could be cut before the removal was considered a material degree? Could ninety-four trees be cut for a six-mile ski trail down Mount Marcy?

Skiers Hal Burton and E. H. Hull helped a crew from the Conservation Department mark the route of the proposed ski trail, which closely followed the Van Hoevenberg trail. People were given a chance to inspect the route, see the ninety-four trees marked for removal, and then attend a public hearing. Since few objections arose, the ski trail project was approved.[22]

Thus, in 1936, the Van Hoevenberg trail was widened in spots for safer and easier skiing. The trail was still considered narrow, only nine to twenty-five feet wide, and had a grade of up to twenty-one degrees. But it offered a descent of 3,189 feet.[23]

The Marcy ski trail is still one of the most popular backcountry ski runs in the state. The difficult, steep sections are interspersed with slower, flat areas. "All in all, this is a classic tour that you will never tire of doing," concludes Tony Goodwin in *Northern Adirondack Ski Tours*.[24]

While as far as anyone knew, there had been no fatalities on Mount Marcy by the late 1940s, some skiers began to be concerned about the potential for such a disaster. Fay Welch met a group of "wretched, bedraggled, hollow-eyed individuals" one warm winter day. "They had attempted the climb the previous day, turned back too late, abandoned their skis near Indian Falls, separated, floundered down through wet snow, followed streams, reached Marcy Dam lean-to, been unable to start a fire, shivered in wet clothing through the remainder of the night when (gratias Dios!) the temperature was only 40° F. If it had been -40°F. (and at that spot in January there probably are more below than above zero nights) they surely would have been badly frozen and might have perished."[25]

Cliff Alexander observed a similar incident: "Last winter [1949], a skier without food or sleeping bags became separated from the rest of his party and made his way down the opposite side of Marcy from his friends. Fortunately he was located in an abandoned lumber camp, although many miles away from the rest of his group. If this person had not been favored by a mild winter, it is quite likely that he never would have survived the first of his two nights out. Such incidents should never happen."[26]

Some winter mountaineers seemed to be taking too many risks. Others were more prudent and adopted winter safety ethics. "Be prepared" and "stay together" were precautions of a party that climbed on January 31, 1949. Richard H. Beck, George Lamb, Irving Lamb, and Thomas A. Ewing packed "sandwiches, chocolate, apples, dried prunes, extra handkerchiefs, safety pins, extra belts, straps, eyedrops, merthiolate, ace bandage, bandaids, lip ice, paraffin, rawhide thongs, flashlight, cigarettes, matches, Phillips-head screws, screw driver, sheath knife, extra cables, compasses, annacin tablets, small flask of brandy, drinking cup, goggles, and clear glasses."[27]

Despite extremely cold temperatures and strong winds, the party did not turn back. Finally they reached a flat spot on the summit and ducked behind a big rock to rest. "Just as were about to leave Irving Lamb looked up and saw a bronze plaque on the side of the rock. We had reached the top of Marcy!. . . . We scraped the ice off the plaque and read it, carved our initials in the ice on the rock, then turned around and started back."[28]

Ten years later, in December 1959, the "Schaefer Expedition" climbed Marcy. The party of four were trained in the "take no chances" attitude of the Wilderness Mountaineering School. They spent days sorting and packing equipment and planning menus. "We knew we had to be prepared for anything the weather might bring, be it thaw, blizzard or below zero temperatures," wrote Mary Schaefer, daughter of Paul Schaefer. The party snowshoed to Indian Falls the first day. The snow was three feet deep and the temperature was well below zero.[29]

It took the entire next day to snowshoe the two miles to Plateau lean-to and set up camp. "It was long after the last tinges of pink and mauve had left the snow of the MacIntyres when we stepped out into the wind for a back straightening and final look around," wrote Schaefer. "We could have reached up and touched the stars, while the cone of Marcy bulked immense in its nearness."[30]

After a comfortable sleep and a breakfast of tea, oranges, hard-boiled eggs, and fortified meatloaf, the foursome took their emergency pack and headed for the summit of Marcy. "The snowshoeing was superb," recalled Schaefer, "and with the aid of ice axes we were able to negotiate the few steep, windblown areas. Too soon we were on the summit. Our Schaefer Expedition Flag made of orange and white parachute flapped in the frigid breeze."[31]

Those who were scared of the forbidding challenge of Marcy in winter did not have to abandon the thrill of skiing on Marcy—they just had to wait for spring. Spring skiing meant sunshine, halter tops, and corn. Above timberline, snow drifted into a huge bowl and "you are offered days of sunbathing and leisure."[32]

The trip was not considered difficult; it was doable between sunup and sundown. But if skiers wanted to spend a few days, they could have supplies dropped at Plateau by the Lake Placid flying club. The summit hut was not recommended since it was usually drifted with snow and it lacked sources of water and firewood.

As for the skiing, the depth of snow and length of season varied. But even in the mildest season, thirty feet of snow remained in the bowl near the top of Marcy in late April. Some years good skiing remained into June. According to *Ski Magazine*, even Whiteface could not match the spring conditions found on Marcy: "Winter or spring, Marcy remains one of the finest ski trips on the continent."[33]

Of course, Marcy offered a different kind of skiing from that found at commercially developed ski centers, like those at Whiteface, Gore, and throughout New England. It was even different from New Hampshire's Mount Washington. The summit of Mount Washington is only five or so miles from a road in any direction while the nearest road to Mount Marcy is seven miles away in one direction and nine to fifteen miles in the other directions.

"Furthermore," says Tony Goodwin, "all sides of Mt. Washington can be readily seen and approached by highway and the skiing in its many ravines, spectacular though it may be, is readily accessible to the masses. Marcy, by contrast, rarely attracts more than a few dozen skiers at a time to ski the trail from Adirondak Loj, and only an elite handful ever skied any other side of the peak."[34]

Some of the "elite handful" from Plattsburgh started skiing whatever was possible to climb and descend on skis. The leader of the group was Geoff Smith and they came to be known as the Ski to Die Club. Members subscribed to the motto "Skiing Is a Controlled Fall." Among their many descents of slides, dykes, and steep faces are descents of Mount Marcy down Johns Brook, Feldspar Brook from Lake Tear, and the slides on the southeast side of Marcy.

Backcountry Boom

The problem is not that Marcy has failed in its role as magnet mountain, but that it has been too successful in attracting hikers, campers and other visitors. . . [s]tate officials are beginning to issue propaganda aimed at undermining the mountain's longstanding reputation as the "Mount Everest of New York."

THE NEW YORK TIMES, MAY 14, 1977

BECAUSE it is the highest of the High Peaks, Mount Marcy has always attracted a large proportion of the Adirondack backcountry visitors. Some people climb it again and again. Paul Smith's College forestry instructor Fred Hunt, known as "The Lone Ranger," climbed Marcy each month for 110 consecutive months.[1]

While there are no long-term data about Mount Marcy visitations, overall trends can be discerned from general data and eyewitness accounts. Very few people climbed Mount Marcy in the early 1800s. However, those who did climb tended to spend two or more nights in the woods, cutting trees for shanties and bonfires. Some even camped on the summit rock, attempting to keep warm from fires of moss and dwarf spruce. The guidebooks of Wallace and Stoddard promoted these mountain adventures and by the end of the century, more people came to Mount Marcy. Permanent shelters, nearby lodges, and cleared trails were the norm.[2]

Climbing parties were not even guaranteed the quiet solitude of the mountaintop. After climbing Mount Marcy in 1898, William James wrote, "As usual, I met two Cambridge acquaintances on the mountain top."[3] And in 1908, two women greeted Governor Hughes' party on the summit.

The introduction of the automobile in the early 1900s brought even more people to the mountains. Now folks from nearby cities could drive to trailheads for weekend climbs. But where should they climb? In the 1920s, the Conservation Commission promoted the park through recreation circulars, including *Trails to Marcy*. They wanted more people to use the Forest Preserve.

Records kept by rangers during the summer of 1932 show 1,000 visitors at Lake Colden and 1,753 at Marcy Dam. In just five years, those numbers more than doubled.[4] A phenomenal 200 people were on the summit on one day—August 5, 1937, for the centennial celebration.

Some hikers were already noticing the changes around Mount Marcy. "When it is written that this country seems untouched, it is quite a joke," wrote Julian W. Schwab in a Letter to the Editor of *The New York Times*. "All one has to do is walk a mile in any direction from the thickest woods to stumble on the customary hotdog stand. . . . There is no longer any solitude and quiet. People leave Placid in cars, run up Marcy and return before lunch any day. The old trails are either cut out or overrun from lack of use. The entire romance of the district has been dissipated."[5]

Maybe the romance was gone, but there was still some solitude. Hiker and scientist Edwin Ketchledge recalls, "Except for mid- or late summer, we were often alone at the top. In spring or fall, we had the place to ourselves, and especially in winter. For that matter, few of us bothered to carry tents in those days; the lean-tos were rarely filled, if occupied at all. . . . We saw more of people's litter left on the summits than we did the people themselves."[6]

Hiker P. Fay Loope was a frequent visitor of Mount Marcy in those days. By 1949, he had scaled the summit sixty-five times, more than half in winter. Why so many times? "Perhaps it is to know the old peak better," he answered, "to discover another mood, and then another and another. One does not really know a mountain until he has stood on it in sunshine and in storm; in rain and in snow; in the summer haze of dog days and in the glistening frost crystals of a sub-zero day; in noonday sun and in inky blackness; in evening's fading light and in the glow of a morning sun still hidden below the horizon."[7]

A moonless November night. An electric storm. A sea of clouds stretching in all directions with mountaintop islands peaking through. A sundog. The snow-field painted red by the rising sun. Frost flowers. These are the "moods" that Fay Loope saw on Mount Marcy.

By 1950, the number of visitors at Marcy Dam had barely risen since 1937. The crowds may not have arrived that year, but a hurricane did. On Saturday, November 25, 1950, gale-force winds and four inches of rain devastated the Adirondack woods. Things were so bad at Adirondak Loj that guest "Ditt" Dittmar feared the roof might blow off.

But imagine how it was on top of Mount Marcy. Robert DeLong and a fellow Explorer Scout climbed out onto the rocks. "We held a conference behind a rock to escape the wind and the flying corn snow which had the effect of BB Shot on one's face," recalled DeLong. They ran from rock to rock until they reached the summit hut. The door wouldn't open, so they crawled through the window. The shelter was disappointing; there was no chance for a fire. So they crawled out and started down. They counted eighteen trees across the trail on the way down.[8]

The blowdown devastated some hiking trails and made others difficult to traverse for a few years. Despite the difficulties, more people were discovering the Adirondacks. Between 1950 and 1959, the number of visitors at Marcy Dam doubled. "What a change in the '50s, and thereafter!" says Ketchledge. "The public lands were becoming public!!"[9]

Grace Hudowalski recalls that when Edmund Hillary, a New Zealander, and Tenzing Norgay, a sherpa, stood atop Mount Everest on May 29, 1953, interest in climbing soared. To investigate the sport of mountain climbing, an Albany newspaper decided to do a story on climbing the "Everest of New York"—Mount Marcy. They chose Grace to arrange the trip. She got permission from the

Conservation Department to do things hikers can't normally do, like drive to Marcy Dam and boat across Lake Colden.[10]

District Forester William E. Petty drove the hikers from Adirondak Loj to Marcy Dam. From there, the hikers climbed the trail. At timberline, they looked up at the mountain. "A hot day in June and we saw snow!" wrote photographer Bernard Kolenberg.[11]

After a snowball fight, the hikers continued to the summit. Kolenberg recalled, "Climbing miles through thick woods, with each step a veritable 'hot foot' of burns, with your body sweating and the 'torch flies' gathering around you, only to have the magnificent climax of scenery from the highest peak in New York State. . . that is the *big pay off!*"[12]

The party descended down the other side to Lake Tear of the Clouds and Lake Colden. A ranger with a boat took them across the lake. Then they walked to Avalanche Lake and took another boat. From there it was two miles to Marcy Dam.

"I went over to the register and gladly signed my name to end the most wonderful and scenic trip I have ever enjoyed," wrote Kolenberg. "No beautiful rock or spot near any city will take the place, for those who see the real mountains and stand up on their peaks and feel the wind through their hair."[13]

Clearly, Kolenberg now understood the sport of mountain climbing, and he understood stewardship. Along the way, Grace picked up gum wrappers and other garbage and Kolenberg was mighty impressed: "The Hudowalskis understand the woods and their paths. They love the smell of the air and the pretty little flowers that you cannot see until you climb a mountain."[14]

George Marshall was that kind of a climber, too. With his brother, Robert, and guide Herb Clark, he was the first to climb all of the forty-six high peaks. He returned in the summer of 1952 to take his son for his first climb of Mount Marcy. "The joys of passing through and experiencing unspoiled forests along the way are perhaps the greatest pleasures of climbing in the Adirondacks and we looked forward to them on the Bushnell Falls and Slant Rock trails," wrote Marshall.[15] They also looked forward to the thrill of standing on a wild mountain peak shrouded in fog.

The woods proved to be as delightful as Marshall remembered them. The drizzle that enveloped them as they reached the top of Panther Gorge only heightened the eerie sense of the mountain.

"We climbed slowly through cold mist towards the top of Tahawus amply prepared for a climatic exaltation," wrote Marshall. "We sensed the outline of the summit dome. Just below it loomed—not delicate alpine vegetation—but trampled ground strewn with orange peels and lunch papers! Disenchantment came heavily upon us, and in our futile search for an unspoiled spot, we found the disintegrating remains of an old shelter literally transformed into a garbage dump!"[16]

Later, from the summit of Basin, he looked down at the Boreas Mountain region west of Elk Lake. "I could not help thinking of the tragedy whereby the people of the State of New York abandoned the southern slopes of the High Peaks and Upper Hudson Valleys to raw material despoiliation [*sic*]—the unique Elk Lake and Boreas basins to lumbering, the once superb Lake Sanford to mining."

He was also disturbed by other examples of "an unnecessary lack of sensitivity to what is appropriate to a wild forest environment." In the Johns Brook valley, new telephone poles for the line to the ranger's cabin ran beside the trail. On the top of Mount Marcy, large white arrows were painted on the rocks when cairns would have been quite adequate.

Marshall appealed to the Adirondack Mountain Club, the Conservation Department, and other groups to develop education programs directed at reversing these unfortunate trends. "[We] must be wary lest we lose the wild forest substance of the Preserve through a continuing process of attrition," he warned.[17]

Whatever measures any organization could have taken in the early 1950s would likely have been far too weak to impact the tremendous boom about to hit the mountains. In the 1960s, the back-to-nature movement spread. College students rediscovered nature. Sales of summer homes rose sharply. There was new interest in winter recreation. Between 1960 and 1965, the number of visitors at Marcy Dam rose from 8,720 to 14,329. At Lake Colden, the increase was even more pronounced. The number went from 5,916 to 12,959.[18] Then, in 1967, the superhighway known as the Adirondack Northway (Interstate 87) was completed between Albany and the Canadian border, putting the Adirondacks within easy reach of millions of people.

In *Adirondack Wilderness*, author Jane Keller observed, "After World War II it was no longer man the exploiter but man the appreciator who had to be watched,

regulated, and warned."[19] Old photos show piles of tin cans, bottle caps, and trash left by hikers. But in fact, "man the appreciator" was not being thoughtless or careless—he was just doing what he was told to do. In those days, lean-tos and established campsites had garbage pits and the ethic was to burn and bury all garbage.

As usage increased, it was recognized that something had to be done; the backcountry needed

Hiking boots at Mount Marcy summit.

a new ethic: "If you pack it in, pack it out!" To promote the new ethic, fourteen volunteers climbed Mount Marcy on Memorial Day, 1966, and hauled out 400 pounds of trash. According to Almy Coggeshall, who headed up the Clean Trailsides committee of ADK, "The Mount Marcy clean-up was designated as a dramatic, highly publicized, symbolic act to kick-off a campaign to gain general acceptance for the carry-out system."[20]

Ray Michalowski, Will Merritt, Clark Gittinger, and Karl Schmieder, all from Schenectady, participating in Operation Can Flattner. Cans were crushed between hinged two-by-fours and carried from Mount Marcy, 1966. Photo by Almy Coggeshall.

An education campaign encouraged the public to carry a litter bag, and there was a noticeable improvement in the state of the woods. But the Conservation Department was reluctant to adopt the carry-out method; it stuck to its policy of garbage dumps. So, many hikers continued to put garbage in the dumps, as policy dictated, and the dumps continued to be eyesores. Finally, the bureaucracy agreed that if campsites were found to be "squeaky clean," then the order would be given to fill over the old dumps.[21]

The final, heroic effort to clean the High Peaks campsites occurred on Memorial Day weekend of 1974. About 280 people came to help, including one worker on crutches. A human chain extended all the way from Indian Falls to Marcy Dam, where trucks carted away four tons of garbage.[22]

Almy Coggeshall recalls, "My moment of triumph came later that summer when I was leaving the parking lot that leads into the Johns Brook Valley and I saw this Department sign at the trailhead:"

> Enjoy the woods and your goodies.
> Leave the woods as they should be—clean!
> Your empties, paper and bottles are light in weight.
> Be good, be strong, considerate and proud.
>
> IF YOU CARRY IT IN,
> PLEASE CARRY IT OUT!

"Seeing this sign meant we had finally prevailed and turned the bureaucracy around," says Coggeshall. "It made it all worthwhile."[23]

Other changes were occurring, too. In 1972, the state adopted the Adirondack Park State Land Master Plan. It classified the High Peaks area as "wilderness" and required the removal of all non-conformances, "those structures, facilities, or uses not compatible with the concept of wilderness."[24] The Marcy summit hut had already been demolished in 1967; now camping facilities in the fragile areas above 3,500 feet began to be removed. By 1976, seven lean-tos in the Marcy area were gone: two at Plateau, two at Indian Falls, and one each at Four Corners, Lake Tear, and Lake Arnold.

Meanwhile, people kept coming. One hiker observed that on the Marcy Dam trail forty people had passed him in less than two hours. "In one sense this was fine," he wrote. "People were enjoying the Adirondack wilderness. On the other hand, such trail erosion contradicts the thesis that forest reserves should be 'forever wild.'"[25]

In 1975, some 28,000 people registered at Marcy Dam, and it was estimated that over 35,000 people visited Mount Marcy that year. Hikers becoming Adirondack Forty-Sixers grew from 15 in 1960 to 70 in 1970 and 126 in 1975. The membership of ADK grew from about 2,000 in 1960 to almost 9,000 in 1975. Today, it has nearly 35,000 members.

The new Department of Environmental Conservation (DEC), which took over the duties of the old Conservation Department, had limited staff and budget; it could not handle the increased usage. Fortunately, volunteer organizations contributed more help. The Forty-Sixers, ADK, and ATIS assisted with trail maintenance, rehabilitation, and rerouting, and offered education programs.

One important step DEC took in 1975 was to hire a ranger for the Marcy area. Peter Fish was to serve as a "wilderness ranger" with a focus on public education. It was the job Fish had dreamed of and the steward Marcy needed.

Peter Fish first climbed Marcy on July 4, 1959. "I climbed it because it was there," he says. At the time, he was twenty-three years old and living in Hartford, Connecticut. After climbing most of the mountains in New Hampshire, he looked at a map one day and found the highest point in New York. Within hours, he arrived at the Adirondak Loj parking area and set out for Mount Marcy.

"Before I walked the two miles to Marcy Dam," he recalls, "I sat down on a rock to rest and knew I was going to die." But, of course, he didn't. He reached Marcy Dam and found an empty lean-to on Fourth of July weekend! The next morning, he climbed Mount Marcy.[26]

Fish went on to climb all forty-six Adirondack high peaks, finishing on Mount Seymour on September 23, 1976. He earned number 1396 from the Forty-Sixers club. He had previously earned the honor of being the twelfth member of the Catskill 3500 club.

When it comes to the Adirondack High Peaks backcountry, Fish, now retired, is probably the most knowledgeable person alive. As of September 1999, he had climbed Mount Marcy 509 times. "Not that I'm counting," he says. Fish climbed it so many times because, for a ranger, it was the place to be. "First-timers do

Marcy and need the education," he says. They needed help with where to camp, how to set up a tent, how to keep their food from bears, etc.

Fish did his ranger job with zeal, journeying over the trails from dawn to dusk, and sometimes into the night. Wherever there was an illegal campsite, an injury, an unruly crowd, a litterbug, he was there. And he came with a helping hand, a sense of humor, or a stern warning.

Even on his day off, Fish hiked Mount Marcy, sometimes in a kilt. People still came up to him with questions. He asked them why they were asking him. "Well, you are a ranger, aren't you?" was the response.

Indeed, he was a ranger. And he was struggling to deal with the new breed of hiker—created and shaped by the new outdoor products industry. Marketers and manufacturers had quickly sprung up to meet the needs of all the hikers and backpackers. Exterior-frame backpacks, down parkas, down sleeping bags, dome tents, freeze-dried food, synthetic clothing, and lightweight boots became available.

It wasn't just the sheer number of people that was a concern; it was the number of inexperienced hikers hitting the trails to Mount Marcy. Besides the problems with litter, destruction of alpine vegetation, trail erosion, and loss of wilderness experience, there were now numerous accidents and lost hikers.

Pete Fish on Mount Marcy for his 509th time, September 1999.

Calamity and Catastrophe

To get lost in such a vast wilderness brings home to one what a small and insignificant thing is a human being in this great universe.

HARRY P. HAYS, 1923.

CALAMITY POND sits beside the trail that goes from the Upper Works to Mount Marcy. Weary hikers might suspect its name describes the condition of the trail or the bumbling manner of some hikers. It doesn't. It is the scene of the first of many mishaps associated with Mount Marcy.

On September 3, 1845, David Henderson, a partner at the Adirondack Iron Works, threw his pistol belt onto a rock. The cocked pistol struck the rock and discharged, killing Henderson. Thereafter, the wilderness pond became known as Calamity Pond. (See "Trips Up the Opalescent" chapter.)

The first mention of a near mishap atop Mount Marcy was made in 1866. Rev. Joseph Twichell found himself on the summit in a thick mist, driving rain, and roaring wind. His skilled guide found the way down to safety. Twichell wrote, "Last summer, a party caught so, with an incompetent guide, nearly perished in the cold and rain."[1]

A few years later, in 1875, Verplanck Colvin's survey crew executed the first known search-and-rescue on the upper slopes of Marcy. Colvin wrote, "On the 25th [of October] we rose at 4 a.m., and resumed the work of leveling. Made search for a short route to the foot of Mt. Skylight. The second growth of evergreen was very dense, and we failed to find a favorable route. The leveler attempting to return along the trail to the nearest bench-mark, lost his way, failing to meet us. Alarmed we searched the trails in both directions, fired pistols, and sent one guide up the Skylight trail, and another up the old slide trail to Marcy. He was finally found near the top of Bartlett mountain—level and man all right—but man somewhat confused in regard to directions and distances."[2]

Colvin was there for the first known injury on Mount Marcy, too. In 1877, during the installation of the signal tower, an explosion occurred and melted lead nearly blinded one of the crew.

Another injury occurred in 1879. A young man from Rochester, Vermont, was camped with two men, and without a guide, near the summit of the mountain. "Toward morning, getting cold, he undertook to chop some wood, cut off three of his toes, and came near bleeding to death," reported the *Plattsburgh Sentinel*. "Fortunately there were some medical students near by, who succeeded in dressing the wound so as to stop the blood. Guides were procured from other parties, who took turns in carrying him down the mountain astride their shoulders."[3]

Guides generally kept hikers safe. But many mountain guides only knew their local regions; they felt quite lost in other territories. The *Plattsburgh Sentinel* reported, "It is stated on good authority that an experienced and well known guide of Long Lake, got lost in attempting to conduct a party to Mount Marcy, and came near perishing, when they were rescued by a guide from Keene Flats."[4]

In 1898, Philosopher William James' guide didn't keep him safe, either. James walked so long that he overexerted himself and suffered permanent heart damage.

Sometimes *not* walking was even worse, especially in winter. One of the guides who accompanied Gifford Pinchot up Mount Marcy stopped below the summit. The guide ended up with a badly frozen foot, "and was lame from it until the following autumn."[5]

These accounts of mishaps or tragedies near Marcy were rare in the 1800s, perhaps because so few people climbed Marcy. Or maybe they were just lucky. For example, A. A. Schenck, Newell Martin, and his brother Pascal came down Marcy in the dark in 1871. "I went ahead with a candle picking out the trail," recalled Schenck.[6]

In the 1900s, more hikers arrived and more mishaps occurred. Evacuation was often a difficult matter. When a hunter was accidentally shot in the leg near Four Corners, it took four men a day and a half to carry him out of the woods.[7]

In another incident, a party came down the Johns Brook trail from Marcy carrying a "litter bearing one who had been hurt on that journey." They met the hiking party of Georgia Pangborn, who wrote that "They rested that night in our camp, and in the morning went on, cheerfully and courageously as became those who made mountains their playmates, and the most cheerful face of all was that of the one who had been hurt in playing that game."[8]

The incident made Pangborn reflect on the danger of mountain climbing. "If one is wounded in the venture it seems a dear price to pay;" she wrote, "but as the young bones weld their edges true and strong again, will there not be large and quieting visions standing about the bed, and calling her to come back again and yet again, even though when next the litter goes down the mountain it should be a funeral march?"[9]

Fatalities were not uncommon on mountains of the northeastern United States. The first documented one occurred on Mount Washington in October 1851. Remarkably, it was over a hundred years later that the first known fatality occurred on Mount Marcy.

Thanksgiving weekend marked the annual High Peaks encampment of several college outing clubs. In 1956, it was held at the Lake Colden lean-tos.

Among the participants were two Cornell hikers, Timothy Bond and Norman Nissan, a young Danish foreign exchange student who was new to cold-weather camping and had limited climbing experience. On Saturday morning, the two men left to check the winter cache at Sno-Bird lean-to, between Marcy and Basin Mountain. This entailed climbing fourteen miles of steep terrain.

They successfully went over Marcy and checked the cache. Nissan moved very slowly on the way back. By the time they reached the side of Marcy, Nissan could not continue. At 6:30, Bond left Nissan and went for help. The rescue team reached Nissan at 1:30 in the morning, but he had been dead for some time.[10]

One lesson learned from this tragedy was that winter parties should consist of at least four persons—one to stay with an injured person and two to go for help.

Winter conditions are not the only reason for accidents. The very next summer another exhausted climber mounted the summit. Theodore McKerron, age 75, arrived at Adirondak Loj wishing to climb Mount Marcy. He brought with him a pile of photographic equipment, a gallon of water, loaves of bread, and a jar of pickles, among other things.

Loj caretaker Homer Beede suggested that he take Skip Nash, age 16, and Foster Beede, age 14, as porters and guides. So the two youths set off for Marcy Dam with the 75-year-old man. It was early afternoon when they arrived at the dam and the boys suggested they turn around and get an early start in the morning.

McKerron refused to go back. "He told us he was bound and determined to climb Marcy and had walked a mile a day for several years to get in shape," recalled Nash.[11]

Although McKerron collapsed several times, he kept climbing. They reached the stone hut on the summit just before sunset and spent a cold and windy night there. A search party reached the summit the next morning and assisted the sick and tired man. It took a few days at the Loj before McKerron recovered from his exhaustion.

Unwillingness to turn back from a summit attempt is the culprit in many mishaps. "Summit fever" is a dangerous ailment.

Steve Clautice and Richard Stepp left Adirondak Loj for a day climb of Mount Marcy in December 1968. They reached Plateau lean-to at 3:15 p. m. and decided to continue for another half-hour. They had still not reached the top after an hour passed. By the time they turned around, it was snowing and the wind had blown snow over their tracks.

They descended to the north but missed the trail and the lean-to. They tried to keep moving in order to stay warm, but the bindings on their modified downhill skis caused them trouble as they walked over blowdown, snowdrifts, and streams. They tried to make a snow cave but were unsuccessful. So, with very little to eat and temperatures around minus twenty degrees Fahrenheit, they started moving again.

Finally they found trail markers along Johns Brook. It was 3:15 p. m. when they reached Johns Brook Lodge. Before they reached the Garden parking lot, it was dark again, but they kept going and reached a house along the road to Keene Valley. Richard Stepp remarked, "This incident convinced me that any day-trip party should carry not only the necessities for bivouac (poncho, rescue blanket, etc., as well as the obvious extra clothing, flashlights, etc.), but should have at least one person with experience in shelter construction."[12]

Besides unpreparedness and poor judgment, there are other reasons for accidents on Mount Marcy. Sometimes the cause is poor physical fitness, weather hardship, or plain ill luck. Sometimes it is inexplicable.

Patrick Griffin, 31, and Chris Beattie, 26, set out to climb all forty-six high peaks in five days. They were both physically tough. They were excellent climbers and knew the Adirondacks well. In addition, they had a support team to work the logistics.[13]

Griffin and Beattie started their trek on Tuesday, June 20, 1972, covering fourteen miles, most of it trailless, and seven peaks in the Seward and Santanoni ranges.

On Wednesday, in torrential rain, they hiked twenty-five miles and eleven mountains. On Thursday, they hiked another twenty-five miles and ten more mountains. However, Beattie's right leg began to hurt from shin splints. Friday morning, Beattie's hiking pace slowed as his pain worsened. After climbing Algonquin, Iroquois, and Colden, he told Griffin that he could not keep up the pace. Griffin went on alone to attempt Redfield, Skylight, and Marcy. The success or failure of the trek now rested with him.

Beattie continued up the trail to Four Corners lean-to. It started to rain heavily as he rested. Then he climbed over Marcy and down to Sno-Bird lean-to where he and Griffin planned to rendezvous with Harry Eldridge, part of the support crew.

Griffin never arrived for goulash dinner that night. The next morning the group walked out via Johns Brook and alerted rangers. Searchers canvassed Griffin's route. His body was found one hundred and fifty yards below Marcy's summit. He had suffered a massive heart attack.

Mount Marcy had claimed a second life. But this one shocked the hiker community. This one occurred in summer. And this man was an athlete and an experienced Adirondack hiker.

But the unexpected happens. Even Good Samaritans are not immune. In September 1975, Dwight Hynick, age 16, was descending from Lake Tear of the Clouds when he met a limping hiker who had twisted his ankle. The helpful Hynick ran ahead to the Lake Colden caretaker's cabin to summon assistance. But the caretaker's St. Bernard would not let the young man near the cabin. He bit Hynick as he approached the door. The next day a DEC helicopter carried the injured hiker and the injured Good Samaritan to the hospital.

Rangers deal with lots of twisted ankles, lost people, and seemingly lost people. One of the busiest years for search-and-rescues in the High Peaks was 1976. Mount Marcy had its share of misadventures. It started in mid-January when two brothers attempted their first winter camping experience. John Barbera, 16, and Joseph, 22, spent the first night in sub-zero temperatures at Indian Falls. The next morning, they headed for Marcy's summit, taking only snowshoes, ski poles, a camera, and a little food. They left their snowshoes at Plateau, thinking they could make better time on the packed snow without them. They made it to the summit amid extremely windy and cold conditions.

Trying to avoid the wind on the descent, they crept around the side of the mountain. The snow was up to their armpits. They stumbled down the steep slope into Panther Gorge as it grew dark. "I had seen a picture of a snow tunnel once before," recalled Joe, "and I tried to duplicate it. We finally dug a pit down to the ground and kicked out some room for our legs. It was cold, but it kept the wind out."[14]

The brothers did exercises to keep warm. They ate some bread and a little chocolate. The next morning they tried to go up the ridge but it was impossible. They decided to descend. They didn't go far before they were forced to spend another night without food or tent or spare clothing.

Fortunately, the weather cleared the next morning and a rescue helicopter was called in. Gary Hodgson, the ranger who spotted the lost climbers, said, "It is foolish to go anywhere in the winter without snowshoes."

Foolish. But recurrent. Ranger Hodgson participated in ten rescues between January and April. Then, along came another—perhaps the most mysterious and famous of all search and rescues on Mount Marcy.

Steven Thomas, a quiet 19-year-old, set out with five other young men for the summit of Mount Marcy. On Monday, April 12, 1976, the group hiked from Indian Falls to Hopkins Lean-to. Despite the wind and cold, Thomas headed for the peak at 3:30 p. m. Alone. He was dressed in jeans, without snowshoes or a pack. That was the last time anyone saw Steven.

Ranger Pete Fish happened to have been on Marcy earlier that afternoon. He recalls, "It was one of the most severe days I've ever experienced on the summit. The winds were so strong that you had to protect your face or lose it."[15] Off the summit, "There was very hard-packed snow that you could walk on," recalls Fish. Although it was dark by the time Fish made his way out of the woods that night, "A full moon was out and shining on the snow. You could see perfectly clearly and walk fast on the crusted snow."

Could Steven Thomas have simply walked out of the woods that night and intentionally disappeared? Ranger Fish thinks it is *possible*. As late as August 1976, Steven's brother, Robert, thought there was a 50-50 chance that Steven was still alive.[16] Of course, it is also possible that he lost his way in the blowing snow on the summit and slipped down the cliff walls of Panther Gorge.

There were helicopter searches and foot searches and even dog searches. After two weeks, all hope of finding the young man alive had vanished, but Robert kept searching for his brother. He eventually moved to Lake Placid and skied and hiked Mount Marcy over and over again (more than 1,000 times as of April 2001).

After Robert had been looking for a few months, he found hiking gear and human bones in Panther Gorge. Steven? No, it was the remains of George Atkinson, 20, of Chicopee, Massachusetts.

Atkinson was last seen alive at Indian Falls on March 14, 1973. He appears to have descended into Panther Gorge and frozen to death. There is a deep valley leading from the summit depression down to Panther Gorge. When winter climbers lose their tracks in whiteouts, the valley is an easy place for them to get into and start descending. Unfortunately, there are straight drops at the end of the valley where it reaches Panther Gorge cliffs.

"Atkinson realized he was at the cliff's edge in time, but lacked the strength to climb back up in the snow," theorized Jim Goodwin.[17]

Perhaps Atkinson could have been rescued from the cliff's edge, but there were many difficulties with the search. Since he had planned a seven-day hike, he wasn't reported missing until he had been gone eight days. It is likely that he was dead by day five or six. His route was not known until a week into the search. Heavy snow fell during the early days of the search, precluding the use of a helicopter and likely burying the body in snow before the search party arrived.[18]

Within weeks of the discovery of Atkinson's body, there were several other accidents. A hypothermic hiker had to be carried out from near Bushnell Falls. Then John Chapman, age 55, from Pittsburgh, attempted to climb a wall near Hanging Spear Falls. Chapman leaned against a tree to rest and the tree gave way. Fortunately he only fractured his right leg and suffered some bumps and bruises. But it took more than a day to evacuate him from the rugged and remote spot.

The same day, a 17-year-old girl took a wrong turn on Mount Marcy and headed for Johns Brook rather than Plateau lean-to. Fishermen from Long Island were lost for two days near South Meadow. Rangers rescued an 18-year-old girl from Colden Dike; a rock had rolled onto her, partially crushing her hand. That same night, a 9-year old boy was burned by hot grease at Marcy Dam.

Eventually the year of 1976 ended. Unfortunately, the mishaps didn't.

In January 1987, Christopher Thomas, age 19, Christopher Rocco, age 19, and Robert Thomas, age 60, from Euclid, Ohio, came to climb Mount Marcy. They were experienced hikers and it was a clear day, so they did not heed the weather report that warned of an approaching storm. The group walked to Indian Falls and left their snowshoes and ice axes there. They took one sleeping bag, some pepperoni, raisins, and chocolate. "We were sucked in by a beautiful day," said Robert.[19]

On top of Marcy, total whiteout conditions existed. They became disoriented and wandered off the summit to the wrong side. Chest-high snow engulfed them. Unable to go on, they prepared for the night. The two younger men crawled in the sleeping bag while Robert covered himself with two parkas. A foot of snow fell during the night. Temperatures dropped below zero.

On Saturday morning, Robert was weak and trembling; hypothermia was setting in. The group decided to separate. The young men left Robert in the sleeping bag and set out to get help. But Chris Thomas and Rocco made a classic mistake. They took the wrong trail and ended up in Panther Gorge. Thomas broke through ice in the brook and soaked his feet. The two young men spent a very uncomfortable night in a lean-to.

Robert Thomas spent the night in the sleeping bag. He knew he was dying. He shivered. He called for help into the whiteness.

On Sunday morning, Chris Thomas and Rocco headed west toward more traveled trails. Two hikers soon found them. Then Dave Dohman, caretaker at the Lake Colden cabin, discovered them and hurried off to retrieve a sled. The two hikers stayed with Chris Thomas and Rocco, put them in sleeping bags, gave them hot tea and soup, and cut away at Thomas' frozen boot.

Meanwhile, Robert prepared for his third night on Marcy.

On Monday morning, Chris Thomas was in a warm hospital while a helicopter crew searched for Robert. They easily spotted the red sleeping bag and the outline of a body that had spent three nights in sub-zero temperatures. The head moved. He was still alive!

Robert Thomas and Chris Rocco recovered. Chris Thomas spent 40 days in hospitals. He had parts of both feet amputated.[20]

Two years later, in March 1989, two men from Pennsylvania, Shawn Dougher, age 25, and Ralph Vecchio, age 29, arrived in the Adirondacks. They intended to ski up Marcy on Sunday and return home on Monday.

Saturday dawned cloudy with flurries and sleet, with worse weather predicted for Sunday. So the pair decided to try for Marcy right away. Dressed in cotton pants and cotton long underwear, and taking only three sandwiches, some water, and a can of beer, they walked into the snowy woods.

At timberline, they met freezing drizzle, wind, and icy conditions. A passing party strongly advised them not to proceed. But Dougher and Vecchio ignored the warning. They left their skis, put on crampons, and headed for the summit. There, they became disoriented in the fog and wind and descended south toward Lake Tear. They bivouacked for the night, trying to start a fire with ten- and twenty-dollar bills. Their 150 dollars lasted about twenty minutes.

Sunday, March 5, brought rain. The two men tried to find their skis. They didn't succeed and spent the night in the open near the summit. Monday dawned clear but cold. Dougher and Vecchio climbed to the summit to wait for a rescue that wasn't underway, since no one knew they were overdue. Finally, the pair decided to descend a steep gully. They made it to Panther Gorge, but fell in the brook several times along the way. They spent the night in a snow cave as temperatures in the open dipped to twenty below zero Fahrenheit.

That night, the White Sled Motel notified authorities that two guests had not returned and all of their camping gear was in their room. A search was organized to begin at nine o'clock Tuesday morning.

On Tuesday, Dougher and Vecchio made their way to Upper Ausable Lake and broke into a camp, hoping to find a telephone. But there was no phone service at the lake. Within a few minutes they heard a helicopter and flagged it down.

Vecchio lost one leg below the knee and the front part of one foot. Dougher lost both legs below the knees and most of his fingertips.[21]

They were lucky to be alive. Even so, they sued the Adirondack Mountain Club for forty-one million dollars. The pair claimed that because ADK had rented them skis, it was ADK's obligation to monitor their whereabouts and to enact a rescue. Recreational clubs across the country watched the legal battle. If the two hikers won, clubs would become the insurers of every ill-prepared hiker. But the hikers didn't win. A federal judge ruled that ADK had no obligation to perform a rescue.

Two years later, a pair of Australian hikers, Rory Doohan, age 33, and Sharon Moore, age 32, began an April hike of Mount Marcy. The weather was unseasonably warm and sunny. Doohan dressed in sneakers, cotton pants, cotton T-shirt, and cotton sweater.

The pair hiked up the Johns Brook trail and spent Monday night at Slant Rock lean-to. A cold front moved in and brought rain and chilly temperatures. Despite the bad weather, they set out for Marcy on Tuesday morning. The snow was crotch-deep along the sides of the trail. They went up the peak and down the other side to Four Corners. By then, they were both quite cold, though Moore had a jacket.

Instead of heading toward Lake Colden and the ranger's cabin, they chose to head toward the Panther Gorge lean-to since it was only a mile away. However, that trail had not been broken; the snow was waist deep with water underneath. They made it half a mile before Doohan could go no farther. He refused to change out of his wet clothes and Moore had a tough time trying to wrap the tent around him. He was dead before morning.

Doohan had reportedly suffered from hypothermia on a previous occasion. Why were he and his partner unequipped to deal with the situation? Why? is always the tragic question.

Cotton clothing, abandoned skis or snowshoes, and Panther Gorge are usually the answers.

Alpine Restoration

Once the hiker breaks out onto the open summit in the Adirondack High Country, he has a front seat to the most spectacular view available in the State, a 360 degree panorama of the 46 highest mountain peaks. . . . Moreover, at his feet is what many of us believe is the rarest, most precious piece of natural real estate left in New York, the truly unique and irreplaceable alpine summit zone.   E. H. KETCHLEDGE,
                    THE CONSERVATIONIST, AUG-SEPT 1970

ALPINE TUNDRA is a rarity in the United States, and the peculiar bog-type alpine ecosystem found on Mount Marcy and a few other Adirondack peaks is especially unique. The twenty or so alpine species that grow in this ecosystem are common plants in Alaska and Newfoundland and the Arctic, but they are rare in New York. They are at their southern limits.

About eighteen acres of Marcy's forty acres of alpine zone are covered with vegetation. It is a small chunk of land but the biggest area of alpine vegetation in the Adirondacks, except for Algonquin Peak, which has an equal amount. Therefore Mount Marcy is a living laboratory for alpine study. Torrey, Parry, Peck, Hashberger, and Adams all conducted scientific studies there. More recently, H. E. Woodin, Orra Phelps, Edwin Ketchledge, R. E. Leonard, and Mike DiNunzio have studied the alpine species atop Marcy.

Except for these few individuals, Mount Marcy's alpine community lay relatively undiscovered by the scientific community. Why? Mount Marcy's remoteness made study difficult. Whiteface was more accessible, especially after the highway was built to its summit. Mount Marcy required walking and lugging equipment at least seven miles over often steep, swampy trails. Scientists had to have the will and the might to get to the remote summit.

But scientists began to find more than vegetation at the summit. Crowds of hikers and backpackers were there. Amid the bare rocks the visitors looked for soft patches to rest on or sheltered ledges to escape the wind. They pitched tents in the grass and moss. They left garbage. They walked over every square foot to get a better view. The fragile summit habitat could not handle the litter, sitters, boots, and abodes. As Adams had reported in 1920, the vegetation was already subject to natural destructive forces.

Thankfully, Dr. Edwin Ketchledge came to the summit. "My first climbs were for purely scientific reasons," explains Ketchledge. "My very first climb up Algonquin was in the summer of 1949. I was exploring for mosses for my graduate work."[1] That work led to a master's degree in botany from SUNY College of

Forestry at Syracuse, a Ph.D. in biology from Stanford University and a position as instructor of forest botany at Syracuse.

In the late 1960s, with support from the United States Forest Service, Ketchledge conducted an ecological study of the summits. He found that some hikers were not just littering; they were trampling. Each careless footstep had the potential to destroy an individual plant and to contribute to widespread erosion by damaging the sphagnum.

As botanist Charles H. Peck had noticed in 1879, sphagnum moss is an important component of the summit environment; it is the dominant ground cover. It holds water that would otherwise be lost to cold, drying winds. It holds a thin layer of soil, mostly dead peat, that may have taken thousands of years to accumulate. It also is a seedbed for other plants, such as cottongrass, Lapland rosebay, leatherleaf, Labrador tea, and alpine bilberry. Some of these seed plants send out strong taproots that take hold in soil pockets. Some roots extend great distances into clefts or crannies between the rocks. The result is a matrix of plant roots that covers summit areas.

However, this matrix is very fragile. Boots easily cut through the shallow turf, allowing water to whisk away the soil. In areas of heavy traffic, the trail wears down to bedrock. Then the trail sides are exposed. The sphagnum gets damaged, the soil washes away, and the plants have no seedbed. What was once an alpine meadow becomes scattered patches of alpine vegetation.

Ketchledge looked for a way to fix the destruction of the rare vegetation. He found no solutions in the scientific literature, so he put his scientific skills to work and developed a method of restoring native alpine vegetation.

His first step was to plant common grass in order to stop the erosion and stabilize the surface. Once the soil was secured, he would figure out a plan to restore the native vegetation. But nature had a plan of its own. As the common grasses died, native species of moss, liverwort and lichen began to invade the surface, without any help from Ketchledge. The mat of mosses then provided the necessary conditions for the slow invasion of plants, such as mountain sandwort, and then three-toothed cinquefoil or Bigelow's sedge.

The early work was done on Dix Mountain. Then, in the 1970s, ADK members and Adirondack Forty-Sixers volunteered to lug eleven-pound restoration kits up other peaks, including Mount Marcy. Since the trek to the Marcy summit was so long, kits and volunteers were sometimes airlifted to Marcy.

Volunteers fertilized, limed, and spread grass seed. The process was successful, if hikers stayed off the site.

To keep hikers away from the restoration areas, the volunteers needed to eliminate the multitude of spur trails. They selected the best trail to the summit, marked it, put loose rocks on the sides, and concealed the spur trails. The restoration site was then treated with the grass mixture. As soon as the sod grew, it held the rocks and stabilized the banks along the trail.

Revegetation area on Mount Marcy.

Ketchledge performed an important study on the summit of Mount Marcy in 1981. He and R. E. Leonard measured the vegetation on the west slope of the summit cone, in a 300-foot triangle of land far from the hiking trails and human disturbances. H. E. Woodin had measured the vegetation in this triangle in 1957, so the new data would provide a long-term comparison of vegetation in the alpine zone.

Woodin had not been so fortunate. He found the work done in 1919 by Adams very inspiring, but he found the data inadequate for comparison since Adams had made no note of exact locations. Thus Woodin decided to establish a permanent transect. He and three other scientists carried supplies and equipment totaling 440 pounds to the top of the mountain in order to measure and mark the transect area.

Woodin established the triangular transect just above timberline, ranging from 4,958 feet to 4,984 feet elevation. He chose this area because it spanned the timberline, and the purpose of his study was to determine whether timberlines in the eastern United States were ascending or descending.[2] But his data proved equally useful in the study of changes in alpine vegetation.

When Ketchledge and Leonard re-examined the site in 1981, they discovered that in twenty-four years there had been only slight changes in the floristic compositions and the percentage of arctic species present. They concluded, "This apparent stability over time of the virgin, alpine community on Mount Marcy stands in sharp contrast to the severe damage occurring along public hiking trails elsewhere on this peak."[3]

This reaffirmed the suspicion that hikers, not environmental factors such as acid rain, were damaging the alpine vegetation. Left alone, the vegetation did fine. The plants seemed to be able to manage the two-month growing season and the natural erosive forces of blizzards, wind, and spring meltwater.

But being left alone was becoming harder and harder. The number of hikers kept increasing. During 1988, more than 50,000 people registered at the trailheads leading to Mount Marcy. The entire mountaintop was covered with boots and fannies and dogs. Restoration wasn't enough; prevention was needed.

In 1989, Professor Ketchledge led an effort to begin the Summit Steward program. The idea was to place naturalists on top of Mount Marcy and Algonquin Peak every day throughout the summer. Their role would be to greet visitors, answer questions, and talk about alpine vegetation and what hikers could do to help protect the summit environment. The Adirondack Nature Conservancy, the state Department of Environmental Conservation (DEC), and ADK joined together to fund, administer, and manage the program.

In 1999, after ten years of the program and continued restoration work, Ketchledge said, "The crisis phase is over. We have stabilized the area. Some test plots that were once bare are now 95 percent vegetated."

Some lowland species have moved up to the summit but are not crowding out the alpine species. No species have been extirpated, according to Ketchledge. "We recently rediscovered one or two we thought were gone," he said. "The truth is the Adirondacks are still unexplored. We only know about the conspicuous places. There are steep rock slides on many peaks that are inaccessible."

There may be species up there that haven't been found yet.

In 1999, the Summit Steward program began a "rock carry project." A ton of fist-sized rocks was dumped at the Adirondak Loj trailhead. A sign asked hikers to "consider carrying a rock" to the summit of Mount Marcy or Algonquin Peak. By the end of the summer, the pile was gone.

The rocks are used by the stewards to build cairns and scree walls, stabilize soil, and cover exposed roots of trampled vegetation. But the rocks did something unexpected. The summit stewards observed that "When the grin-bearing, rock-carrying hiker presents their gift to the steward, that hiker leaves the summit with a higher level of awareness and a personal incentive to pass on the stewardship message."[4]

A Management Plan

One of the biggest challenges in wilderness management is how to keep the "wildness" in wilderness and yet, still make it available for public use and enjoyment under today's heavy recreational pressures.
HIGH PEAKS UNIT MANAGEMENT PLAN, MARCH 1999

TODAY the cry is: the trails are too crowded. But what does that mean? Are there too many people on the trail? Is the parking lot full? Are the lean-tos and campsites full? Is someone jabbering on a cell phone?

Eighty years ago, Conservation Commissioner George Pratt was concerned that the Forest Preserve was too little known and too little used. Forest Preserve managers sought ways to make the High Peaks area more accessible and more convenient. They improved trails, built lean-tos, and published brochures promoting the trails to Marcy.

During the 1960s and 1970s, the number of visitors increased dramatically. There was litter, untended outhouses, trash, muddy trails, and camping above timberline with no concern for rare vegetation. During the last twenty years or so, most of the abuse has been eliminated, and a new, more environment-friendly ethic has developed. Still, the number of visitors is large. Unlike Pratt, today's administrators seek ways to limit use and to disperse use.

Visitor Use By Trailhead[1]

Trailhead	Visitors Registered	
	1988	**1998**
Adirondak Loj	31,822	46,549
South Meadow	4,492	9,745
Johns Brook	11,101	19,680
AMR	incomplete	11,755
Elk Lake	135	1,285
Upper Works	3,635	6,050

When people say "the trails are too crowded," I suppose they mean that in some way their experience has been unsatisfactory. For me, it is not the number of hikers I meet, but where I meet them, what they say, and what they leave behind. One group of six obnoxious hikers could ruin a hike, while the pleasant passing of thirty might be a joy.

Some hikers actually like meeting other people. They feel desolate if they don't see a person every twenty minutes.

Those who want total solitude should search for another mountain or carefully select their day and route. Early one Sunday morning in June 2000, I walked the entire Van Hoevenberg trail to the summit of Mount Marcy without seeing another person. I shivered atop the summit, completely shrouded in fog and solitude.

It is not the sheer number of hikers that determines the feeling of overuse. Nor is it the number that determines the level of damage inflicted by hikers. Two irresponsible hikers can cause more harm than an army of amenable ones.

There are far greater numbers of visitors to Mount Marcy today than there were thirty years ago, but there is far less damage. Why? The hardening of the trails and the addition of rock steps and boardwalks. The summit stewards. The education programs.

Is that enough? Is Mount Marcy the way it should be?

Mount Marcy is part of the High Peaks Wilderness Area, the state's largest designated wilderness area: 197,685 acres. According to the Adirondack Park State Land Master Plan prepared by the Adirondack Park Agency and adopted in 1972, a wilderness area is a place not controlled by humans. It is a place where the land's primeval character and influence are retained and natural processes are allowed to operate freely; it is not occupied or modified by humans. It is a place where humans are visitors and the imprint of their work is substantially unnoticeable. A wilderness area has outstanding opportunities for solitude or a primitive and unconfined type of recreation.

This is the kind of place Mount Marcy should be.

How do we accomplish that? The State Land Master Plan (SLMP) "authorized and directed" the DEC to develop management plans for all ninety Adirondack Preserve land units. The Unit Management Plans (UMPs) would designate what activities are permissible in areas of the land unit, and must conform to the SLMP. In 1977, the DEC began work on the High Peaks UMP. The plan was released for review in December 1978, and widely criticized. The DEC withdrew it and worked on plans for other areas, the first of which was completed in 1983.[2]

After years and years of debate, the High Peaks UMP was completed in March 1999. The plan recognizes that "One of the biggest challenges in wilderness management is how to keep the 'wildness' in wilderness and yet, still make it available for public use and enjoyment under today's heavy recreational pressures."

Unfortunately, in portions of the eastern High Peaks (from the eastern extremity to west of the Indian Pass Trail, including Mount Marcy) natural processes are not allowed to operate freely. The land has been, and is being, occupied and modified by humans. Wilderness standards are not being met.

Therefore, the plan creates stricter rules for this fragile area. Day use group size is limited to fifteen. Campsite or lean-to use is limited to eight persons. Camping in the South Meadow-Flowed Lands high-use corridor is allowed at designated campsites and lean-tos only. No at-large camping is allowed in this area. And, no campsite or lean-to can be occupied for more than three consecutive nights.

Campfires are prohibited. Backcountry stoves are required for cooking meals. Glass containers are prohibited. Pets must be leashed on all marked trails, at campsites, and at elevations above 4,000 feet. Cell phones are allowed, to aid in search and rescue.

In addition, the "Leave-No-Trace" outdoor ethic is being promoted. It encourages hikers and campers to minimize their impact and soften their presence—to leave no trace of their visit.

The plan mandates that these measures receive a fair trial for five years before rationing and reservation systems are considered. To prevent more restrictive access measures in the future, it is hoped that all visitors to the eastern High Peaks will obey the stated rules.

In addition to the problems of overuse, accidents, vegetation trampling, and trail erosion, there is the lack of access to the Mount Marcy trails. The state owns only one of the major entrances: South Meadow. The entrances at Adirondak Loj, Keene Valley (the Garden), Ausable Lakes, Elk Lake, and Upper Works are still all privately owned. While the state has easements and public use is allowed at these locations, fear of liability may cause private owners to close trails.

Parking is another issue at these trailheads. A limited number of spaces are available at most locations. On holidays and summer weekends, where does the overflow go? At the Garden parking lot in Keene Valley, the situation became so bad that the town of Keene instituted a $5-per-day parking fee at the Garden and shuttle bus service from Marcy Field on Route 73. Conversely, some people see limited parking as the solution. If the parking lot is full, then the woods are full and no more hikers should enter.

The eastern High Peaks wilderness area is a special place—not only to New York State but also to the entire eastern United States. And Mount Marcy is the primary attraction. For more than 160 years, geologists and guides, botanists and backpackers, authors and artists have visited Marcy. All left with some sense of a wilderness experience.

Wilderness settings are becoming rare commodities. "The demands on New York's wilderness resources will intensify over time as resources like clean air and water become more precious," states the UMP. "There will be requests for use of wilderness that cannot even be envisioned now, but they will certainly come. When natural resource managers decide what to approve and what to deny, their foremost goal must be the protection of the wilderness resource itself. The wilderness resource in all its many facets is fragile and can be lost through the effects of seemingly inconsequential decisions."

The decisions made every day by every resource manager, every ranger, and every visitor determine the quality of the wilderness setting. Everyone must be conscious of those "seemingly inconsequential decisions" that greatly influence the fragile and feral environment of Mount Marcy.

Should you climb Mount Marcy? That is a personal decision. It depends on your physical condition, your ambition, and your goals.

You can still have a wonderful Mount Marcy experience without climbing the mountain. Grace Hudowalski recalled such a day in 1952:

> Last fall, as we relaxed at Indian Falls before our ascent of Tabletop, we ran into a group from the Outing Club of the University of Vermont. "Climbing Marcy?" they inquired confidently. "No," we replied, "Tabletop." They were stupefied.
>
> We tried to explain why Tabletop but, of course, it didn't register. How could they know we *knew* the challenge of the highest, or that we could see Marcy, glittering with early frost in the late morning sun as we pushed up trailless Tabletop. How could they know we still kept tryst with "The Cloud Splitter" whether we stood on its summit or saw it from Algonquin or the rock ledges of Phelps or the tree-covered summit of Redfield or scrambling up the Panther Gorge-side of Haystack![3]

I hope more people will realize that they can still "keep tryst" with Marcy from afar. One of my most memorable experiences was on TR Mountain in September 2000. On a whim, two mountaineers invited me to join them on a trailless adventure up the newly named summit. It was a cool crisp morning. When we reached a slight opening in the forest, I stood on a fallen tree and spotted the summit of Mount Marcy. The season's first frosting of rime ice sparkled across the rocky cone in the far distance.

Other days I have appreciated Mount Marcy from Mount Jo, Baxter Mountain, the lookout near Newcomb, John Brown's Farm, and the center of Heart Lake. From any perspective, there is no mountain in the world quite like it. And the plan is to keep it that way.

Fare-Thee-Well

My time is fast passing to view these grand mountains,
And the grand scenes of Nature that about them I see,
Of great boulder rocks and sweet crystal fountains,
Fresh from their Creator they have all come to me.
And I must soon leave to unborn generations,
Those scenes that so long have been dear to my sight,
Who will hereafter view them with varied emotions,
And volumes about them great Authors will write.
Oh! the old feldspar mountains, with their sweet crystal fountains,
The evergreen mountains we all love so well!

ORSON S. PHELPS, "MOUNTAIN SONG"

IF I let my imagination run free, I can suppose that little has changed since Old Mountain Phelps viewed "the grand scenes of Nature" about Mount Marcy. When I stand on the summit, I still get that "heaven up-h'isted-ness" feeling. I still see the great boulders and the brilliant waterfalls. I see the feldspar and the acres upon acres of evergreens. And they seem fresh and vibrant and pristine.

But the reality is that the scene has greatly changed. Ninety percent of the forest is second growth, not old growth. Thousands upon thousands of human feet have stepped onto the anorthosite since Phelps' generation. Many simply admired the scene. But some trampled alpine flora. Some pitched tents. Some strapped on skis while others wore snowshoes. A few died. One became President of the United States.

Horses hauled stones and generators up the mountain. Huts and signal towers were built and later destroyed. Fires and axes assaulted the slopes. More recently, hikers hauled out garbage and hauled in grass seed and rocks to restore the summit vegetation. The improvements over the last twenty years are tremendous. Mount Marcy has undergone much change—change for the better. It is one of the few places on earth where "the grand scenes of Nature" have been restored.

But like Phelps, I wonder what the next generation will think of these scenes. Will they be able to feel the natural rhythms of the mountain?

Last summer, I took my daughter Marcy on her first trip up Mount Marcy. I wanted to show her the place that I love so well. Though she was only eight years old, she was eager to follow the footsteps of Old Mountain Phelps along Johns Brook to Slant Rock and beyond. When we reached the timberline, Marcy turned into a mountain goat and climbed on all fours over the wrinkled rocks.

I led her to the bronze plaque and she read the words out loud. Then we climbed to the top of the rock slab and stood on the highest point of the mountain. Marcy spread her arms and leaned into the wind.

Mount Marcy
by Marcy Weber

The wind lifts my soul.
My soul lifts my spirit and makes me rise, too.
I fly with the falcon.
I zoom through the water with the otter and beaver.
I fly again.
I fly over many mountains.
I land and zoom back down on the wings I have.
Down to the valley.

Marcy Weber, age 8, on Mount Marcy
by William L. Weber, III.

Mount Marcy is a space where even the youngest of souls can feel the elements and connect with natural forces. They can see the wildlife, rivers, forests, and fragile alpine ecosystem that once dominated the whole countryside. They can enjoy a sense of timeless landscape. This is a rare experience in today's world.

The "old feldspar mountain" that we call Mount Marcy is invaluable and irreplaceable terrain. There is no mountain in the world quite like it. We must safeguard it. We must preserve it for unborn generations. So the wind can lift their soul. So they can spread wings and split clouds.

Notes

Origins

[1] Alfred L. Donaldson, *A History of the Adirondacks* (New York: Century, 1921; reprint, Fleischmanns, New York: Purple Mountain Press, 1992), vol. I, 159.

[2] "Gleanings From Old Fields," *Plattsburgh Republican* (March 27, 1875).

[3] Y. W. Isachsen et. al., editors, *Geology of New York: A Simplified Account* (Albany: New York State Education Department, 2000), 24-42.

[4] George B. Cressey, "Chapter 1: Land Forms," in *Geography of New York State*, edited by John H. Thompson (Syracuse: Syracuse University Press, 1966), 19.

[5] "Gleanings From Old Fields."

[6] Howard W. and Elizabeth B. Jaffe, *Geology of the Adirondack High Peaks Region* (Lake George, New York: The Adirondack Mountain Club, 1986), 10.

[7] Ibid.

[8] Y. W. Isachsen et. al., *Geology of New York*, 42.

[9] William C. Redfield, "Some Account of Two Visits to the Mountains in Essex County, New York, In the Years 1836 and 1837; With a Sketch of the Northern Source of the Hudson," *The Family Magazine* (1838; reprinted from the *American Journal of Science and Arts*, July-December 1837), 350.

[10] Robert H. Boyle, *The Hudson River, A Natural and Unnatural History* (New York: W. W. Norton & Company, Inc., 1969), 28.

Iron Works

[1] Russell Carson, *Peaks and People of the Adirondacks* (1927; reprint, with preface by George Marshall, introduction by Philip G. Terrie Jr., and map by Jerome S. Kates, Glens Falls, New York: The Adirondack Mountain Club, 1973), 3.

[2] Mary MacKenzie, *History of the Village of Lake Placid, New York* (reprinted from *The Placid Pioneer*, Autumn 1970), 1.

[3] David Henderson to A. McIntyre, October 14, 1826, *The Story of Adirondac*, by Arthur H. Masten (Syracuse: Syracuse University Press, 1968), 23.

[4] Redfield, *The Family Magazine*, 347.

[5] Census figures from Winslow Watson, *A General View and Agricultural Survey of the County of Essex* (Albany: 1853), 713.

[6] David Henderson to A. McIntyre, October 14, 1826, *The Story of Adirondac*, 18.

[7] Ibid., 21.

[8] Ibid., 26.

[9] Masten, *The Story of Adirondac*, 32-34.

[10] A. McIntyre to Duncan McMartin, June 6, 1833, *The Story of Adirondac*, 58.

[11] David Henderson to A. McIntyre, September 8, 1833, *The Story of Adirondac*, 61.

[12] Ibid.

[13] A. McIntyre to Duncan McMartin, September 19, 1834, *The Story of Adirondac*, 58.

The First Ascent

[1] Ira J. Friedman, *History of the State of New York, Volume Nine: Mind and Spirit* (Port Washington, New York: Empire State Historical Publication, 1962), 112. Governor Clinton had pushed the survey in the hope of finding coal. More than $250,000 had been wasted

1 in the search for it in New York State; now no more capital would be spent on that hope.

2 William Stanton, *American Scientific Exploration, 1803-1860* (American Philosophical Society, 1991). Online at http://www.amphilsoc.org/library/guides/stanton/3644.htm

3 Redfield, *The Family Magazine*, 346.

4 Ibid.

5 Ibid., 347.

6 Ibid.

7 Ibid.

8 A. McIntyre to D. McMartin, November 15, 1836, *The Story of Adirondac*, 73.

9 The Historical Society of Pennsylvania (HSP), Gratz Collection, Ebenezer Emmons to Governor William Marcy, October 12, 1836.

10 Ebenezer Emmons, "First Annual Report of the Second Geological District of the State of New-York," in *State of New York Assembly Document No. 161* (February 11, 1837), 98-9.

11 Later, Slide Mountain was found to be 4,180 feet high. Still, several Adirondack peaks rise higher than the highest Catskill peak.

12 Emmons, "First Annual Report," 99.

13 Ibid., 104.

14 John Miller diary, 1837. John Miller Papers, Princeton University Library.

15 William C. Redfield, *New York Journal of Commerce* (August 24, 1837).

16 James Hall, letter to editor, Mount Marcy, Essex County, August 5, 1837, *Albany Daily Advertiser* (August 15, 1837).

17 Redfield, *New York Journal of Commerce* (August 24, 1837).

18 Ibid.

19 Ibid.

20 Redfield, *The Family Magazine*, 350.

21 Ibid.

22 "Excerpts from Manuscript of William C. Redfield on the Adirondack Region," (Copied April 4, 1926 by Russell Carson and recopied June 8, 1940 from Mr. Carson's copy by G. L. Hudowalski; made from certified copy made by Mills Blake from original manuscripts and papers loaned by Charles B. Redfield to Verplanck Colvin).

23 Redfield, *New York Journal of Commerce* (August 25, 1837).

24 Hall to editor, August 5, 1837, *Albany Daily Advertiser*.

25 Redfield, *New York Journal of Commerce* (August 25, 1837).

26 Ibid.

27 "Excerpts from Manuscript of William C. Redfield."

28 John Torrey to Benjamin Silliman, August 23, 1837, *John Torrey: A Story of North American Botany* by Andrew Denny Rodgers III (Princeton, New Jersey: Princeton University Press, 1942), 131.

29 Charles Lanman, *A Tour to the River Saguenay, in Lower Canada* (Philadelphia: Carey and Hart, 1848), 79.

30 Ebenezer Emmons, report, in *Assembly Document No. 200* (February 20, 1838), 241.

31 Redfield, *The Family Magazine*, 353.

32 Nettie Holt Whitney, "Reminiscences of Keene Valley and the Pioneer Holt Family" (1925), 61. Keene Valley Library.

33 Redfield, *The Family Magazine*, 347-8.

34 Hall to editor, August 5, 1837, *Albany Daily Advertiser*. Mount McIntyre (now called Algonquin Peak) is west of Mount Marcy.

35 Rodgers, *John Torrey*, 131.

36 Emmons, *Assembly Document No. 200* (February 20, 1838), 242.

37 Redfield, *New York Journal of Commerce* (August 25, 1837).

38 Redfield, *The Family Magazine*, 351.

39 The Historical Society of Pennsylvania (HSP), Gratz Collection, John Torrey to Archibald McIntyre, August 1, 1838.

40 Redfield, *The Family Magazine*, 345.

41 The Historical Society of Pennsylvania (HSP), Gratz Collection, Benjamin Silliman to John Torrey, September 22, 1837.

For Marcy's Sake

1 Richard Henry Dana Jr., "How We Met John Brown," *Atlantic Monthly* (July, 1871), 3.

2 William Marcy, journal, 1836. Marcy Papers, Library of Congress, Manuscripts Division.

3 David Henderson to A. McIntyre, March 27, 1837, *The Story of Adirondac*, 77.

4 John Bassett Moore, *A Secretary of State from Brown, William Learned Marcy: an Address* (Providence, Rhode Island: Palmer Press, 1915). Ivor D. Spencer, *The Victor and the Spoils* (Providence, Rhode Island: Brown University Press, 1959).

5 John Bassett Moore, "The Name of Marcy," *The Sun* (July 9, 1919).

6 Moore, *A Secretary of State from Brown*, 6.

7 "Hands Off Mount Marcy!," *The Sun* (June 29, 1919).

8 Moore, "The Name of Marcy."

9 Warder Cadbury, "The Improbable Charles C. Ingham," *Adirondac* (August 1987), 25.

Call It Tahawus

1 Joel T. Headley, *The Adirondack; or, Life in the Woods* (Harrison, New York: Harbor Hill Books, 1982; a facsimile of the 1849 edition, with later added chapters; and a new introduction by Philip Terrie), 46.

2 Robert F. Lucid, editor, *The Journal of Richard Henry Dana, Jr.* (Cambridge: Belknap Press of Harvard University Press, 1968), 366.

3 Lanman, *Tour to the River Saguenay*, 79.

4 Charles Fenno Hoffman, "Scenes at the Sources of the Hudson," *The New-York Mirror* (October 21, 1837), 132.

5 Quoted in Russell Carson, "The FootPath" (June 21, 1929).

6 Arthur H. Masten, *Tahawus Club, 1898-1933* (Burlington, Vermont: Free Press Interstate Corp., 1935), 3. George Marshall, "Phelps, Holton and the Phonic Mountaineers," *Adirondac* (January-February 1954), 6.

7 Philip Terrie, unpublished manuscript in his possession. No title, undated.

8 Wallace Bruce, "The Adirondacks," *Outing* (June, 1883), 35. Wallace Bruce, *The Hudson* (New York: Bryant Literary Union, 1894), 285.

9 Alfred Billings Street, *The Indian Pass* (New York: Hurd and Houghton, 1869; reprint, Harrison, New York: Harbor Hill Books, 1975), xiv.

10 "Gleanings From Old Fields," *Plattsburgh Republican* (March 27, 1875).

11 *Victory Mountain Park* (New York: The Association for the Protection of the Adirondacks, 1919).

12 Donaldson, *A History of the Adirondacks*, vol. I, 47.

13 "An Aged Indian Hunter," *The Sun* (July 22, 1900). "Some Forgotten Place Names. . .," *The Journal of American Folk-lore*, (1900), page 126, says the early name for Mount Marcy, which probably included the neighboring peaks, was Wawobadenik, meaning White Mountains.

14 Russell Carson to W. Scott Brown and others, March 16, 1924. Carson

Papers, Adirondack Museum Library.

15 John Howard Redfield, *Recollections of John Howard Redfield* (Private printing, 1900), 317-8.

16 Verplanck Colvin, *Report on the Progress of the Adirondack State Land Survey to the Year 1886* (Albany: Weed, Parsons and Company, 1886), 56.

17 Carson to Brown and others, March 16, 1924. Carson Papers, Adirondack Museum Library.

Measuring Up

1 John Howard Redfield, *Recollections*, 308.

2 Thomas F. Gordon, *Gazetteer of the State of New York* (Philadelphia: T. K. and P. G. Collins, 1836), 448.

3 E. F. Johnson, "Mountains in New York," *The American Journal of Science* (July 1839), 84. According to *Assembly Document No. 50* (January 24, 1840), 338, this measurement was published on January 30, 1839, in Johnson's report to the New York legislature.

4 Ebenezer Emmons, "Third Annual Report of the Survey of the Second Geological District," in *State of New York Assembly Document No. 275* (February 27, 1839), 202n.

5 Johnson, "Mountains in New York," 89.

6 *Assembly Document No. 50* (January 24, 1840), 336-7. Warder H. Cadbury, "Men and Mountains," *Adirondack Life* (July/August 1984), 40.

7 Headley, *The Adirondack; or, Life in the Woods*, 100-1.

8 *Assembly Document No. 50* (January 24, 1840), 336.

9 Colvin, *Report on the Topographical Survey* (1874), 32-35.

10 O. S. Phelps, "Finding the True Height of Tahawus," *Plattsburgh Republican* (November 20, 1875).

11 Colvin, *Report on the Topographical Survey* (1879), 94-5.

Trips Up the Opalescent

1 Ebenezer Emmons, *Assembly Document No. 275* (February 27, 1839), 26.

2 Hoffman, "Scenes at the Sources of the Hudson," *The New-York Mirror* (October 21, 1837), 132.

3 "The Wilds of Northern New York," *Putnam's Monthly* (September 1854), 266. Reprinted, with Preface by Sandra Weber (Fleischmanns, New York: Purple Mountain Press, 2001). Most scholars conclude the author is Benedict.

4 Ibid.

5 H. (Joel Headley), "Life in the Adirondacks," *The New York Times* (August 5, 1858).

6 Headley, *The Adirondack; or, Life in the Woods*, 46.

7 Ibid., 53-5.

8 Ibid., 56 and 60-1.

9 Jervis McEntee, diary, 98. Adirondack Museum Library.

10 Headley, *The Adirondack; or, Life in the Woods*, 54.

11 *Plattsburgh Republican* (September 13, 1845).

12 Lucid, editor, *The Journal of Richard Henry Dana, Jr.*), 368.

13 Cadbury, "The Improbable Charles C. Ingham," 25.

14 Louis Legrand Noble, *The Life and Works of Thomas Cole* (Cambridge: The Belknap Press of Harvard University Press, 1964), 280.

15 Lanman, *A Tour to the River Saguenay* (1848), 79, says Cole climbed Marcy, but no other evidence supports this claim.

16 Lanman, *A Tour to the River Saguenay*, 78.

17 Ibid., 78-9.

18 Ibid., 79-80.

19 Charles Lanman, *Adventures of An Angler in Canada* (London: Richard Bentley, 1848), 100.

20 Hoffman, "Scenes at the Sources of the Hudson," *The New-York Mirror* (October 14, 1837), 124.

21 Barbara McMartin, *To the Lake of Skies* (Canada Lake, New York: Lake View Press, 1996), 143.

22 Carson, *Peaks and People*, 267.

23 Ibid., 268.

24 George Marshall, "Phelps, Holton and the Phonic Mountaineers," *Adirondac* (January-February 1954), 4. Marshall's article was based on information told to Verplanck Colvin by Orson Phelps.

25 Ibid., 5.

26 Ibid., 6. Dana, "How We Met John Brown," 3.

27 Lucid, editor, *The Journal of Richard Henry Dana, Jr.*, 365.

28 Ibid., 365-6.

29 Ibid., 369.

30 Ibid., 373.

31 McEntee diary, 92. Adirondack Museum Library.

32 Ibid., 94.

33 Ibid., 94-5.

34 Ibid., 96.

35 Ila Weiss, *Poetic Landscape: The Art and Experience of Sanford R. Gifford* (Newark: University of Delaware Press; London and Toronto: Associated University Presses, 1987), 109.

36 "The Wilds of Northern New York," 269.

Coming Round the Mountain

1 T. Addison Richards, *Appleton's Illustrated Hand-Book of American Travel* (New York: D. Appleton & Co., 1857), 170.

2 T. Addison Richards, "A Forest Story: Part II-The Adirondack Woods and Waters," *Harper's New Monthly Magazine* (September 1859), 460.

3 Ibid., 464-5.

4 Ibid., 465.

5 T. Addison Richards, *The Romance of the American Landscape* (New York: Leavitt and Allen, 1855), 7.

6 Ibid., 236.

7 Benson J. Lossing, *The Hudson: From the Wilderness to the Sea* (New York: Virtue and Yorston, 1866), 36.

8 Carson, *Peaks and People*, 67 and 68n.

9 Harold E. Mahan, *Benson J. Lossing and Historical Writing in the United States* (Westport, Connecticut: Greenwood Press, 1996), 2.

10 *Essex County Republican* (September 22, 1870 and September 29, 1870).

11 Lossing, *The Hudson*, 27-8.

12 Ibid., 32.

13 Ibid., 33-4.

14 Ibid., 27.

15 John Burroughs, *The Writings of John Burroughs: Wake Robin* (Boston and New York: Houghton, Mifflin and Company, 1923), 97-8.

16 Ibid., 94.

17 Ibid., 101-2.

18 The Historical Society of Pennsylvania (HSP), Dreer Collection, John Brown Papers, Ruth (Brown) Thompson to John Brown Jr., August 17, 1859.

19 Street, *The Indian Pass*, 80.

20 Ibid., 84.

21 Marshall, "Phelps, Holton and the Phonic Mountaineers," 4.

22 Street, *The Indian Pass*, 88.

23 Ibid., 95.

24 Ibid., 89.

25 S. R. Stoddard, *The Adirondacks: Illustrated* (Albany: Stoddard, 1874), 123-7.

26 Ibid., 125-26.

27 *Among the Adirondacks*, unpublished manuscript (about 1870), 42. MS 61-60. Adirondack Museum Library.

28 Ibid.

29 *A Descriptive and Historical Guide to the Valley of Lake Champlain and the Adirondacks* (R. S. Styles' Steam Printing House, 1871), 99.

30 Colvin, *Report on the Topographical Survey* (1874), 40.

31 "Adirondack Park," *Plattsburgh Sentinel* (August 22, 1879).

32 Ibid.

33 Stoddard, *The Adirondacks: Illustrated* (1885), 137.

Mercy Climbs

1 "The Adirondack Region," *The New York Times* (August 20, 1875).

2 Charles Dudley Warner, *In the Wilderness* (Houghton, Osgood and Company, 1878; reprint, with Introduction by Alice Wolf Gilborn, Syracuse: The Adirondack Museum and Syracuse University Press, 1990), 55.

3 Orson S. Phelps, "Mountain Camp Building," *Plattsburgh Republican* (July 3, 1875).

4 Wallace, *Descriptive Guide* (1872), 362.

5 Margaret Goodwin O'Brien, *Women Artists* (unpublished manuscript). Keene Valley Library.

6 *Essex County Republican* (September 29, 1870).

7 Orpha Bruce is listed in the 1860 census as the 22-year-old daughter of Chester Bruce. No daughter named Teresa is listed in 1850 or 1860. Perhaps the other companion was Mary T. Bruce, age 15 in 1860. Her middle name may have been Teresa.

8 Rev. J. H. Twichell, *Extract from Scrapbook*, 21. Saranac Lake Library.

9 "Gleanings From Old Fields," *Plattsburgh Republican* (March 27, 1875).

10 Lucia Pychowska, "Sketches of American Life and Scenery: To Saranac and Back," *The Continental Monthly* (December 1864), 675.

11 Lucia Pychowska, "Walking-Dress for Ladies," *Appalachia* (1887), 28-30.

12 Pychowska, "To Saranac and Back," 670.

13 Ibid., 664.

14 Pychowska, "Walking-Dress for Ladies," 29. November 5 is known as Guy Fawkes Day, and all over England people shoot off fireworks, light bonfires, and march through the streets with a dummy of "the Guy" dressed in old clothes. Fawkes tried to blow up a government building in 1605 but his plot was discovered.

15 Twichell, *Extract from Scrap-book*, 18-9. Saranac Lake Library.

16 Pychowska, "To Saranac and Back," 671.

17 Ibid., 671-2.

18 Ibid., 672-3.

19 Ibid., 673.

20 Ibid., 674.

21 Ibid., 675.

22 Twichell, *Extract from Scrap-book*, 20. Saranac Lake Library.

23 Orson Phelps, "In the Wilderness," *Plattsburgh Republican* (June 3, June 17, and June 24, 1876).

24 Ibid.

25 Donaldson, *A History of the Adirondacks*, vol. I, 360.

26 Henry van Dyke to Alfred Donaldson, July 22, 1919. Donaldson Collection. Saranac Lake Library.

27 Twichell, *Extract from Scrap-book*, 4. Saranac Lake Library.

28 "The Adirondacks," *The New York Times* (August 11, 1875).

29 Ibid.

30 *New-York Daily Tribune* (July 13, 1870).

31 Ibid.

32 Ibid.

33 Ibid.

34 Rev. F. H. Twichell, "In the Adirondacks," in *Noah Porter: A Memorial by Friends* by George S. Merriam (New York: Charles Scribner's Sons, 1893), 154.

35 "One of the Many Mountain Trips," *The New York Times* (August 1, 1877).

36 Street, *The Indian Pass*, 97.

37 Ibid., 103.

38 *Essex County Republican* (November 21, 1872) in *Glenn's History of the Adirondacks: Volume 2 - The Keene Flats* by Morris F. Glenn (Alexandria, Virginia: by author, 1987), 35.

39 Stoddard, *The Adirondacks: Illustrated* (1874), 138.

40 Ibid., 143. Guidebook author E. R. Wallace reported seeing the same spectacle, "thrilling and magnificent in the highest degree." Wallace, *Descriptive Guide* (1872), 361.

41 Stoddard, *The Adirondacks: Illustrated* (1879), 172.

42 Ibid.

43 "The Adirondack Region," *The New York Times* (August 20, 1875).

44 Warner, *In the Wilderness*, 52.

45 Ibid., 60.

46 Ibid., 61.

47 Charles Brumley, *Guides of the Adirondacks: A History* (Utica, New York: North Country Books, Inc., 1994), 148.

48 Ibid., 147-8.

49 Carson, *Peaks and People*, 74n.

Lake Tear of the Clouds

1 Nina H. Webb, *Footsteps Through the Adirondacks: The Verplanck Colvin Story* (Utica, New York: North Country Books, 1996), 12.

2 Ibid., 18.

3 Verplanck Colvin, 1871 Report, quoted in *The Adirondack Park: A Political History* by Frank Graham Jr. (Syracuse: Syracuse University Press, 1978), 70-1.

4 Colvin, *Report on a Topographical Survey* (1873), 19-20.

5 Ibid., 8.

6 Ibid., 21.

7 Verplanck Colvin, "The Discovery of the Sources of the Hudson," in Carson, *Peaks and People*, 143.

8 Colvin, *Report on a Topographical Survey* (1873), 21.

9 Ibid.

10 Verplanck Colvin, in Carson, *Peaks and People*, 143.

11 Boyle, *The Hudson River*, 71.

12 Colvin, *Report on a Topographical Survey* (1873), 40.

13 Colvin, *Report on the Topographical Survey* (1874), 159.

14 Phelps, "Mountain Camp Building."

15 Ibid.

16 Stoddard, *The Adirondacks: Illustrated* (1874), 146.

17 Orson S. Phelps, *Mountain Song*. Donaldson Collection. Saranac Lake Library.

18 Phelps, "Mountain Camp Building."

19 Ibid.

20 Colvin, *Report on a Topographical Survey* (1873), 35.

21 Bruce, *The Hudson*, 282.

22 "Correspondence. New Trails," (July 8, 1875), in *Glenn's History*, 54-5.

23 "Adirondack Park," *Plattsburgh Sentinel* (August 22, 1879).

24 Jim Goodwin to author, June 14, 1999.

25 Colvin, *Report on the Topographical Survey* (1874), 160.

Heart Lake

1 Lossing, *The Hudson*, 44.

2 *Essex County Republican* (May 27, 1871), in *Glenn's History*, 23.

3 Stoddard, *The Adirondacks: Illustrated* (1874), 120.

4 "Retrospect of Lake Placid," *Lake Placid News* (December 14, 1917), 10.

5 Ibid.

6 For more details about Scofield, Van Hoevenberg, and the Adirondack Lodge, see *The Finest Square Mile: Mount Jo and Heart Lake* by Sandra Weber (Fleischmanns, New York: Purple Mountain Press, 1998).

7 Wallace, *Descriptive Guide* (1872), 160(b).

8 Godfrey Dewey, "The Adirondak Loj of Long Ago," *Adirondac* (July/August 1963), 53. Maitland C. De Sormo, Biographical Sketch, in *Told Around the Campfire* (Saranac Lake, New York: Adirondack Yesteryears Inc., 1967), 6. Dewey names the chief guide as Peter, presumably Peter McCree.

9 Wallace, *Descriptive Guide* (1882), Hotel and other changes.

10 Laura Waterman and Guy Waterman, *Forest and Crag* (Boston: Appalachian Mountain Club, 1989), 279.

11 Karl Baedeker, *The United States with an Excursion into Mexico, Handbook for Travellers* (Leipsic: Karl Baedeker, 1893), 175-6.

12 George Roberts to Russell Carson, March 16, 1928. Carson Papers,

Adirondack Museum Library.

13 Waterman and Waterman, *Forest and Crag*, 216.

14 Henry James, *The Letters of William James* (Boston: The Atlantic Monthly Press, 1920), 75.

15 Ibid.

16 Ralph Barton Perry, *The Thought and Character of William James* (Cambridge: Harvard University Press, 1948), 375.

17 James, *The Letters of William James*, 76-7.

18 Ibid., 77.

19 Ibid., 95.

20 William G. Distin, "Heart Lake Before the Big Fire," *Adirondac* (March-April 1964), 24-25.

Johns Brook

1 Waterman and Waterman, *Forest and Crag*, 738, notes for 210.

2 Carson, *Peaks and People*, 267.

3 Walter Lowrie, "Marcy Reminiscences," *Adirondac* (March-April 1956), 31. In *Mountain Climbing in Keene Valley in the Latter Part of the Eighties and Later* (unpublished, 1933), Keene Valley Library, Walter Lowrie wrote that Phelps' first trail followed the Johns Brook route. No other accounts support this; they state that Phelps' first trail went via the Ausable Lakes and was built in 1861.

4 Pychowska, "To Saranac and Back," 669.

5 Carson, *Peaks and People*, 76.

6 Wallace, *Descriptive Guide* (1872), 361.

7 Walter Lowrie, "Walter Lowrie: Theologian in the Adirondacks," *Adirondac* (September-October 1969), 91. (Reprint of a letter written by Lowrie in January 1928.)

8 Lowrie, "Marcy Reminiscences," 33, note 3.

9 Lowrie, "Walter Lowrie: Theologian in

the Adirondacks," 92-3. Lowrie, "Marcy Reminiscences," 31 and 33, note 3. Glover said it was Mr. Bahler's son Adrian who led the group.

[10] Stoddard, *The Adirondacks: Illustrated* (1878), 162n.

[11] Wallace, *Descriptive Guide* (1894), 306-7.

[12] Lowrie, *Mountain Climbing in Keene Valley*, 1-3.

[13] Ibid., 4.

[14] Lowrie, "Marcy Reminiscences," 31. This differs from *Mountain Climbing in Keene Valley*, 8, which says it was the same year.

[15] Lowrie, *Mountain Climbing in Keene Valley*, 8.

[16] Lowrie, "Walter Lowrie: Theologian in the Adirondacks," 92.

[17] Lowrie, *Mountain Climbing in Keene Valley*, 9.

[18] Lowrie, "Marcy Reminiscences," 31-2.

[19] Lowrie, *Mountain Climbing in Keene Valley*, 11.

[20] Frank W. Freeborn, "Some Adirondack Paths," *Appalachia* (July 1891), 231.

[21] "For a Trail Up Mount Marcy," *The New York Times* (August 6, 1895).

[22] Meade Dobson, "Mel Hathaway's Clearing," *Adirondac* (March-April 1964), 26.

[23] "A Winter Trip Up Marcy," newspaper clipping (December 1903). Loomis Scrapbook #2, Keene Valley Library.

[24] Dobson, "Mel Hathaway's Clearing," 26.

[25] Billy Burger, "The Adirondacker, Up Mount Marcy in 1909," *The Record-Post* (Ausable Forks, New York: April 2, 1942).

[26] Ibid.

[27] Ibid.

[28] Georgia Wood Pangborn, "From an Adirondack Note-Book," *Outlook*

(September 2, 1911), 29.

[29] Ibid., 28-9.

[30] Ibid., 30.

[31] Lowrie, *Mountain Climbing in Keene Valley*, 6-7.

[32] Goodwin letter, June 14, 1999.

[33] Ibid.

[34] Ibid.

Mud Pond or Elk Lake

[1] Redfield, *The Family Magazine*, 348.

[2] Street, *The Indian Pass*, 173.

[3] Ibid., 176-7.

[4] Orson Phelps, *Essex County Republican* (June 8, 1871), in *Glenn's History*, 23.

[5] Ibid. Wallace, *Descriptive Guide* (1872), 379.

[6] Stoddard, *The Adirondacks: Illustrated* (1874), 194-5.

[7] "Adirondack Park," *Plattsburgh Sentinel* (August 22, 1879).

[8] C. B. Going, "Climbing Mount Marcy," *The Evening Post* (New York: September 15, 1894).

[9] Ibid.

[10] Ibid.

[11] Ibid.

[12] Ibid.

[13] Wallace, *Descriptive Guide* (1894), 341. Wallace (1887), 272n.

[14] Lucy Bohrman, "A Trip Up Mt. Marcy, Sept. 2-6, 1896," unpublished manuscript, 1.

[15] Ibid., 5.

[16] Ibid., 9.

[17] Ibid., 14-5.

[18] Ibid., 19.

[19] Kate Field, "The Bloomer Girls," in *The Adirondack Reader* (Glens Falls, New York: The Adirondack Mountain Club, Inc., 1983), 99. (Reprinted from

The Atlantic Almanac from 1870).

20 Howard Goodwin, "Three Adirondack Summers: 1895, 1901, 1903," *Adirondac* (September-October 1971), 97.

Winter Ascents

1 Colvin, *Report on a Topographical Survey* (1884), 160-1.

2 Carson, *Peaks and People*, 65.

3 W. Scott Brown, in Brian W. Swinn, "Mills Blake," *Adirondac* (October 1982), 12.

4 "Snow Climbing in the Adirondacks," *High Spots* (January 1932), 3.

5 C. Grant LaFarge, "A Winter Ascent of Tahawus," *Outing* (April 1900), 69.

6 Ibid., 73.

7 Gifford Pinchot diary. Gifford Pinchot Papers, Library of Congress.

8 LaFarge, "A Winter Ascent of Tahawus," 75.

9 "A Winter Trip Up Marcy," (December 1903).

10 Ibid.

11 Ibid.

12 *Lake Placid Club Notes* (March 2, 1908), 38.

13 Lewis A. Wells, "A January Ascent of Mount Marcy," *Appalachia* (June 1908), 343.

The Alpine Zone

1 John Torrey to Benjamin Silliman, August 23, 1837, in Rodgers, *John Torrey*, 131.

2 Hall to editor, August 5, 1837.

3 Hoffman, *The New-York Mirror* (October 21, 1837), 132.

4 William A. Weber, *King of Colorado Botany* (Niwot, Colorado: University Press of Colorado, 1997), 5.

5 Joseph Ewan, *Rocky Mountain Naturalists* (Denver: University of Denver Press, 1950), 34.

6 "The Wilds of Northern New York," 268.

7 *New-York Daily Tribune* (July 13, 1870).

8 "Gleanings From Old Fields."

9 Orson Phelps, in Bill Healy, *The High Peaks of Essex: The Adirondack Mountains of Orson Schofield Phelps* (Fleischmanns, New York: Purple Mountain Press, 1992), 27.

10 George T. Stevens, M.D., *The Flora of the Adirondacks* (Albany: Joel Munsell, 1868; read before the Albany Institute, February, 1867), 16-7. *Essex County Republican* (October 10, 1872), in *Glenn's History*, 33.

11 Stevens, *The Flora of the Adirondacks*, 14.

12 Charles H. Peck, "Botany: Plants of the Summit of Mount Marcy," in Colvin, *Report on the Topographical Survey York* (1879), 401-6.

13 Ibid.

14 Ibid.

15 E. H. Ketchledge and R. E. Leonard, "The Impact of Man on the Adirondack High Country," *The Conservationist* (October-November 1970), 17.

16 Carson, *Peaks and People*, 138.

17 Colvin, *Report on the Topographical Survey* (1879), 365-6.

18 Elon Howard Eaton, *Birds of New York* (Albany: University of the State of New York, 1910), 42 and 50.

19 John W. Harshberger, "Alpine Fell-Fields of Eastern North America," *Geological Review* (April 1919), 239.

20 Ibid., 239-40.

21 "Mount Marcy," *American Scenic and Historic Preservation Society* (1920), 318.

22 Charles C. Adams, George P. Burns, T. L. Hankinson, Barrington Moore, and Norman Taylor, "Plants and

Animals of Mount Marcy, New York," *Ecology* (1920), 225-6.

[23] Ibid., 216-18.

Roosevelt's Ride

[1] Theodore Roosevelt, *Theodore Roosevelt's Diaries of Boyhood and Youth* (New York: Charles Scribner's Sons, 1928), 242-54.

[2] "The Case Against Czolgosz," *The New York Times* (September 11, 1901).

[3] Masten, *Tahawus Club, 1898-1933*, 54.

[4] Ibid., 55-6.

[5] Richmond B. Williams, "TR receives his summons to the presidency," *Bell Telephone Magazine* (Autumn 1951), 197-200.

[6] Masten, *Tahawus Club, 1898-1933*, 55.

[7] "President Doomed and Had No Chance of Recovery From the Start," *New York Herald* (September 15, 1901).

[8] Harry V. Radford, "President Roosevelt's Ascent of Mt. Marcy," *Forest Leaves* (Winter 1904), 6. Quoted from *New York Herald*.

[9] Ibid.

[10] Eloise Cronin Murphy, *Theodore Roosevelt's Night Ride to the Presidency* (Blue Mountain Lake, New York: Adirondack Museum, 1977), 15.

[11] Williams, "TR receives his summons to the presidency," 202.

[12] Theodore Roosevelt, *An Autobiography* (New York: The MacMillan Company, 1919), 379.

[13] Murphy, *Theodore Roosevelt's Night Ride*, 16. Williams, "TR receives his summons to the presidency," 202.

[14] Edward A. Harmes, "2:15 A.M.: T.R.'s Ride from Tahawus to North Creek," *Adirondac* (November-December 1963), 90. Murphy, *Theodore Roosevelt's Night Ride*, 34, note 15.

[15] Harmes, "2:15 A.M.: T.R.'s Ride," 90.

[16] Murphy, *Theodore Roosevelt's Night*

[17] Masten, *Tahawus Club, 1898-1933*, 55.

[18] "Roosevelt on his Way," *Washington Post* (September 14, 1901).

[19] Harmes, "2:15 A.M.: T.R.'s Ride," 90.

[20] Murphy, *Theodore Roosevelt's Night Ride*, 20-1.

[21] Ibid.

[22] Harmes, "2:15 A.M.: T.R.'s Ride," 92.

[23] "President Doomed," *New York Herald*.

[24] Harmes, "2:15 A.M.: T.R.'s Ride," 92.

[25] "President Doomed," *New York Herald*.

[26] Murphy, *Theodore Roosevelt's Night Ride*, 25.

[27] "President Doomed," *New York Herald*.

[28] Col. G. W. Townsend, *Our Martyred President. . .Memorial Life of William McKinley* (1901), 471. "Roosevelt's Trip to Buffalo," *The Sun* (September 15, 1901).

[29] *Selections From the Correspondence of Theodore Roosevelt and Henry Cabot Lodge, 1884-1918* (New York: Charles Scribner's Sons, 1925), 506.

[30] Masten, *Tahawus Club 1898-1933*, 57.

[31] William Chapman White, *Adirondack Country* (1954; reprint, New York: Alfred A. Knopf, 1987), 159.

[32] Mary Jane Nardacci, "Comments," *Adirondack Life* (Summer 1976), 62. Murphy, *Theodore Roosevelt's Night Ride*, 31.

A New Century

[1] William D. Glover, "Climbs With Walter Lowrie," *Adirondac* (November-December 1956), 110.

[2] H. M. Suter, *Forest Fires in the Adirondacks in 1903* (Washington, D. C.: U. S. Department of Agriculture, Bureau of Forestry, 1904).

3 Sharp Swan, "Roots, Boots, and Routes," in *Of the Summits, of the Forests*, 89.

4 Goodwin, "Three Adirondack Summers: 1895, 1901, 1903," 97.

5 Seneca Ray Stoddard, "In the Beginning, The Oldest Mountain on Earth," *Stoddard's Northern Monthly* (May 1906), 4.

6 Ibid., 6.

7 Ibid.

8 L. E. Shattuck, "Up Mount Marcy After Governor Hughes," *New-York Tribune* (August 16, 1908).

9 Ibid.

10 Ibid.

11 McEntee diary, 77-78. Adirondack Museum Library.

12 Edith Pilcher, *Up the Lake Road* (Keene Valley, New York: The Adirondack Mountain Reserve, 1987), 5-7.

13 Street, *The Indian Pass*, 139.

14 "Adirondack Park," *Plattsburgh Sentinel* (August 22, 1879).

15 Mary MacKenzie, to author, March 7, 2001.

16 Goodwin letter, June 14, 1999. James A. Goodwin, "Lumbering High on the High Peaks," *Adirondac* (September 1982), 3.

17 Shattuck, "Up Mount Marcy After Governor Hughes." Charles L. Brayton, "The 1914 'Fast Marcy,'" *Adirondac* (May-June 1968), 46.

18 Swan, "Roots, Boots, and Routes," 90.

19 Carson, *Peaks and People*, 80.

20 Henry Van Hoevenberg, letter about Adirondack Camp & Trail Club, April 25, 1911. Lake Placid-North Elba Historical Society.

21 Hicks, "Camps and Trails Near Lake Placid," *Lake Placid News* (November 11, 1921), 2.

22 Goodwin letter, June 14, 1999.

23 Stoddard, *The Adirondacks: Illustrated* (1892), 131.

24 Goodwin letter, June 14, 1999. Swan, "Roots, Boots, and Routes," 90.

25 "Mount Marcy," *American Scenic and Historic Preservation Society* (1920), 313-4.

26 Goodwin letter, June 14, 1999.

27 Pilcher, *Up the Lake Road*, 49.

28 Ibid., 46 and 93. Apperson to Theodore Anthony, May 15, 1928. Apperson Papers, Adirondack Research Library.

29 John T. Carr Lowe, "A Change of Worlds on Marcy," *Adirondac* (July-August 1950), 83.

30 Goodwin, "Lumbering High on the High Peaks," 4.

31 Ibid.

32 Goodwin letter, June 14, 1999.

Victory Mountain Park

1 E. H. Hall, "Victory Mountain Park," notes from meeting held January 10, 1919. Association Archives, Adirondack Research Library.

2 *Victory Mountain Park* (New York: The Association for the Protection of the Adirondacks, 1919).

3 Ibid.

4 Goodwin letter, June 14, 1999.

5 T. Morris Longstreth, "The Great Memorial," *The Conservationist* (April 1920), 57.

6 "Hands Off Mount Marcy!," *The Sun* (June 29, 1919). "Mount Marcy Remains," *The Sun* (July 4, 1919).

7 John Bassett Moore, "The Name of Marcy," *The Sun* (July 9, 1919).

8 Goodwin letter, June 14, 1999.

9 State of New York Conservation Commission, *Annual Report for the Year 1919* (Albany: J. B. Lyon Company, 1920), 99.

10 "Addition to the State Forest," *State Service* (January 1921), 431.

11 Harold Hochschild, *The MacIntyre Mine—From Failure to Fortune* (Blue Mountain Lake, New York: Adirondack Museum, 1962), 13.

12 "Gleanings From Old Fields."

13 Harold Weston, *Freedom in the Wilds*, (St. Huberts, New York: Adirondack Trail Improvement Society, 1971), 53.

14 Colvin, *Report on the Topographical Survey* (1874), 266. Colvin, (1879), 106.

15 Commissioner Alexander MacDonald to Dr. Hall, November 4, 1922. Adirondack Research Library.

16 Essex County Deed Record, Book 172, 289.

17 "State Now Owns Its Mountain Tops," *The New York Times* (February 21, 1923), 20.

The 1920s

1 James M. Glover, *A Wilderness Original: The Life of Bob Marshall* (Seattle: The Mountaineers, 1986), 32.

2 Carson, *Peaks and People*, xii and xxvii.

3 T. Morris Longstreth, *The Adirondacks* (New York: The Century Co., 1920), 261-4.

4 Longstreth, "The Great Memorial," 55.

5 T. Morris Longstreth, *The Lake Country* (Lake Placid Club, New York: Adirondack Camp and Trail Club, 1922), 48-9.

6 Longstreth, "The Great Memorial," 55.

7 Arthur S. Knight, editor, *The Adirondacks: Guide and History* (Lake George, New York: Lake George Printing Co., 1921), 92.

8 H. S. Douglas, "Climbing the 'Cloud-Cleaver,'" *The Vermonter* (1923), 4.

9 Ibid., 6.

10 A. S. Hopkins, *The Trails To Marcy* (Albany: State of New York,

Conservation Department, 1927), 12.

11 Lowrie, *Mountain Climbing in Keene Valley*, 15.

12 Waterman and Waterman, *Forest and Crag*, 213.

13 Hopkins, *The Trails To Marcy*, 13.

14 Harry P. Hays, "On Adirondack Trails" (Times Tribune Company, 1923; reprinted from *Altoona Tribune*), 7-8. The sequence of events in the account is sometimes mixed-up and inaccurate.

15 Ibid., 11.

16 Ibid., 12.

17 Ibid., 5.

18 Ibid., 21.

19 Ibid., Preface.

20 Goodwin letter, June 14, 1999.

21 Hopkins, *The Trails To Marcy*, 5.

22 Jim Goodwin to author, April 4, 2001.

23 *New York Evening Post* (June 26, 1926).

24 Ibid.

25 Grace Hudowalski, "My Pappy Done Tole Me," *Cloudsplitter* (July-August 1944), 3.

26 Gertrude H. Carragan, "The Trip to Marcy," unpublished manuscript (1923).

27 Hudowalski, "My Pappy Done Tole Me," 4.

28 Ibid.

29 Mary Arakelian, *Doc: Orra A. Phelps, M.D.* (Utica, New York: North Country Books, 2000), 72.

30 Ibid.

31 Ibid., 75.

32 Ibid., 93.

33 Professor Edward Everett Hale, "The Old Trails Up Marcy," original manuscript of article prepared in December 1925. Adirondack Museum Library.

34 George Marshall, in Carson, *Peaks and People*, xxv.

35 Jerod Rosman, e-mail to author, November 1, 1998. According to Jed's grandson, Jerod Rosman, the family name has often been misspelled "Rossman" because of a clerical error by the U. S. Army during the Civil War.

36 H. W. Hicks, "Great Adirondack Guides, Jed Rossman," *High Spots* (January 1933), 16.

37 "The Hunter Home From the Hill, Jed Rosman," *High Spots* (April 1937), 16-7.

38 T. Morris Longstreth, *The Sky Through Branches* (New York: The Century Co., 1930), 58-9. The mountaintop is not named in the poem, but tradition says it is Marcy.

39 Carson, *Peaks and People*, xxi.

40 Ibid.

Built On High

1 Colvin, *Report on a Topographical Survey* (1873), 35.

2 Colvin, *Report of the Adirondack Survey* (1879), 156-7.

3 Ibid., 170.

4 Ibid., 31.

5 Webb, *Footsteps Through the Adirondacks*, 60.

6 Bohrmann, *A Trip Up Mt. Marcy*, 8.

7 La Farge, "A Winter Ascent of Tahawus," 75.

8 Longstreth, *The Lake Placid Country*, 50.

9 Pirie MacDonald, "MacDonald Hospice on Mount Marcy," *Cloudsplitter* (1942, no. 3), 2-3.

10 Ibid.

11 "Marcy Shelter Opponents Err, Sponsor Insists," (May 15, 1928). MS 63-270, Box 4, Adirondack Museum Library.

12 W.G. Howard, "Mount Marcy Shelter," *New York Herald Tribune* (May? 1928). MS 63-270, Box 4, Adirondack Museum Library.

13 Goodwin letter, June 14, 1999.

14 C. G. Suits, "The Marcy Summit-February, 1933," *Adirondac* (February/March 1989), 14.

15 "Shelter House On Mt. Marcy Is Protested," *New York Herald Tribune* (May 14, 1928).

16 Theodore Dreier, "Mount Marcy Shelter," *New York Herald Tribune* (May 20, 1928).

17 Editorial, *New York Herald Tribune* (May 18, 1928).

18 J. S. Apperson, "Shelter on Mount Marcy," *New York Herald Tribune* (May 21, 1928).

19 Apperson to Johannsen. July 23, 1928. Apperson Papers, Adirondack Research Library.

20 Goodwin letter, June 14, 1999.

21 Waterman and Waterman, *Forest and Crag*, 276.

22 Terris Moore, "A Midwinter Sleep on Marcy's Summit," unpublished manuscript (January 1, 1929). Adirondack Museum Library.

23 Ibid.

24 Conservation Department, *Annual Report for 1929*, 67.

25 Goodwin letter, June 14, 1999.

26 George Marshall, "Imperishable Freshness!," *Adirondac* (March-April 1953), 28.

27 Gary Hodgson to Jim Bailey, February 7, 2001.

28 J. S. Apperson to W. G. Howard, June 20, 1928. Alexander MacDonald to J. S. Apperson, June 14, 1928. Apperson Papers, Adirondack Research Library.

The 1930s

1 Helen Menz, "Marcy in the Early '30s," *Adirondac* (May/June 1997), 16.

2 Ibid., 17.

3 Paul Schaefer, *Defending the Wilderness* (Syracuse, New York: Syracuse University Press, 1989), 177.

4 Robert Marshall, "Fourteen in One," in *The Adirondack Reader* (Glens Falls, New York: The Adirondack Mountain Club, Inc., 1983), 417-8. (Reprinted from *High Spots*, October 1932.)

5 Schaefer, *Defending the Wilderness*, 178.

6 Marshall, "Fourteen in One," 416.

7 Schaefer, *Defending the Wilderness*, 178-9.

8 Grace Hudowalski, "Marcy Kaleidoscope," *Adirondac* (March-April 1953), 26.

9 Sharp Swan, "The Mount Marcy Centenary Celebration," in *Of the Summits, of the Forests* (Morrisonville, New York: Adirondack Forty-Sixers, 1991), 100-102.

10 "Seaver Fay Recalls Historic Mt. Marcy Broadcast," *The Lake Placid News* (August 11, 1977).

11 Ibid.

12 "Speech of Lithgow Osborne," *High Spots* (December 1937), 11.

13 Ibid.

14 Swan, "The Mount Marcy Centenary Celebration," 102.

15 Grace Hudowalski, interview with author, Guilderland, New York, March 25, 2000.

16 Russell M. L. Carson, "The Adirondack Mountain Club," *High Spots* (December 1937), 20.

17 Frank Graham Jr., *The Adirondack Park: A Political History* (Syracuse: Syracuse University Press, 1978), 208-9.

Winter Adventures

1 "The Adirondacks: A Winter Holiday Out of the Beaten Paths," *Boston Transcript* (February 1, 1911).

2 Alexander F. Ormsbee, "Another Winter Ascent of Mount Marcy," *Appalachia* (July 1910), 136.

3 Dick Tucker, chairman of the Adirondack Research Library in Schenectady, has researched the first ski ascents of the high peaks and has a forthcoming book on the history of ski mountaineering.

4 William M. White, "Mount Marcy—Winter 1911, A First Ascent on Skis," *Adirondac* (January 1984), 5.

5 Apperson to Orlando Beede, February 8, 1922. Apperson Papers, Adirondack Research Library.

6 Waterman and Waterman, *Forest and Crag*, 339.

7 Brian Powell, compiler, *Jackrabbit: His First Hundred Years* (Don Mills, Ontario: Collier Macmillan Canada, Ltd., 1975), 172.

8 Alice E. Johannsen, *The Legendary Jackrabbit Johannsen* (McGill-Queens Univ. Press, 1993), 204.

9 Ibid.

10 Powell, *Jackrabbit: His First Hundred Years*, 55.

11 Waterman and Waterman, *Forest and Crag*, 339-40.

12 C. G. Suits, "The Marcy Summit-February, 1933," *Adirondac* (February/March 1989), 15.

13 Vincent J. Schaefer, "Letters," *Adirondac* (September-October 1971), 98.

14 Suits, "The Marcy Summit-February, 1933," 16.

15 Ibid.

16 *Of the Summits, of the Forests*, 95. Goodwin letter, June 14, 1999.

17 *Of the Summits, of the Forests*, 95.

18 Russell Carson, "From the Winter Camp to the Top of Marcy," *High Spots* (March 1930).

19 Ibid., 12.

[20] A.T. Shorey, "Mount Marcy in the Deep Winter Snow," *ADK Bulletin* (April-May 1939).

[21] Ibid.

[22] New York State Conservation Department, *Annual Report for the Year 1936* (Albany: J. B. Lyon Company, 1937), 43.

[23] New York State Conservation Department, *Ski Trails of New York State* (Albany: J. B. Lyon Company, 1939), 5.

[24] Tony Goodwin, *Northern Adirondack Ski Tours* (Glens Falls, New York: Adirondack Mountain Club, Inc., 1981), 58.

[25] Fay Welch, "Mount Marcy in Winter," unpublished manuscript (October 1948). Adirondack Museum Library.

[26] Cliff Alexander, "Some Notes on Winter Camping," *Adirondac* (Jan-Feb. 1950), 16.

[27] Richard H. Beck, George Lamb, Irving Lamb, and Thomas A. Ewing, "Mt. Marcy," unpublished manuscript (January 31, 1949). Adirondack Museum Library.

[28] Ibid.

[29] Mary Schaefer, "Schaefer Expedition, December 1959," *Adirondac* (January-February 1961), 4.

[30] Ibid., 5.

[31] Ibid.

[32] William Irvin, "The Mountain that Stays Open Late," *Ski Magazine* (February 15, 1950), 7.

[33] Ibid., 22.

[34] Tony Goodwin, "Challenge Skiing: High Peaks Adventures," *Adirondack Life* (January/February 1985), 26.

Backcountry Boom

[1] Waterman and Waterman, *Forest and Crag*, 643.

[2] An AMC cylinder that was on Mount Marcy from 1888 to 1890 contained records from 20 parties who ascended from Cold Slough and 11 parties from Adirondack Lodge. From Freeborn, "Some Adirondack Paths," 232.

[3] James, *The Letters of William James*, 75.

[4] Conservation Commission, *Annual Report* (1932 and 1937).

[5] Julian W. Schwab, "Mount Marcy Not 'Untouched'," *The New York Times* (August 12, 1937).

[6] Edwin H. Ketchledge, with Kathleen D. Regan, "Adirondack Insights #26: Managing the High Adirondack Summits," *Adirondac* (September/October 1993), 22.

[7] P. Fay Loope, "Moods of Marcy," *Adirondac* (January-February, 1949), 4.

[8] Robert DeLong and A. G. Dittmar, "Marcy in the Hurricane," *Adirondac* (May-June 1951), 54.

[9] Ketchledge and Regan, "Managing the High Adirondack Summits," 22.

[10] C. R. Roseberry, *Albany Times Union* (June 28, 1953)

[11] Bernard Kolenberg, "Mount Marcy and I," *Adirondac* (September-October 1953), 97.

[12] Ibid., 98.

[13] Ibid., 99.

[14] Ibid., 94.

[15] Marshall, "Imperishable Freshness!," 28.

[16] Ibid.

[17] Ibid., 34.

[18] Conservation Department, *Annual Report for 1960*, 33, and *Annual Report for 1965*, 53. Stated figure is the number of hikers counted by caretakers or rangers.

[19] Jane Eblen Keller, *Adirondack Wilderness, A Story of Man and Nature* (Syracuse: Syracuse University Press, 1980), 198.

[20] Almy Coggeshall, e-mail to author,

May 3, 2001.

[21] Almy Coggeshall, e-mail to author, May 7, 2001.

[22] Ibid. Eleanor F. Brown, *The Forest Preserve of New York State* (Adirondack Mountain Club Inc., 1985), 177.

[23] Coggeshall e-mail, May 7, 2001.

[24] *High Peaks Unit Management Plan* (March 1999), 88.

[25] James Marshall, "Letters," *Adirondac* (September-October 1971), 99.

[26] Pete Fish, interview with author, August 31, 1999.

Calamity and Catastrophe

[1] Twichell, *Extract from Scrapbook*, 22. Saranac Lake Library.

[2] Colvin, *Report of the Adirondack Survey* (1879), 96.

[3] "Adirondack Park," *Plattsburgh Sentinel* (August 22, 1879).

[4] Ibid.

[5] LaFarge, "A Winter Ascent of Tahawus," 75.

[6] A. A. Schenck, letter to editor, *High Spots* (January, 1933), 12.

[7] Douglas, "Climbing the 'Cloud-Cleaver'," 7.

[8] Pangborn, "From an Adirondack Note-Book," 30.

[9] Ibid.

[10] Willem Lange, "A Death on Marcy," *Adirondack Life* (November/December 1981), 14-17.

[11] Skip Nash, "Mt. Marcy Adventure," *Adirondac* (October 1979), 105.

[12] Richard Stepp, "Lost on Marcy," *Adirondac* (May-June 1969), 55-6.

[13] Winthrop A. Rockwell, "The Challenging Mountains: Two Men Attempt 46 Peaks in 5 Days," *The New York Times* (February 18, 1973).

[14] Kathryn M. Roberts, *Lake Placid News*

(1976).

[15] Fish interview.

[16] E. H. (Ed Hale), "The Searcher," *Lake Placid News* (August 26, 1976).

[17] Goodwin letter, June 14, 1999.

[18] Chris Carpenter, "Marcy in Winter," *Adirondack Life* (November-December 1977), 35.

[19] Liza Frenette, "No Margin for Error," *Adirondack Life* (February 1988), 50-3.

[20] Ibid.

[21] Tony Goodwin, "Accident Report," *Adirondac* (June 1989), 10.

Alpine Restoration

[1] Dr. Edwin Ketchledge, interview with author, May 2, 1999. Sandra Weber, "Dr. Edwin Ketchledge," *Adirondack Explorer* (July 1999).

[2] Howard E. Woodin, "Establishment of a Permanent Vegetational Transect Above Timberline on Mt. Marcy, New York," *Ecology* (April 1959), 320.

[3] E. H. Ketchledge and R. E. Leonard, "A 24-Year Comparison of the Vegetation of an Adirondack Mountain Summit," reprinted from *RHODORA* (October 1984), 439 and 443.

[4] Melissa Buckler, *Summit Steward Program July Report* (August 18, 1999).

A Management Plan

[1] *High Peaks Unit Management Plan* (March 1999), 48.

[2] Eleanor F. Brown, *The Forest Preserve of New York State* (Conservation Committee, Adirondack Mountain Club, Inc., 1985), 188-9.

[3] Grace Hudowalski, "Marcy Kaleidoscope," *Adirondac* (March-April 1953), 33.

Index

About the author

SANDRA WEBER has written for *Backpacker, Adirondack Life, The Conservationist, Adirondack Explorer, Adirondac, Highlights For Children, Wild Outdoor World,* and other publications. She is also the author of *The Finest Square Mile: Mount Jo and Heart Lake* (Purple Mountain Press, 1998) and *The Lure of Esther Mountain: Matriarch of the Adirondack High Peaks* (Purple Mountain Press, 1995).

Sandra, her husband, and her two daughters reside in southeastern Pennsylvania but spend as much time as possible at their old log cabin just a few miles from the Mount Marcy trailhead.

About the Publisher

PURPLE MOUNTAIN PRESS, established 1973, is a publishing company committed to producing the best original books of regional interest as well as bringing back into print significant older works. It also publishes under the Harbor Hill imprint. For a free catalog of more than 300 hard-to-find books about New York State, write Purple Mountain Press, Ltd., P.O. Box 309, Fleischmanns, New York 12430-0309 or call 845-254-4062 or fax 845-254-4476 or email purple@catskill.net. Visit the website at http://www.catskill.net/purple.